International Econor

International Economics

Theory, Evidence and Practice

Peter Wilson

Lecturer in Economics
University of Bradford

Wheatsheaf
Books

DISTRIBUTED BY HARVESTER PRESS

First published in Great Britain in 1986 by
WHEATSHEAF BOOKS LTD
A MEMBER OF THE HARVESTER PRESS GROUP
Publisher: John Spiers
Director of Publications: Edward Elgar
16 Ship Street, Brighton, Sussex

British Library Cataloguing in Publication Data
Wilson, Peter
  International economics: theory, evidence and practice.
  1. International economic relations
  I. Title
337   HF1411
ISBN 0-7108-0790-2
ISBN 0-7108-0006-9 Pbk

Typeset in 10pt Times by M.C. Typeset, Chatham, Kent
Printed and bound in Great Britain by
Biddles Ltd, Guildford and King's Lynn

THE HARVESTER PRESS PUBLISHING GROUP
The Harvester Press Publishing Group comprises Harvester Press
Limited (chiefly publishing literature, fiction, philosophy,
psychology, and science and trade books), Harvester Press
Microform Publications Limited (publishing in microform
unpublished archives, scarce printed sources, and indexes to these
collections) and Wheatsheaf Books Limited (a wholly independent
company chiefly publishing in economics, international politics,
sociology and related social sciences), whose books are distributed
by The Harvester Press Limited and its agencies throughout the
world.

To My Father

Contents

List of Tables and Figures

Figure

Preface

It is my intention in this book to provide the essential ingredients of modern international economics in a predominantly descriptive style for those students who are opting to study international economics, but who possess only a rudimentary understanding of economic theory; and for those students who are taking courses in economics, but who are not specialising in international trade.

I hope to cater for the first group by combining some trade theory with a lively treatment of issues relating to the contemporary world, including the international debt crisis, reforms of the international monetary and trading system, and the relations between developed and developing countries. As far as the second group is concerned, I have tried to isolate the most important aspects of international economics for students who do not wish to work out every caveat and theorem in international trade theory, but at the same time do not want to be presented with an over-simplistic treatment of the subject.

There are many good textbooks which provide a thorough analysis of the principles of international economics and illustrate them with examples drawn from the real world, and there are many texts which offer a simpler version of the same material. There seems, however, to be a dearth of books which provide a balance between some basic theory, a 'taste' for more complex analysis, and sufficient applied material to enable students to get to grips with issues of current relevance.

Finally, I have tried to introduce a higher proportion of material relating to the developing countries than is conventional practice in textbooks of this sort. This is partly because the specialist literature on trade and development has undergone considerable expansion in the last two decades or so, but also because many of the important issues in the international arena concern these countries.

In writing this book I have accumulated a number of debts of gratitude, not least to my former teachers at the universities of Exeter and Warwick, including Nick Crafts for stimulating my interest in economics as an undergraduate, and Alec Ford and John Williamson for continuing this process at postgraduate level.

I am also grateful to the cohorts of students at the universities of Sussex and Bradford who have attended my courses on international economics, and to my colleagues at Bradford, especially to Brian Burkitt and Fred Singleton, whose zest for life remains a constant source of inspiration to me. Peter Holmes was also kind enough to read and comment on parts of the original manuscript, although the responsibility for any remaining errors remains, of course, exclusively mine.

Finally, an extra special thank you to my wife Hazel for putting up with considerable inconvenience during the last year and for shouldering a disproportionate amount of the household chores.

1 Introduction

1.1 THE STUDY OF INTERNATIONAL ECONOMICS

International economics is concerned fundamentally with the study of trade between nations in a world which is growing ever more interdependent in its economic relations.

Although the contrast between an open trading economy and a closed autarkic economy has only been used for theoretical convenience, since in reality no economy is entirely self-sufficient, in recent decades it has become even less prudent to divorce domestic economic questions from their international ramifications. The spread of multinational corporations and the increasing sophistication of international marketing and communications networks after the second world war are two examples of this process of integration.

There has in consequence been a subtle re-thinking of the links between international trade theory and economic theory in general, away from the practice of building models for closed economies which are then opened up to foreign trade almost as an afterthought, towards an approach which attempts to integrate international trade more fully into national models at the outset. Much of this re-thinking owes its inspiration to the revival of monetarism, a doctrine which amongst other things has always stressed the links between international trade and the domestic economy through the money supply, especially in a world of flexible exchange rates and mobile international capital. These issues will be discussed in more detail in Part 3.

There are, none the less, some practical reasons for the development of a distinct branch of economics dealing with international trade.

To begin with international economics has, over the years, developed some separate tools of analysis and has addressed itself to different problems. Although in one sense it represents an extension of economic theory to the specific problems encountered in trade between nations, many important insights were first developed in the international sphere. A good example of this is the theory of comparative advantage which we shall discuss in Chapters 2 and 3. Moreover, issues in international economics, such as those arising from the settlement of debt between countries or from the operation of the foreign exchange market, could be classed as distinct problems for which separate tools of analysis might be required.

The major reason, however, probably relates to the existence of independent sovereign states determining political boundaries between nations. Although national political centres may have surrendered some authority to regional or supranational bodies (such as the European Commission), and the growth of the multinational corporation has somewhat blurred the question of who controls economic activity, the nation-state is still the dominant political entity.

One consequence of this is the existence of barriers between countries which prevents the complete mobility of goods and factors to a much greater degree than between regions within a country. Immigration laws, customs duties, trade restrictions and exchange controls are all obvious impediments to international mobility. There are, however, more subtle methods of restricting imports, including health and quality regulations. Whatever their form, all these barriers tend to create an economic climate which is more homogeneous within a country than between countries, although as we shall see in Part 2, they do not rule out important movements of capital and labour. There are also classic cases of inter-regional inertia such as that between the north and south of Italy and between the north and south of Brazil.

Some of these international differences can, of course, occur even in the absence of government controls in so far as consumer tastes, languages and cultures vary more between countries than between regions and give rise to different economic structures. Despite the tendency towards standardised consumption patterns in the modern world, epitomised by 'Coca Cola' and 'fast food', the British still prefer tea to coffee and drive on the left, while their Common Market partners the French prefer coffee and drive on the right!

An important corollary to political sovereignty is the right of a country to determine its own independent monetary system. The problem which arises is not so much a result of different types of money *per se*, but of differences in economic conditions and policies between countries leading inevitably to fluctuations in the value of their currencies. These in turn manifest themselves in surpluses and deficits on the balance of payments and necessitate some adjustment mechanism between countries. There is no obvious counterpart to this problem between regions sharing a common currency.

Thus although in recent years there have been attempts to integrate international economics more directly into models of domestic economic activity, and many of the distinctions we have drawn between nations differ only in degree from differences between regions, there is still a strong case for the study of international economics as a discipline in its own right.

1.2 SOME METHODOLOGICAL PROBLEMS

When studying international economics, two methodological problems cannot be ignored: the division of international trade theory into the pure theory of international trade and the monetary theory of international trade; and the positive–normative distinction.

The pure theory of international trade calls upon microeconomic theory and focuses on relative prices or values. For example, how many potatoes can be exchanged for a pound of salt? How many hours of work will earn a loaf of bread? The situation is thus analogous to a non-money or barter world where real and not money magnitudes are important and it is the *relative* exchange value of things which is paramount. We shall use this approach to explain the pattern of trade in Chapters 2 and 3, and the effects of tariffs in Chapter 5.

The monetary theory of international trade (sometimes called international finance), on the other hand, relies upon a macroeconomic framework to introduce trade into models describing the relationships between such factors as national income, employment, the general price level and the money supply. We shall call upon this approach in Part 4 when we discuss the balance of payments and the foreign exchange market.

This separation into pure and monetary theory is dictated more by the sheer practical difficulties involved in dealing simultaneously with changes in income and relative prices, rather than by any deep-seated theoretical convictions. Ideally we would want a synthesis between the two, and much discussion in contemporary economic theory centres on trying to improve on this uneasy marriage. In practice, however, many of the topics we shall discuss in this book will utilise insights derived from both these approaches.

The distinction between positive and normative statements in international economics is perhaps part of a more fundamental debate within the social sciences. The convention in economics is to define a positive statement (or theory) as being concerned with what 'is' rather than what 'ought to be'. For example, what factors determine the pattern of trade between countries? Are tariffs and quotas equivalent in their effects? Normative statements, however, involve recommendation and therefore value-judgements. For instance, is free trade better than no trade? Will the imposition of a tariff by a country benefit its consumers?

This dichotomy is part and parcel of the commitment by economists to a scientific methodology which involves, amongst other things, the testing of positive theory against data and the recognition that disagreements over normative issues cannot be settled by an appeal to the facts. There is by no means universal acceptance for this methodology, but the prevalent feeling amongst economists is that it is sensible to try to separate positive and normative statements and to adopt a scientific approach. The importance of separating matters of fact from matters of opinion will become clearer as we explore the subject-matter of international economics.

1.3 OUTLINE OF THE BOOK

In Part 1 we consider trade theory predominantly from a pure theory point of view, starting with a review of some earlier theories, including Ricardo's principle of comparative advantage. We then survey the modern theory of international trade, and in Chapter 4 focus specifically on its implications for the developing countries. In Part 2 we switch our attention to trade policy. The first chapter looks generally at the effects of barriers to trade and the case for protection, Chapters 6 and 7 then look more at policy issues surrounding the formation of cartels, international commodity agreements and integration movements, illustrating the theory with examples from the contemporary world. Part 3 examines international factor movements, beginning with a general discussion of the relationship between trade and factor markets, and then dealing more specifically with foreign direct investment and foreign aid. In Part 4 our analysis is firmly within the monetary theory of international trade as we investigate the balance of payments, both as an accounting framework and as a theoretical framework upon which to base policies. We look at both the traditional approach to payments policies in Chapter 12, and at more recent contributions, including the monetarist and structuralist approaches to the balance of payments, in Chapter 13. We then complete this part of the book with a discussion of the foreign exchange market, including the perennial issue of fixed versus flexible exchange rates. Finally, in Part 5, we analyse the international monetary system, beginning with a general discussion of the role of money in the international context, followed by a history of the international monetary system since 1870, including the evolution of relations between the North and South and the proposals for a new international economic order.

FURTHER READING

Some early reflections on the methodology of international economics can be found in Viner (1937, pp. 594–601) and Caves (1960, Ch. 1). For a good summary of the conventional view of economics as a social science, see Friedman (1953) and Lipsey (1983, introduction). A critique of this view from a radical perspective can be found in Green and Nore (1977). Some examples of the attempt to integrate trade theory with models of domestic activity can also be found in Lipsey (1983), and a collection of views on the current state of international economics is contained in Ohlin *et al.* (1977).

PART 1

The Theory of International Trade

2 The Theory of Comparative Advantage

In this first part of the book we concentrate our attention on the pure theory of international trade using the theory of relative prices developed in microeconomics, although we shall refer to insights from the monetary theory of international trade, especially in Chapter 4.

In particular, we shall address ourselves to two questions. The first is a positive question about why international trade occurs, namely, what explains the pattern of international trade? This will lead us on to a discussion of the gains from trade, i.e. the advantages from engaging in trading relations with other countries. Since the interpretation of these gains (or losses) involves opinions about the desirability of trade, we shall need to go beyond positive theory to consider a normative question: how *should* a country conduct its trading relations?

In this chapter we analyse these questions by looking at some early theories of trade including the Ricardian theory of comparative advantage. In Chapter 3 we show how this simple principle has been extended by later theories. Finally, in Chapter 4 we reconsider these questions explicitly in terms of the developing countries.

2.1 MERCANTILISM

The growth in international trade and the rise of a powerful merchant class in Europe led to the emergence of a body of thought between the middle of the sixteenth century and the late seventeenth century which was primarily concerned with the relationship between a country's wealth, identified by its stock of precious metals, and its balance of trade.[1] This doctrine, known as mercantilism, represents one of the earliest justifications for

9

international trade.

Although mercantilism involved more than just a discussion of the role of trade, it was primarily an interventionist philosophy advocating government regulations to achieve a surplus on the balance of trade in order to accumulate precious metals. This was seen as a means of increasing national wealth and prestige. As a result, the mercantilists saw no virtue in a large volume of trade *per se* and recommended policies to maximise exports and minimise imports. In order to achieve this, tariffs and other import restrictions were enforced, while exports were subsidised. In addition, bullion exports were controlled and navigation laws ensured that, if possible, goods were transported in ships owned or manned by the home country.

An inherent inconsistency in mercantilist thinking was pointed out by the classical economist David Hume as long ago as 1752.[2] Hume based his explanation in terms of a simple quantity theory of money and the free mobility of gold between countries operating under fixed exchange rates.[3] If England had a surplus on the balance of trade with France, i.e. its merchandise exports exceeded the value of its merchandise imports, the resulting inflow of gold would swell the domestic money supply, and in accordance with the quantity theory, generate inflation in the domestic price level. In France, however, the outflow of gold would have the reverse effect. This change in relative prices between England and France would encourage the French to buy less English goods and the English to buy more French goods, thus leading to a deterioration in the English balance of trade and an improvement in that of the French until England's surplus advantage was eliminated. Hence, in the long run, no country could sustain a surplus on the balance of trade and so accumulate gold and other precious metals as the mercantilists had envisaged. We shall return to this 'price specie flow' model in Chapter 13 when we look at the monetarist approach to the balance of payments, and again in Chapter 16 as a description of the gold standard, a fixed exchange rate system which operated roughly between 1870 and 1914, and in a modified form after the first world war.

Hume's demonstration of the futility of mercantilism is based upon a crude model and it would be insufficient on its own to explain balance of payments adjustments between countries, yet it retains enough general validity to remain a persuasive critique of the mercantilist viewpoint. Mercantilism is not an entirely absurd doctrine and it still thrives in a more refined form in modern thinking, yet it misses the whole point of trade and fails to recognise that policies to restrict imports and encourage exports are only valid in certain circumstances. For example, countries often restrict imports to protect strategic industries or to enable them to finance a foreign war, but the wholesale adoption of trade restrictions is unlikely to benefit the country in the long run, and will certainly be detrimental to the world as a whole. We shall consider the case for protection in more depth in Chapter 5.

Mercantilism as a trade strategy is essentially self-defeating, not least because it is impossible for all countries simultaneously to achieve surpluses on the balance of trade. It only makes sense to pursue it if one believes that trade is a zero sum game, i.e. what one country gains another country necessarily loses. It was Adam Smith and David Ricardo who showed the shortsightedness of this approach and the potential for trade to benefit all countries at the same time, even if some countries benefited more than others. It is to these views that we now turn our attention.

2.2 ABSOLUTE ADVANTAGE

The classical economist Adam Smith wrote a famous book in 1776 in which he established a basis for trade between countries as an extension of the principle of specialisation and division of labour between individuals or households.[4] According to this principle, if one country could produce a good cheaper than a second country, and if the second country could produce a different good more cheaply than the first, then it would be to the advantage of both countries to specialise on the good which they could produce cheaper, and trade.

This principle, which has become known as absolute advantage to distinguish it from comparative advantage (which we shall discuss in section 2.3), represents a fundamental attack on the mercantilist idea that trade is a zero sum game:

It is the maxim of every prudent master of a family, never to attempt to make at home what it will cost him more to make than to buy. The tailor does not attempt to make his own shoes, but buys them from the shoemaker . . . . What is prudence in the conduct of every private family can scarce be folly in that of a great kingdom.[5]

Since both the tailor and the shoemaker gain from specialisation and exchange then, by analogy, countries can also gain by specialisation and trade. According to Smith, the whole point of trade is not to export for its own sake but to be able to import goods and increase consumption possibilities. Self-sufficiency reduces specialisation and division of labour and therefore reduces the wealth of nations.

To explain why this is the case, imagine there are two countries, England Portugal, two goods, cloth and wine, labour is the only factor of production, and labour is mobile domestically but cannot move between countries. The data in Table 2.1 show the production possibilities for the two countries prior to international trade. The maximum England can produce of cloth per unit of labour is 30 units if all of its labour force is engaged in cloth production. If, however, England transferred its labour into wine production, then 15 units could be produced per unit of labour. The maximum outputs for Portugal are 5 and 50, respectively.

Table 2.1: Absolute advantage in England and Portugal

	Output per unit of labour	
	Cloth	Wine
England	30	15
Portugal	5	50

Clearly, England has an absolute advantage in the production of cloth, i.e. it can produce more per unit of labour than Portugal, while Portugal, on the other hand, has an absolute advantage in wine production. Absolute advantage in this sense means more output for the *same* resources.

The *positive* implication of this theory is that countries will tend to export goods for which they have an absolute advantage and import those for which they have an absolute disadvantage. Hence England will specialise on cloth exports to Portugal in exchange for imports of wine. The *normative* implication of Smith's theory is that countries *should* specialise on goods for which they have an absolute advantage and engage in free trade, i.e. exchange goods in international markets which are as free as possible from restrictions on competition.[6]

Although it is ultimately a matter of opinion as to whether free trade is a desirable policy, we can use the data in Table 2.1 to show how both England and Portugal could benefit from trade.

Consider the case where both countries agree to swap cloth and wine on a one-to-one basis, so 1 unit of cloth exchanges for 1 unit of wine. If England swaps 30 units of cloth for 30 units of wine she gains 15 units of wine over and above what she could get by giving up 30 units of cloth and transferring the labour into domestic wine production instead. Portugal, on the other hand, obtains 25 more units of cloth through trade, i.e. 30 from England minus the 5 it could produce instead at home.

Hence, both countries obtain more of the other commodity through trade than they could get by remaining closed economies. Furthermore, the total production of cloth and wine is higher with trade and specialisation. To show this, assume that we transfer 1 unit of labour from wine to cloth production in England, and 1 unit from cloth into wine in Portugal. The increase in the outputs of the two goods are shown in Table 2.2

Table 2.2: Increased world output with absolute advantage

	Change in output	
	Cloth	Wine
England	+30	−15
Portugal	− 5	+50
Total	+25	+35

2.3 COMPARATIVE ADVANTAGE

The principle of absolute advantage suffers from the drawback that it only applies when both countries have an absolute advantage in one commodity. But what if one country can produce both commodities absolutely cheaper than another? The USA, for example, can produce many goods cheaper than most other countries. It was Ricardo in 1817 who showed that there might still be a basis for trade as long as each country had a *comparative* advantage, i.e. its advantage is greater in one commodity than in the other.[7]

Ricardo's theory of comparative advantage states that a country will (or should?) export a good for which it has a comparative advantage (where its relative cost of production is lower) and import a good for which it has a comparative disadvantage. Trade will be mutually advantageous as long as there are differences in *relative* cost ratios between countries.

As with absolute advantage there is both a positive and a normative side to the theory and it has never been entirely clear which was uppermost in Ricardo's mind, i.e. whether he was presenting a positive explanation of the pattern of trade in terms of differences in comparative costs, or advocating free trade.[8] In this chapter we shall confine ourselves to a simple exposition of Ricardo's principle and defer until Chapter 3 a fuller treatment of the positive and normative implications of specialisation according to comparative advantage.

The data in Table 2.3 show the maximum outputs of cloth and wine per unit of labour in England and Portugal prior to trade.[9] Note that England has an absolute advantage (can produce more of both goods per unit of labour) in the production of both goods. However, if we look at *relative* efficiency, the theory of comparative advantage predicts that England will export cloth to Portugal in exchange for wine. This is because England can produce cloth 600 per cent as efficiently as Portugal (i.e. $30/5 \times 100$) but is only 150 per cent as efficient at producing wine ($15/10 \times 100$). Hence England has a *comparative* advantage in the production of cloth. Portugal, on the other hand, is *relatively* more efficient at producing wine.[10]

Table 2.3: Comparative advantage in England and Portugal

	Output per unit of labour	
	Cloth	Wine
England	30	15
Portugal	5	10

We can now show, as in the case of absolute advantage, how trade can be mutually advantageous if both countries specialise and export the good for which they have a comparative advantage.

Assume that before trade each country possesses 6 units of labour and uses 3 in each activity. World output and consumption of cloth (105) and wine (75) are shown in Table 2.4. In the absence of trade, both countries must consume what they produce. Now if England specialises on cloth and moves 1 unit of labour from wine to cloth production, and Portugal moves all its labour from cloth to wine, the new production and consumption possibilities are shown in Table 2.4. World production and consumption of cloth (120) and wine (90) are higher as a result of specialisation.

Table 2.4: Trade and specialisation between England and Portugal

	Cloth	Wine	Total consumption
Prior to specialisation and trade			
England	90 (3 × 30)	45 (3 × 15)	135
Portugal	15 (3 × 5)	30 (3 × 10)	45
Total production	105	75	180
After specialisation			
England	120 (4 × 30)	30 (2 × 15)	150
Portugal	—	60 (6 × 10)	60
Total production	120	90	210
After specialisation and trade			
England	(90) 120 − 20 = 100	(45) 30 + 20 = 50	
Portugal	(15) 0 + 20 = 20	(30) 60 − 20 = 40	

Not only is world output higher, but both countries can benefit from trade. If England and Portugal swap wine and cloth on a one-to-one basis, with both countries choosing to exchange 20 units of their export for 20 units of the import, Table 2.4 also indicates that both countries are able to consume more of both commodities after specialisation and trade than in their absence. (The figures prior to trade are reproduced in brackets for comparison.)

This is only one of a number of possible trades, but in general, trade and specialisation will be mutually advantageous as long as there exists a comparative cost difference between the two countries, i.e. the ratio of 30/5 in Table 2.3 does not equal 15/10. It is important to note that there is no basis for trade if these ratios are the same since the 'deal' a country could get in the international market would be no better than it could get in the domestic market. Also, we have used our example to show the benefits of trade for both countries by allowing England to continue to produce some of *both* commodities while Portugal specialises completely on wine. In fact, Ricardo's model would suggest that both countries will specialise entirely on the good for which they have a comparative advantage. We shall raise this question again in Chapter 3.

To conclude this chapter it is important to emphasise the simplicity of Ricardo's exposition of comparative advantage as opposed to its more thorough treatment in modern economic theory. The following represent the most important limitations of Ricardo's model:

1. The model is static and assumes given resources.
2. There are only two countries, two goods, and one factor of production—labour.[11]
3. Labour is mobile nationally but not internationally.
4. Costs per unit of output are constant, i.e. specialisation by England or Portugal has no effect on costs per unit and, therefore, on output per unit of input (efficiency).
5. Transport costs between countries are zero.
6. Trade is determined by supply (cost) factors and demand (consumption) has no apparent role.
7. The mechanism whereby the relative prices at which countries exchange exports and imports (the terms of trade) is determined is not explained; we simply assumed arbitrarily that England and Portugal exchanged on a one-to-one basis and directly bartered cloth for wine.[12]
8. The effects of trade on income distribution are ignored.
9. Comparative advantage determines trade, as dictated by relative labour costs, but there is no explanation for these differing costs.

We shall relax many of these assumptions in the next chapter.

NOTES

1. The terms balance of trade and balance of payments were used synonymously here, although they are not the same. See Chapter 11.1
2. See Hume (1969).

3. In its extreme form, the quantity theory postulates that a change in the money supply will lead to an equiproportional change in the general price level when the economy is fully employed and the velocity of circulation of money is fixed.
4. See Smith (1937).
5. Smith (1937, pp. 424–5).
6. Although Smith is often presented as the champion of free trade, he was not always in favour of it. For example, he advocated a gradual movement towards free trade to mitigate any effects on workers currently benefiting from protected industries; and he considered the Navigation Acts in England as justifiable restrictions on trade for purposes of national defence.
7. See Ricardo (1963). Other writers before Ricardo had realised the principle of comparative advantage, but he was the first to provide a systematic explanation of it. See Viner (1937).
8. Bhagwati (1964) suggests that he viewed it primarily as a normative theory.
9. We have used output per unit of labour (efficiency) rather than labour costs to facilitate the extension of Ricardo's work in Chapter 3. Ricardo himself, however, compared the ratio of the labour costs of production of cloth in England and Portugal with the ratio of the costs of wine. Because these two ratios were different, each country had a comparative advantage in one of the goods.
10. $10/15 \times 100 = 67$ per cent in wine, which exceeds $5/30 \times 100 = 17$ per cent in cloth.
11. When Ricardo was writing, the labour theory of value was popular. This theory has many variations but it essentially argues that the value of output is proportional to the amount of labour or labour time involved in its production. Ricardo did not believe that labour represented the only cost of production but he chose to ignore the others for simplicity.
12. Although most discussions of Ricardo invoke this barter situation, Ricardo himself did consider the role of national money. It turns out that the addition of money costs does not invalidate the idea of comparative advantage. We shall return to this point in Chapter 3.1.

FURTHER READING

A mercantilist view of trade can be found in Newman *et al.* (1954). For Smith and Ricardo's work, see Smith (1937) and Ricardo (1963). An excellent exposition of the classical theory of comparative advantage is available in Harberler (1936) and Viner (1937). For a survey of early trade theory, see Ellsworth and Leith (1975).

3 The Modern Theory of International Trade

3.1 COMPARATIVE ADVANTAGE

In this chapter we show how Ricardo's simple principle has been absorbed into the more general neoclassical pure theory of international trade. It turns out that many of the restrictive assumptions listed in section 2.3 above can be relaxed to give a more complete explanation of the pattern of trade and yet the basic idea behind comparative advantage is retained intact. In addition, we can use modern welfare theory to provide us with a more precise appraisal of the normative implications of specialisation according to comparative advantage.

Although the neoclassical generalisation of comparative advantage presents a useful starting point for studying international trade, it is by no means a complete explanation, and in section 3.3 we explore post-Ricardian contributions to trade theory, including the well-known Heckscher–Ohlin model. In most cases these theories do not contradict Ricardo's principle, but offer a more detailed explanation of the factors which lie behind it, or extend it into new areas. We shall defer until Chapter 4 a discussion of theories which have been presented more specifically for developing countries.

We begin by returning to our England–Portugal example from Chapter 2. The pre-trade production possibilities for cloth and wine are reproduced in Table 3.1. Note that the data now refer to the maximum outputs of the two commodities given *all* available resources, including land, labour, capital and the current level of technology; and not just to labour input. This is the first generalisation of Ricardo's model.

A second generalisation invokes the concept of opportunity costs to explain comparative advantage, rather than the ratios of labour productivity used in Chapter 2. This concept is fundamental

Table 3.1: Production possibilities for England and Portugal

	Maximum output per unit of resources	
	Cloth	Wine
England	30	15
Portugal	5	10

to economic theory and involves the valuation of economic activities in terms of the opportunities forgone.[1] In our case the value of cloth is defined in terms of the wine production forgone in order to produce 1 unit of cloth. Since the production of 30 units of cloth in England requires the giving up of 15 units of wine, the opportunity cost of cloth in terms of wine is 0.5. In Portugal it is 2 units of wine (i.e. 10/5). Hence, since the opportunity cost of cloth in England is lower than in Portugal, England has a comparative advantage in cloth and exports it to Portugal, as Ricardo supposed.

The production possibilities for England are shown in Figure 3.1. If all resources are put into cloth production, a maximum of 30 units can be produced. If, however, they are put into wine instead, 15 units can be produced. The line between these two maximum points shows the efficient combinations of cloth and wine that can just be produced with given resources and technology, and is known as the production possibility frontier (PPF). A point within the line, such as x, is not efficient in the sense that resources are lying idle or are not being combined in the most efficient way. A point beyond the frontier, such as y, is not attainable.

We can now use this PPF to explain how trade between England and Portugal can be mutually advantageous. Prior to trade, England can choose any point on the solid frontier in Figure 3.2 and remain efficient. Assume combination **P** is selected. Since England is closed to trade, **P** also represents its consumption possibilities. If England now engages in trade and specialises in cloth, it will move to **P***.[2] If the PPF somehow represents the domestic trade-off between cloth and wine for England, we need to represent the deal which it can obtain in the international market by trading with Portugal. Let this be represented by the dotted international terms of trade line in Figure 3.2. This implies, as in Chapter 2, that wine and cloth are exchanged on a one-for-one basis, i.e. 30 units of cloth exchange internationally

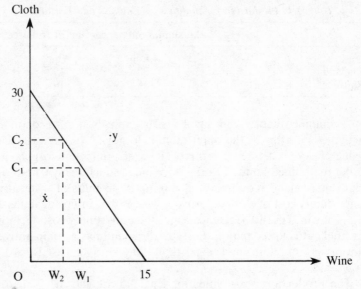

Figure 3.1: The production possibility frontier for England

for 30 units of wine.

The advantage of trade for England is now clear. Although it is specialising exclusively on cloth, its consumption possibilities are no longer constrained to coincide with P^* but are given by the international terms of trade line. It is possible, therefore, for England to choose a point such as C^* which contains more of both commodities than at **P**. As long as the international terms of trade fall between the two pre-trade opportunity cost ratios of 0.5 and 2, both countries can benefit from trade by increasing their consumption possibilities. If another point such as D were chosen, containing more of one commodity but less of the other compared with **P**, trade may still be justified if compensation is possible. We shall return to this case in section 3.2 below.

Figure 3.2 can also be used to explain the pattern of England's trade. If it is producing OP^* of cloth but only consuming OA^*, then P^*A^* must be exported to Portugal. Similarly, if England is not producing any wine itself but is consuming A^*C^*, then it must be importing A^*C^* from Portugal. The same analysis could be applied to Portugal using Portugal's PPF. Clearly, in this simple

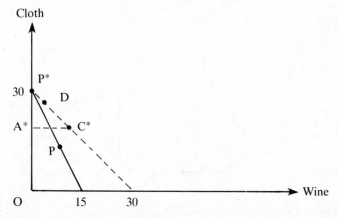

Figure 3.2: The pattern of trade for England

bilateral case, England's exports would be Portugal's imports, and vice versa.

The next step is to show how this simple reinterpretation of Ricardo's principle can be further generalised to give a more complete explanation of the pattern of trade within the Ricardian tradition.

The first assumption to releax refers to the shape of the PPF. In Ricardo's presentation, costs were assumed constant over the entire range of output, and this is indicated in Figure 3.1 by a straight line PPF. This implies that as England specialises on cloth production C_1, C_2, the amount of wine forgone W_1, W_2, always remains in the same proportion for *equal* increments of cloth up the vertical axis no matter how many units of cloth England produces.

Figure 3.3 shows how the shape of the frontier will vary with decreasing opportunity costs (a) and increasing opportunity costs (b). Repeating the experiment carried out earlier and moving up the cloth axis, the amount of wine given up for each successive unit of cloth gets smaller and smaller in the case of decreasing costs and larger and larger in the case of increasing costs.

The former could arise in the early stages of specialisation from the benefits of large-scale production, while the latter might reflect diminishing returns to scale as more and more resources are transferred out of wine and into cloth production. Non-constant opportunity costs could simply reflect the fact that a given factor is

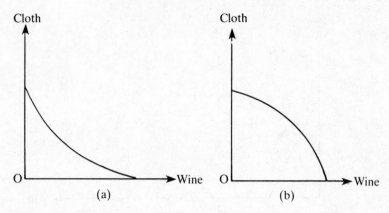

Figure 3.3: Two cases of non-constant opportunity costs

not equally efficient in cloth and wine production. In general a country's PPF is derived from information on total factor availabilities and on the production functions which relate factor inputs to output in various industries. A detailed discussion of the factors which determine the shape of the frontier is beyond the scope of this book and we shall follow the convention of assuming (b) to be the more general case. This is likely to occur quite often even if returns to scale are constant as long as different goods require factor inputs in significantly different proportions. For example, imagine that wine uses relatively more land and less labour than cloth and resources are being transferred from cloth production into wine. Since resources are being used in different proportions in the two industries the clothing industry will release a lot of labour and not much land compared to the proportions required in wine production. Hence to absorb these inputs the wine industry must shift towards more labour-intensive methods of production and the effect of the resource transfer is similar to that experienced with diminishing returns in so far as the addition of labour to the relatively fixed factor – land – raises costs in the wine industry.

The important conclusion which follows from this is that specialisation need not be complete in England and Portugal, and both may continue to produce some of both commodities. This is because the further advantages from specialisation are lost before specialisation is complete as opportunity costs begin to rise.

So far we have concentrated, as Ricardo did, on the supply side of international trade and arbitrarily chosen C* as the consumption point. We can, however, represent the community's preferences between cloth and wine by community indifference curves, as depicted in Figure 3.4. A community indifference curve shows combinations of the two commodities between which the community is indifferent, i.e. they find equally desirable. For example, at point x consumers choose OC_0 of cloth and OW_0 of wine. A point such as y would give equal satisfaction, but consumers are content subjectively to trade off less cloth (C_0–C_1) for some more wine (W_1–W_0). An important property of these curves is that a curve to the right-hand side of another, such as I_2, represents combinations the community would choose if possible. For example, z on I_2 in Figure 3.4 would represent a higher level of welfare than y on I_1 even though it involves less wine and more cloth. However, whilst one might be confident in interpreting the move from y to z as a welfare improvement in the context of an individual consumer's indifference map, it is much more difficult to do so when the curves represent the community's preferences. This is because it involves the explicit comparison of the welfare levels of different consumers, but who can say that the community is better-off at z compared to y if some consumers are better-off and others are worse-off. One way round this is to assume that the tastes of the community are identical to the tastes of an individual, that they do not change over time, and that income distribution remains constant. These assumptions are clearly unrealistic but community

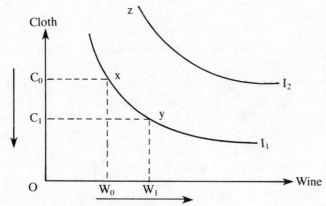

Figure 3.4: Community indifference curves

indifference curves turn out to be very useful, as we shall see, for illustrating the demand side of the economy. They should not, however, be taken literally.[3]

We are now in a position to reformulate Ricardo's principle in terms of the neoclassical pure theory of trade. Figure 3.5 incorporates both the supply and demand sides of the economy using the PPF (exhibiting increasing opportunity costs) to represent the supply side, and community indifference curves to represent demand.

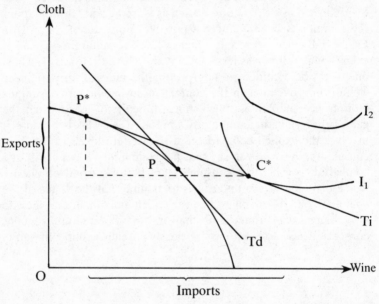

Figure 3.5: Supply and demand in international trade for England

Prior to trade, England is producing at P, where the domestic terms of trade line Td (representing the relative prices of the two goods domestically) cuts the PPF. At this point the allocation of resources is in equilibrium with the relative costs of production. When the economy is opened up to trade at the international terms of trade Ti (representing international prices), production is reorganised to P* where Ti cuts the PPF. In other words, at the new set of international prices, production is rearranged so that England specialises on cloth, although this specialisation is not complete. It continues until the opportunity cost of cloth production rises to meet the international relative price of cloth.

As far as consumption is concerned, this is given by C* where the highest community indifference curve cuts the Ti line indicating the consumption possibilities available with trade. To bring the production of cloth and wine at P* into balance with consumption at C*, trade occurs given by the pattern of exports and imports shown in figure 3.5. The same analysis could be applied to Portugal using its PPF and community indifference map.

Thus, given different pre-trade opportunity cost ratios between England and Portugal reflected in the shapes of their respective PPFs, and increasing opportunity costs, the two countries produce and consume at a point (P in the English case) where the domestic relative prices of the two goods equate to marginal opportunity costs. This follows from the assumptions of perfect competition, otherwise there would be an incentive for producers to switch from one commodity to another to take advantage of the higher price. With trade, however, and a new set of international prices, England and Portugal specialise on the good for which they have a comparative advantage (moving to P*) up to the point at which Ti cuts the PPF. Then given consumption preferences in the two countries, the pattern of trade is defined as the difference between domestic production of the good and consumption preferences. The pattern of trade is therefore determined by *both* production costs and demand. As long as Ti falls between the limits set by the pre-trade opportunity cost ratios, trade is mutually advantageous, but specialisation need not be complete if costs are non-constant.

Although this represents the basic neoclassical treatment of comparative advantage, there are many other ways in which it has been extended. To begin with, both domestic and international relative prices might be explained by applying the theory of competitive markets rather than assuming, as we did, that these prices are arranged arbitrarily. Similarly, although we have assumed two countries and two commodities, the model can be generalised to cover many countries, many goods and many factors of production.

The basic idea of comparative advantage is also not lost if *money* costs are introduced rather than relative costs. It is still possible to construct a list of commodities for which a country has a comparative advantage, but the role of money costs is to determine where in the chain the link is broken, i.e. the number of goods which a country will actually export. For example, at a given wage rate England may export five goods to Portugal, with the fifth good being the least efficient. If the wage ratē in England now rises it may lose comparative advantage in the fifth good and will import it instead.

Similarly, if the value of the English currency rises (equivalent to a devaluation in Portugal) the effect is the same as for the rise in money wages. It will cost foreigners more to purchase English exports and thus makes them less competitive. In Appendix 3.1 we show in more detail how the Ricardian model can be generalised to include many commodities and the effects of changes in money wages and exchange rates. In general, the higher the money wage rate and the value of the country's currency, the more goods will be imported rather than exported, but the *particular* goods involved will still be defined by comparative advantage in production.

Finally there are questions relating to uncertainty and resource immobility. So far we have assumed that all the relevant information is available to ensure the equilibrium pattern of trade is obtained and factors of production are perfectly mobile domestically. In practice, however, decisions are made under varying degrees of uncertainty and resources can be highly immobile. We shall discuss cases of factor immobility in Chapter 4 when we investigate the relationship between trade and development and again in Chapter 5 in connection with protection. As far as uncertainty is concerned, this is a difficult area but in recent years much of economic theory, including that pertaining to international trade, has been rewritten using the tools of uncertainty analysis. For further details on this, see Batra (1975) and Helpman and Razin (1978).

3.2 THE GAINS FROM TRADE REVISITED

We turn our attention in this section to the modern neoclassical interpretation of the gains from trade. These are illustrated in Figure 3.5. The *static gains* are obtained by comparing the position before trade with the position after trade has taken place. The

static *production* gain is represented by the move from P to P*
reflecting the improved efficiency due to specialisation. The static
consumption gain is implicit in the ability of English consumers to
reach a higher community indifference curve than at P by
consuming at new international prices.[4] Hence, the static gains
from trade refer to the increased real income or consumption
implicit in the ability to reach a higher indifference curve and
potentially consume more of both cloth and wine compared with a
closed economy.

These gains are static in so far as the economy is on the PPF
given *fixed* endowments and known technology. If, however, we
were to move beyond the static framework of traditional comparative cost theory, it becomes immediately apparent that the
opening-up of the economy to trade is likely to generate *dynamic
gains* resulting from a shifting-out of the PPF and an increase in
the quality and quantity of the country's factors of production. In
Figure 3.6 these dynamic gains enable the country to produce
more of both commodites, but the growth-induced effects of trade
could be biased towards either commodity, in which case the PPF
would shift out more in the direction of one commodity than the
other.

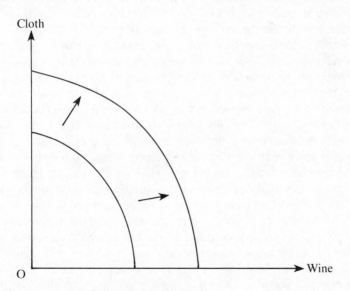

Figure 3.6: The dynamic gains from trade

Dynamic gains could arise from a number of factors. For example, there might be economies from large-scale production as trade expands the size of the market, or trade might make available better technology or increased supplies of capital and labour from abroad. It is even possible that the sudden opening-up of the economy to foreign competition might stimulate increased efficiency, or the demonstration of foreign consumer goods encourage people to work harder to be able to afford them, according to the so-called 'international demonstration effect'. Trade in this sense is acting as an 'engine of growth'; but these dynamic effects could be quite small in practice or unevenly distributed between countries, and they might even be negative in their impact. We shall return to this subject in the next chapter.

Although we have shown that there *may* be gains from trade, it by no means follows that free trade is the most desirable state of affairs, and modern welfare economics has done much to clarify the sense in which countries and individuals may be better-off with trade.[5] Using the neoclassical tools of the PPF and community indifference curves we have shown that it is possible for a country to increase its consumption possibilities by engaging in trade, but in order to evaluate these gains from trade we need to assess their effects on income distribution. This need arises because trade is bound to change the welfare positions of most individuals and for some the effects may be negative. For example, if cloth production is relatively labour-intensive in England and trade encourages a movement along the PPF in the direction of cloth, then according to the Stolper—Samuelson theorem, this will tend to benefit labour at the expense of other factor-owners. We shall discuss the reasoning behind this conclusion when we look at the effects of trade on factor-owners in more detail in Chapter 8, but if trade makes some people better-off and others worse-off, in what sense can the welfare of the country as a whole be said to have increased as a result of trade? To answer this question we need to consider some propositions from modern welfare economics.

To begin with, if neoclassical assumptions about the economy apply and all countries engage in free trade, then it can be shown that the world as a whole is most efficient in the sense of reaching a point on the world PPF. Free trade is better than no trade or restricted trade in so far as it is *possible* to choose a position on the frontier such that all individuals are better-off and it would be impossible to make one individual any better-off without making someone else worse-off. The world as a whole is said to be 'Pareto-optimal'.

However, having said this, not all individuals must necessarily be better-off with free trade and there is nothing in the analysis to suggest that all countries will gain equally. Governments may wish, therefore, to violate the principle of free trade in order to change the distribution of the gains from trade, either within a particular country, or between countries.

An alternative way of thinking about the welfare implications of trade was put forward by Kaldor (1939) and Hicks (1939) and is known as the compensation criterion. According to this, trade would have increased the welfare of the country as a whole even if some people lost, as long as it were *possible* for the gainers to fully compensate the losers and still be better-off themselves. Whether compensation should in fact be paid is a matter of ethical judgment, but one could say that trade had at least increased *potential* welfare.

It is not possible, therefore, to evaluate the gains from trade without specifying the criteria upon which the gains are to be assessed. The Pareto and Kaldor-Hicks criteria are only representative of a number of such criteria which are discussed in welfare economics in order to judge the implications for the welfare of a community of a change in circumstances, such as when a country is opened up to trade, but for our purposes it is perhaps enough to say that trade can improve *potential* welfare. If, however, neoclassical assumptions about the economy are violated, for example when markets are imperfectly competitive, then it is *also* no longer possible to conclude that free trade is better than no trade, or that free trade is always superior to restricted trade, such as when a county imposes tariffs on imports. We shall need to examine the implications of relaxing these assumptions when we discuss the theory of protection in Chapter 5.

3.3 POST-RICARDIAN TRADE THEORY

In the Ricardian world, the pattern of trade is determined by international differences in the relative productivity of different industries within countries. Neoclassical theory treats this as a special case and generalises to differences in opportunity costs as the basis of comparative advantage, allows for more countries, more factors of production, more goods, and for the effects of demand on trade as well as supply.

Post-Ricardian trade theory takes comparative advantage as the starting point and investigates all those factors which determine differences in comparative costs other than productivity. These differences are then viewed as emanating either from endowments of factors of production or primary inputs, or from the nature of production functions relating inputs to outputs. We have already referred to the influence of consumer tastes and economies of scale on comparative advantage, so we concentrate here on the effects of factor endowments as represented in the so-called Heckscher–Ohlin theory of trade, and a number of factors which have been put forward in more recent years to account for trade in modern sophisticated consumer goods. Under this latter heading we shall look at the availability, technological gap and product-cycle models, and the theory of representative demand.

One of the most important explanations for comparative advantage was put forward by Eli Heckscher (1919) and reinforced by Bertil Ohlin (1933). The Heckscher–Ohlin theory argues that comparative advantage arises from the different relative factor endowments of the countries trading. Consequently, a country will export those commodities which are relatively intensive in their most abundant factor.

For example, if wheat farming is relatively intensive in land (uses relatively more land in its production) compared with cloth production, which is relatively labour-intensive, and the USA is relatively land-abundant compared to India, which is labour-abundant, then the Heckscher–Ohlin theory predicts that the USA will export wheat to India in exchange for cloth.

The common-sense reasoning is that one might expect land to be relatively cheap in the USA, giving it a comparative advantage in the land-intensive commodity, while India would have a comparative advantage in cloth. Note that it is *relative* not absolute endowments which are important: one country may well have larger absolute amounts of land and labour than another country, but be *relatively* abundant in one of them. Similarly, there is a distinction between relative abundance and cheapness. The price of a factor depends upon demand as well as supply, and if the influence of demand outweighs that of supply, then a country apparently well endowed with land might find that its price is high compared to labour (if the demand for land-based products is high), so that it exports labour and not land-intensive goods.

The crucial difference, therefore, between this theory and that of Ricardo is its stress on factor endowments as the determinant of comparative advantage rather than on differences in productivity. Given any product with a particular factor intensity requirement, for Ricardo, differences in labour productivity between countries determines comparative advantage. For Heckscher–Ohlin, however, labour is equally efficient in both countries, but comparative advantage is still defined if one country is relatively abundant in the factor used most intensively in that commodity.

A number of economists have expressed dissatisfaction with the Ricardian and Heckscher–Ohlin theories of trade, especially with regard to manufactured goods. Kravis (1965) emphasises the availability of scarce natural resources, including specialised knowledge, as a determinant of the pattern of trade. This might help to explain why Kuwait exports oil, the Soviet Union exports diamonds and Scotland exports whisky. Comparative advantage is irrelevant if the country is only able to produce certain goods with these specialised inputs. In this sense a country produces and exports what it has available.

The importance of the availability of specialised knowledge of technology is also stressed in the technological-gap and product-cycle approaches. The former suggests that trade may occur simply as a result of technical progress taking place in country A rather than in country B, since the innovator can take advantage of its early start to gain economies of scale and the benefits of 'learning by doing'. Hence, a comparative advantage exists until foreign producers succeed in eliminating the gap through imitation. This process is particularly prevalent in areas such as synthetic materials and electronics, which are research-intensive. For more details on the technological-gap concept, see Posner (1961).

Product-cycle theory builds upon this innovation–imitation process by describing the cycle in the life of a new product. Innovation takes place in one country and, assuming it cannot be easily imitated by competitors, production is initially confined to the home market. This is because the market for this product is likely to be quite small in the first instance and small-scale production will be more appropriate. Once the product has become established the country enjoys a comparative advantage and exports it. However, imitation occurs in the industrial economies as the production technology becomes standardised, and the first country may even become a net importer of the good. Ultimately the rest of the world catches up, and comparative advantage is dictated by other factors, including resource endowments.

Hence, unless the first country has a continuing comparative cost advantage in this product, production shifts elsewhere as the product matures. However, unlike in the technological-gap theory, a country can maintain its lead in new products by engaging in research and development. An example of this process might be where the USA carries out the original innovation, but the product is ultimately developed in another country, such as Japan, where there is a relative abundance of unskilled labour. So as the product goes through the cycle of being intensive in research and development and skilled labour to being intensive in capital and unskilled labour, its main production location shifts. Examples of relevant products might be computers, electronics and automobiles. For a good example of this approach, see Vernon (1966).

Finally, there is the question of demand patterns. It is a fact of modern life that most trade in manufactures takes place between countries whose factor endowments and technologies are *similar* and not, as the Ricardian and Heckscher–Ohlin models might suggest, different. The importance of similarity in demand patterns was pointed out by Linder (1961). Linder's representative demand hypothesis suggests that a country will only successfully export a sophisticated manufactured good if it has a buoyant domestic market to provide the jump-off to make it competitive, i.e. can take advantage of economies of large-scale production, and if it exports to an economy displaying similar tastes and income levels. In this sense, England is more likely to export television sets to Germany than to Sri Lanka. In addition, unlike in the case of primary goods where production would tend to be closely related to factor endowments, the most important determinant of the pattern of trade in manufactures is the level of income *per capita*. Countries with high incomes do not only consume more

TVs, but higher quality TVs. Hence, according to Linder's approach, each country would tend to produce TVs appropriate to their income levels and *then* would export them to countries with similar income levels once the jump-off had been established.

3.4 EMPIRICAL EVIDENCE

Rather like Pythagoras's Theorem, the comparative cost *theorem* is not really a testable proposition, but one can attempt to test a *theory* which states that actual trade flows are related to comparative costs. A pioneering attempt to do this was carried out by MacDougall (1951) using data for 1937 from the USA and Britain. The hypothesis under test was whether differences in relative labour productivity in the two countries could explain their export shares since, according to comparative advantage, one would expect differences in labour productivity to influence relative costs and thus export prices. MacDougall found that British and American relative export shares in manufactured goods in third markets (i.e. not with each other) were indeed correlated with relative labour costs. Since wage rates were at the time approximately twice as high in the USA as in Britain, the USA should be the major exporter to third markets of products in which its labour productivity was more than twice that of Britian; and Britain should be the major exporter where it was less than twice. This is indeed what he found. The fact that when costs were the *same* in the two countries American exports were only two-thirds those of the British (when they should be equal), was explained by MacDougall in terms of the competitive advantage given to Britain under the system of Commonwealth Preference concluded between Great Britain and her colonial associates in 1932, which involved the lowering of tariff rates on goods which the countries concerned imported from each other.

Stern (1962) repeated MacDougall's analysis with more extensive data and for a later time period (1950), and Balassa (1963) also repeated the analysis for 1950. Both of these studies confirmed MacDougall's findings of a high correlation between labour productivity and export shares.

Although these results provided some support for the theory of comparative advantage, the analysis was still at a relatively high level of aggregation, and when Bhagwati (1964) reworked the data using more sophisticated statistical techniques, he was unable to find any significant relationship between labour costs and relative export prices. This was puzzling given the results of MacDougall, Stern and Balassa. In addition the theory was generally incomplete as an explanation of trade since it took no account of transport costs, protection, imperfect competition and non-traded goods; and it didn't actually explain *why* differences in labour productivity occurred. Attention therefore switched to testing the Heckscher–Ohlin model, which attempted to explain the basis of comparative advantage, and therefore the pattern of trade, in terms of relative endowments of capital and labour.

Leontief (1954) set out to do just this using American data for 1947, but to everyone's surprise, including his own, he found that the USA was exporting labour-intensive goods to the rest of the world in exchange for capital-intensive imports, despite the fact that it was conventional wisdom that the USA was endowed with more capital per worker than any other country. This subsequently became known as 'the Leontief paradox'.

Naturally this stimulated considerable debate and a spate of further empirical studies. Japan—which was generally considered to be labour-abundant—was found to be exporting capital-intensive goods; and India's exports to the USA turned out to be more capital-intensive than her imports, although her exports to the rest of the world were, as expected, labour-intensive. Finally, capital-rich Canada's exports were in general relatively capital-intensive, but her exports to the USA were relatively *more* capital-intensive than her imports from the USA.[6]

Since the Leontief paradox first appeared there has been considerable discussion in international economics as to the validity of the Heckscher–Ohlin model. The conclusion seems to be that, although it is broadly correct in emphasising the role of relative factor endowments in explaining comparative advantage, the interpretation given to factor endowments requires considerable elaboration. In particular, one needs to distinguish between skilled and unskilled labour, to include natural resources in the analysis, and to view specialised technological advances as relative resource endowments in knowledge and skills. Simply using aggregate measures of capital and labour is far too crude.

Once the definition of factor endowments becomes broader,

then the Leontief paradox becomes more explicable. For example, the USA may in fact be relatively abundant in *skilled* labour and in natural resources and research and development, as well as being a relatively capital-rich country. In addition, US tariffs may tend to exclude labour-intensive imports, thus making it *appear* that labour-intensive industries are not especially competitive. Finally, 'factor intensity reversal' may cause the goods which are capital-intensive exports of the USA to compete with labour-intensive production in the importing countries. In other words, the USA exports goods which are labour-intensive in the USA, while it imports goods which are labour-intensive abroad. This conflicts with the original Heckscher–Ohlin assumption that goods are unambiguously capital- or labour-intensive.

Once the Heckscher–Ohlin model is expanded to include specialised technological advances as resource endowments in knowledge and skills, then it also becomes compatible with the evidence supporting those theories emphasising the role of technology and innovation, especially in the area of modern consumer durables. One simply cannot explain the production pattern in developed countries without looking at the origin of the technological gap which gives a country an initial lead in a particular product, and at the way in which this knowledge is gradually diffused to the rest of the world. A good example here is provided by Hufbauer's (1966) study of synthetic materials. As expected, the USA exports a larger share of its production of new products rather than older ones which have become subject to imitation by foreigners.

Similarly, the product-cycle theory has been particularly useful in explaining how changes in the pattern of production and trade occur in goods such as electronics. Here, production tends to originate in a country such as the USA or Japan and spreads (with a lag) to other developed industrial countries, and subsequently to the newly industrialising countries of the Third World, as factor proportions required in production change away from skilled labour and knowledge towards automatic factory processes using relatively more capital and unskilled labour. For further elaboration on this process, see Hirsch (1967).

It is unclear how important Linder's theory of representative demand is in the modern world where large corporations are more foot-loose than they might have been in the past, and less afraid of venturing abroad and altering their products to suit tastes in foreign markets. Similarly, demand patterns have become much more standardised and the local firm no longer has quite the same advantage over its foreign rivals than it might have enjoyed in the past. None the less, the use of the domestic market as the base from which to export to countries with similar demand patterns may still play a role in trading decisions. We shall look more closely at the motivation for setting up production abroad in Chapter 9, when we consider the multinational corporation.

The modern theory of international trade is therefore rich in theoretical insights, but still relatively weak in empirical generalisations outside the case-study framework. Nevertheless, the theory of comparative advantage provides a persuasive general explanation for trade, especially when Ricardo's simple principle is expanded within the neoclassical tradition to include differences in opportunity costs, more factors of production, more goods and countries, and the effects of demand patterns on trade as well as of costs. Modern welfare theory also offers a more qualified explanation of the gains from trade and the normative implications of free trade policies. The Heckscher–Ohlin model goes some way towards explaining the basis of comparative advantage, as long as the definition of factor endowments is broadened to incorporate skilled labour and natural resources as well as simple aggregates of capital and labour; and specific attention is given to goods which embody specialised knowledge and technology. This then makes the Heckscher–Ohlin approach compatible with theories stressing the role of technology and innovation. Comparative advantage, Heckscher–Ohlin and later theories, therefore, tend to merge into one another within the modern theory of international trade.

APPENDIX 3.1

Comparative advantage with many goods, money costs and exchange rates

	A	B	C	D	E	F	G	H	I	J
England	100	100	100	100	100	100	100	100	100	100
Portugal	200	180	160	140	120	100	80	60	40	20

The theory of comparative advantage can be generalised to

incorporate many commodities, money costs, and money exchange rates.

The data above rank goods A–J for England and Portugal in terms of their constant unit labour costs such that England is *relatively* most efficient at producing A (i.e. 100/200), then B (100/180), and so on. If the prices of these goods are taken as equal to their production costs and money wages are £1 per unit in England and $1 per unit in Portugal, and the exchange rate between the two currencies is £1 = $1, then (measuring international prices in terms of £) the prices of the goods will be:

	A	B	C	D	E	F	G	H	I	J
England	£100	£100	£100	£100	£100	£100	£100	£100	£100	£100
Portugal	£200	£180	£160	£140	£120	£100	£ 80	£ 60	£ 40	£ 20

The principle of comparative advantage then implies that England will export Goods A–E, and Portugal will export goods G–J, with F not being traded. The role of money wages is to define money costs and to determine where in the chain of comparative advantage the link is broken. In other words, wage rates determine the number of goods a country will export, but not the ranking itself, which depends on *relative* prices or labour costs.

For example, let the wage rate in England rise to £1.1 so that the price of good F now costs £110. F will now be exported by Portugal to England. Moreover, as wages continue to rise, England will lose its comparative advantage progressively back along the chain to the left-hand side and will import these goods. Thus, once we know the good whose price is the same in both countries—F in this case—we also know the pattern of trade: A–E will be exported by England, and G–J by Portugal.

A rise in the value of the pound in England of 10 per cent is equivalent to a devaluation of the Portuguese currency. In other words, £1.1 now exchanges for $1. The effect is the same as for the rise in money wages in England.

In general, therefore, we can conclude that the higher the money wage rate in England and the higher the value of its currency, the more goods it will import rather than export, but the specific goods concerned will still be determined by the principle of comparative advantage in production.

NOTES

1. The application of this concept to comparative advantage is attributed to Haberler (1936). For some background on this, see Lipsey (1983, ch. 4).
2. Since the pre-trade opportunity cost ratios are different in England and Portugal, each country has a comparative advantage in one of the commodities, and there is a basis for trade. This is shown by the fact that the slopes of the PPFs in the two countries are different. If they were identical, but England's frontier was further away from the origin, England would have an absolute advantage in both goods, but no comparative advantage. Trade would only be profitable in this case if demand patterns were different in the two countries.
3. For a more detailed, but well explained, analysis of community indifference curves, see George and Shorey (1978).
4. Even if the economy stayed at P, there is still the possibility of consumption gains arising from cheaper imports.
5. A good survey of modern welfare theory is available in George and Shorey (1978). The specific welfare implications of trade are raised in Findlay (1970, p. 120).
6. For a recent review of these paradoxes, see Baldwin (1979).

FURTHER READING

A more detailed treatment of the theory described in this chapter, especially for those with a grounding in intermediate microeconomics, can be found in Kindleberger and Lindert (1978) and Caves and Jones (1981). The latter also includes a useful review of the empirical evidence, especially with respect to the more recent theories discussed in this chapter. Findlay (1970) is also a good text for bringing out the links between the various strands of the literature, including the refinements to the basic Ricardian model.

4 International Trade and Economic Development

In this chapter we turn our attention specifically to what are generally known as the less-developed, or developing countries (LDCs) and examine the relationship between international trade and economic development. An important question here which was raised by Gerald Meier (1968, ch. 8) in 1968 is whether there might be a conflict between trade and development, i.e. whether free trade (or more trade) brings LDCs closer to their development targets, or whether development is incompatible with a pattern of resource allocation based upon free trade and comparative advantage.

We begin in section 4.1 by returning to the neoclassical interpretation of comparative advantage and the gains from trade which provided the underpinning for outward-looking, free trade policies in the period following the second world war. We contrast this with views associated with the so-called new trade theorists, who were strongly critical of the neoclassical approach and highly influential in encouraging LDCs to adopt a more protectionist, inward-looking stance in the 1960s and early 1970s. Finally, in section 4.3 we attempt to synthesise these different views on trade and development from the perspective of the 1980s.

4.1 COMPARATIVE ADVANTAGE AND THE DEVELOPING COUNTRIES

The neoclassical synthesis of trade theory after the second world war, in which classical writings on trade were reformulated and extended within the neoclassical general equilibrium framework, including the Heckscher–Ohlin approach, appeared to suggest little conflict between trade and development. As we saw in Chapter 3, trade would achieve domestic production efficiency and was also 'an engine of growth'.[1] Specialisation according to comparative advantage would enable a country to reach the production possibility frontier and maximise both the static and dynamic gains from trade. Trade and development would thus proceed hand-in-hand, and free trade would ensure the highest level of real consumption for each country and for the world as a whole. Moreover, evidence could be adduced from economic history to support the positive role that trade might play in the development process. Countries such as Canada, Australia and the United States had all apparently enjoyed export-led growth in the nineteenth century, and even a relative latecomer such as Japan is said to have benefited from silk exports.[2]

It would be an exaggeration to suggest that neoclassical economists were in favour of absolute free trade as the path to development, but perhaps typical of the advice given to LDCs in the 1950s was that offered by Gottfried Haberler:

my conclusion is that substantially free trade with marginal, insubstantial corrections and deviations, is the best policy from the point of view of economic development.[3]

4.2 THE NEW INTERNATIONAL TRADE THEORISTS

In the late 1950s and early 1960s, many economists had expressed concern about the association of free trade policies with development and with the apparent lack of conflict between trade and development within the neoclassical approach. This protest culminated in a meeting of the United Nations conference on trade and development (UNCTAD) in 1964 and the publishing of a document outlining a 'New Trade Policy for Development'.[4]

The new trade theorists were essentially arguing that the neoclassical model was talking about what ought to be, and not what actually happens. Trade, they suggested, has not been an 'engine of growth' for most LDCs in the twentieth century despite specialisation according to comparative advantage and, moreover, specialisation and free trade could well conflict with other development objectives.[5] A good example of these sentiments can be found in Nurkse (1967), who suggested that although trade in the nineteenth century might have been an engine of growth, it had not been so in the twentieth century, with the exception of the oil-exporting countries. This attack on free trade can be seen as an amalgamation of a number of views on the relationship between trade and development, which we shall discuss in turn.

Economists such as Chenery (1961) attacked the neoclassical approach from within economic theory by suggesting that it was starting from a model which was singularly inappropriate for LDCs. Although dynamic gains were talked about, the mainstay of the free trade approach was a static theory of resource allocation based upon *given* resources and tastes, and a model of perfect competition.[6] The static bias of the model meant that it was more useful in showing where a country had been than in indicating where it might go, and the application of perfect competition was particularly unrealistic since imperfections in markets were a characteristic feature of these economies. The neoclassical model was, according to Chenery, inappropriate for countries involved in a process of rapid structural change and concerned with long-run development.

Another facet of this protest, influenced strongly by the writings of Myrdal (1957) and Singer (1950), emphasised the cumulative 'backwash' effects that trade might bring to a country and the possibility of a widening of the gap between the rich and poor countries of the world. Instead of trade generating dynamic gains or 'spread effects', as the neoclassical model suggested, trade had often in practice exacerbated income disparities between countries and between regions within a country. For example, an enclave export sector, possibly dominated by expatriates, might expand at the expense of traditional agriculture by drawing away scarce skilled labour and other resources, leaving the traditional sector more underdeveloped than before. Similarly, the gains from trade in the form of export earnings could well be lost to the domestic economy through 'leakages' of expatriated profits. The impact of trade on development could, therefore, be highly uneven, with some regions and countries (usually the richer ones) benefiting from trade whilst leaving other regions lagging further behind.

These sentiments are also shared by neo-Marxist 'exploitation' theories stressing the unequal exchange between rich and poor countries associated with the historical experience of colonialism, or the neo-colonial behaviour of multinational corporations in the modern world. Although these radical theories are not homogeneous and there are important differences between them, they stress the dependence of LDCs on trade with developed countries (DCs) and the essentially exploitative nature of this relationship as the 'surplus' is transferred from poor to rich countries.[7]

Another important dimension of the protest by the new trade theorists relates to the idea of 'unequal shares', closely allied to the concept of the terms of trade. Although the neoclassical model never claimed that all countries would gain equally from trade, it became clear to some economists, such as Balogh (1963), that the pattern of specialisation open to many LDCs might be unacceptable on *normative* grounds, especially if it meant the perpetual production of primary products:[8]

The antiseptically neutral process envisaged in the usual blackboard diagram in which country A moves further along the commodity x axis of its transformation curve while B moves further along the commodity y axis (both parties gain by exchange) may look very different when it is realised that x may involve back-breaking labor in the cane fields and y automated factory production.

The dispute here is not over the possibility of gains from trade but over the fairness of their distribution if countries pursued comparative advantage. The future was seen to be particularly bleak if LDCs were typically primary producers and their terms of trade (usually taken here to be the barter terms of trade, or the ratio of an index of export prices to an index of the prices of imports) were expected to deteriorate over time. This decline in the terms of trade for the 'periphery' (LDCs) *vis-à-vis* the 'centre' (DCs) represented an important part of the new trade theorists' case, and was forcefully expounded by both Prebisch (1964) and Singer (1950).

For Prebisch the prospects for exporting primary products would inevitably be poor compared with manufactures as a result of Engels' law which postulated a decreasing proportion of income spent on basic foodstuffs and raw materials as countries became richer.[9] The primary terms of trade were also expected to fall over time in as much as factor incomes in LDCs would be constrained by population pressures and excess labour supplies, which would put less pressure on final goods prices than in DCs. Moreover, even if primary prices did rise there was always the danger of encouraging the production of synthetic substitutes in other countries—rubber and cotton being two cases which come to mind in the last two decades.

The idea that the benefits of specialisation might well accrue to the industrial countries rather than to primary producers in LDCs had also been given some theoretical weight by Bhagwati (1958) under the case of 'immiserising growth'. He demonstrated within the neoclassical framework that rapid technical progress in primary production could lower prices sufficiently to outweigh the real income gains from specialisation. In this sense, the benefits of trade and specialisation are transferred from the periphery to the centre.

As far as the evidence is concerned, there has been considerable debate as to the appropriate way to measure the terms of trade, and whether in fact they have deteriorated for LDCs. For a review of the evidence on the terms of trade, see Spraos (1980). It seems that, although there has been a diversity of experience between countries, reflecting their different commodity composition of exports and imports, the long-run terms of trade of primary commodities has been declining relative to manufactures; and the position of non-oil-exporting LDCs has generally deteriorated. As Table 4.1 shows, the purchasing power of primary exports (except oil) has declined since 1960, especially in beverages and agricultural raw materials; and on average the barter terms of trade have fallen for non-oil-exporting LDCs, leaving aside the boom between 1971 and 1974.

It has been suggested that a more appropriate measure of the terms of trade is the income terms of trade. This calculates the ratio of export to import prices multiplied by the quantity of exports, and allows for the possibility that an increase in export volume may offset any decline in price. On this score, Wilson *et al.* (1969) found that the income terms of trade for LDCs grew more slowly than for DCs over the period 1957 to 1965, especially when both sets of countries were adjusted for differences in population growth. They also suggested that the picture has probably got worse since 1965 since the barter terms of trade have deteriorated for LDCs, and LDC exports have grown more slowly than those of DCs. Nevertheless, some countries including the oil exporters have experienced an improvement in their terms of trade, and it is

Table 4.1: The terms of trade for non oil-exporting developing countries and primary exports 1960–81

Year	Developed countries[1]	Developing countries[2]	Primaries[3]	Food[4]	Beverages[5]	Raw materials[6]	Metals[7]
1960	107	108	115	83	133	158	121
1961	—	—	109	79	124	145	119
1962	—	—	106	80	120	138	115
1963	107	100	113	96	118	142	114
1964	110	102	118	90	133	139	139
1965	109	105	112	82	118	132	149
1966	107	107	114	81	121	133	157
1967	109	102	106	81	119	119	132
1968	109	109	105	79	120	116	137
1969	109	109	110	82	121	119	145
1970	111	113	107	82	129	103	145
1971	110	106	96	78	112	96	118
1972	111	106	100	83	113	116	109
1973	110	109	132	110	120	178	137
1974	97	109	138	144	117	141	140
1975	100	100	100	100	100	100	100
1976	99	99	112	81	189	123	105
1977	98	105	125	72	302	117	104
1978	100	98	103	71	190	109	95
1979	97	90	106	71	177	117	109
1980	—	—	104	86	140	110	108
1981	—	—	94	79	115	105	99

Notes:
[1,2] Unit value index of exports divided by a unit value index of imports (1975 = 100).
[3] Total index of 30 primary commodities exported by developing countries, excluding gold and crude petroleum, deflated by the United Nations index of manufactures exported by developed countries (1975 = 100).
[4,5,6,7] Index of commodities by major groups deflated by the United Nations index of manufactures exported by developed countries (1975 = 100).

Sources: [2] UNCTAD (1991), 3,4,5,6,7 International Monetary Fund (1982).

by no means clear that the fault always lies with external factors outside the control of the LDCs themselves. We shall return to this point in section 4.3.

A further potential conflict between trade and development refers to the idea of an ever-widening trade gap between developed and developing countries. This approach stresses the difficulties that many LDCs face when competing with DCs in manufactured goods. These difficulties arise from their initial technological inferiority and the lack of sufficient purchasing-power in their domestic markets to provide a jump-off to enable them to compete effectively with DCs. A balance of payments constraint on development can then arise if traditional export receipts are not enough to purchase essential imports from abroad necessary to fully utilise domestic resources and stimulate growth in manufactured exports.

According to this approach, therefore, a conflict can emerge between short-run balance of payments stability, which may require the cutting-back of imports (in the absence of protectionist measures or foreign assistance), and long-run development, for which some types of import may be essential. This school of thought, owing much to the work of the Swedish economist Linder (1967), thus adds a balance of payments dimension to the debate, and is part of the 'structuralist two-gap' approach to trade and development. By explicitly incorporating a balance of payments constraint into models of growth and development, these models generate conclusions which justify protectionist policies as a means of changing the structure of production. We shall return to this school of thought when we look at the structuralist approach to the balance of payments in Chapter 13, but for a good review of these models, see Thirlwall (1983, ch. 13).

One final ingredient in the new trade theorists' case relates to the risks associated with concentrating on a narrow range of primary commodities. The argument is that primary products exhibit strong fluctuations in price compared with industrial goods; LDCs depend heavily for their export revenue on primary goods; and fluctuations in export revenue impose significant costs on the countries concerned.

This problem of export instability has been an important issue in North–South relations ever since the 1964 UNCTAD meeting, and it has formed the basis for demands by LDCs for international commodity agreements and compensation schemes. We shall examine these policy issues in more detail in Chapter 6, and the international relations aspects in Chapter 17, but there seems to be little doubt that many primary products (for example coffee and cocoa) do exhibit severe fluctuations in price, and some support for the view that primary commodities are more unstable in this respect than manufactured goods.[10]

The causes of this phenomenon seem to lie in the inherent characteristics of the markets for primary·goods, including low price elasticities of supply and demand, and the propensity to display 'cobweb' cycles, where lags in supply generate cyclical effects on prices. Problems arise where there are frequent shifts in supply and demand and there is not much scope for altering output once the trees have been planted, or the crops sown. Primary commodities are particularly prone to shocks caused by the weather, disease, etc. and are especially vulnerable to destabilising speculative pressures.

It is also generally accepted that LDCs are *relatively* more dependent for their export revenue on a narrow range of primary products, even though DCs produce more primary products in total, and some newly industrialising countries, such as Taiwan and South Korea, have established a manufacturing base. Even these countries, however, tend to be narrowly specialised within the manufacturing sector, concentrating on light engineering or textiles. Classic cases of dependence are Ghana (cocoa), Sri Lanka (tea) and Zaire (copper).

As far as the costs of export instability are concerned, private costs are seen as arising principally from fluctuations in export receipts, causing hardship for producers if their incomes vary, and introducing an element of uncertainty into planting or investment decisions. Most stress, however, has fallen on the supposed social costs of unpredictable fluctuations in government revenue; on the uncertainty generated in development planning; and on the forced cancellation of important investment programmes and other forms of crisis adjustment when export shortfalls raise balance of payments problems.

There has now been a significant amount of empirical research on the export instability issue, some based upon highly aggregative cross-section analysis, and some looking more closely at particular case studies. Early work, stimulated by MacBean's (1966) pioneering study, tended to suggest that the problem might have been exaggerated and that remedial action, especially at the international level, might not *in general* be justified. Subsequent research, however, has tended to make the picture far less clear-cut, and some researchers believe that export instability is a serious problem for many poor countries. For a review of the literature in this area, see Wilson (1983).

These views on the potential conflict between trade and development were strongly influential in encouraging many LDCs to adopt an inward-looking trade bias in the 1960s and early 1970s. Prebisch, for example, was a prominent member of the United Nations Economic Commission for Latin America. LDCs felt justified in adopting protectionist policies to offset the backwash effects of trade, and the risks associated with having all their eggs in one primary commodity basket.

These policies were also defended on the grounds that they were designed to alter the distribution of the gains from trade by switching to new lines of production, either for the domestic market to substitute for imports, or for potential export. If free trade was seen as working in favour of DCs by virtue of the products LDCs seemed destined to produce and trade, then the answer was to change the structure of production and the composition of imports and exports, even if this conflicted with short-run comparative advantage. Moreover, there was some justification for protectionist policies within neoclassical theory itself, particularly in relation to the so-called 'infant industry' case. We shall consider this case, together with other arguments for protection, in Chapter 5.

4.3 TRADE AND DEVELOPMENT IN THE 1980s

The new trade theorists' protest was successful in so far as it clarified the implications of comparative advantage and free trade for LDCs, established the possibility of a conflict between trade and development (especially in the longer run), and stimulated the construction of models relevant to LDCs. It had been too easy, as Diaz Alejandro (1972) pointed out, to jump from the sensible proposition that some trade can make everyone better-off, to the conviction that more trade will always do just that. As we saw in Chapter 3, modern free-traders are careful to point out that free trade is only *potentially* superior to no trade, and requires the conditions of the neoclassical model to apply. 'Second best' (which we shall discuss in the next chapter) now becomes a valid area of inquiry and free trade is neither necessarily superior to no trade nor always superior to restricted trade. In this sense, the debate is no longer simply about free trade versus protection, but under what circumstances LDCs are justified in interfering with trade. This means, as we shall see in Part 2, that the policy options open to LDCs have become much wider.

It is also hard not to conclude that trade has been an engine of 'low horse power rating' for many LDCs in the twentieth century. As Table 4.2 suggests, exports have been growing much more slowly for LDCs in the post-war period than for DCs, especially when you take into account the oil-exporting countries. The share of the total value of world trade accruing to non-oil-exporting *LDCs* fell from 27.33 per cent in 1951 to 15.67 per cent in 1970 and 15.56 per cent in 1980. Most trade, it seems, takes place in industrial goods between DCs.[11]

Table 4.2: The growth of exports in developed and developing countries compared 1950–77

	Annual average growth in the value of exports		
	1950–60 %	1960–70 %	1970–77 %
World	7.0	7.1	7.3
Developed market countries	7.6	7.6	7.8
Developed socialist countries	8.0	8.0	10.4
Less developed countries	4.0	5.0	3.0

Source: World Bank (1978a, Annex, table 6).

None the less, it has been argued that LDCs have themselves often been to blame for this poor record, especially when set against relatively outward-looking countries such as Taiwan,

Puerto Rico, Singapore and South Korea, which have been successful in achieving a measure of industrialisation. Although protectionist policies, if carefully selected and implemented, could form part of a sensible development strategy, the experience of many LDCs in the 1960s and 1970s was that they generally did not work very well and could be very costly. The adoption of import-substitution policies in parts of Asia and Latin America in the late 1950s and early 1960s were successful only because they involved the production of relatively unsophisticated non-durable consumer goods, such as textiles and simple household goods. As these goods were generally intensive in unskilled labour and required small-scale production units, production for the home market proved to be fairly easy.

However, when countries such as Brazil and India tried in the 1960s to push import substitution a stage further and produce consumer durables as well as steel and petrochemicals, problems began to arise. The production of these goods tends to require a large market to reap the benefits of economies of scale, and is dependent on a steady supply of spare parts and other inputs, as well as scarce capital and skilled labour. What countries such as Brazil and Ghana discovered was that domestic purchasing power was insufficient, and costs were kept very high by shortages of essential inputs (often imported) and low productivity. This was often made worse by excessive bureaucracy and corruption. An influential study on the problems associated with protectionist policies in LDCs is that of Little *et al.* (1970).

As a result, many LDCs have come to recognise their neglect of comparative advantage, and in the 1970s adopted a more liberal approach to trade policy. Less emphasis was now placed on blaming external factors emanating from the demand side, and more time was spent on identifying supply bottlenecks originating from within LDCs themselves and adopting positive policies to overcome these obstacles. A good example of this was Sri Lanka's decision to adopt a more outward-looking trade policy in 1976. In addition, many countries in South-East Asia and Latin America have begun actively to pursue an outward-looking strategy based upon the expansion of non-traditional manufacturing exports; a strategy which has been encouraged by the World Bank.[12]

As far as the historical context is concerned, Myint (1958) has consistently argued that in many countries trade acted as a 'vent for surplus', i.e. as a means of overcoming surplus domestic capacity and ensuring the full utilisation of domestic resources. Instead of starting from a position on the production possibility frontier as comparative advantage presumes, trade enables a country to reach a point on the PPF from a position *inside* the frontier. Thus if the real choice is not between using these resources for domestic production or for export, but between using them for export or leaving them idle, then the opportunity costs of trade might well be lower than 'exploitation' arguments have suggested.

Myint believes that the vent for surplus approach is more appropriate than comparative advantage in explaining the rapid growth of exports in many parts of the developing world in the nineteenth century, but unfortunately it is not always clear whether trade is diverting domestic resources or venting them. The latter is probably more relevant where there were under-utilised resources with no obvious alternative uses, such as mines and fishing grounds, or where the domestic market would have been saturated in the absence of trade. Comparative advantage is, however, still relevant when deciding on the *type* of product to trade.

From the vantage point of the 1980s, therefore, the theory of trade with respect to the developing countries has moved away from its earlier free trade axis to a more sophisticated level, recognising the possibility of a conflict between trade and development. Free trade is no longer seen as a panacea for development, and a much wider range of policy tools are available to Third World governments to tailor trade policy to their particular needs and to the diversity of their historical experience. In this sense, there has been a conceptual synthesis between the neoclassical approach and the writings of the new trade theorists, and to this extent the protest by the new trade theorists was successful.

On the other hand, there has been somewhat of a neoclassical resurgence in the 1970s and 1980s based upon a less pessimistic scenario than that of the new trade theorists. This view emphasises the advantages which many LDCs have gained by dismantling much of their earlier protectionist armour and the benefits to be derived from pursuing a more outward-looking trade policy. There remain, however, important practical differences between a strategy which is geared essentially towards the elimination of impediments to free trade and the maximisation of 'carry-over' from trade, and one based upon a more independent inward-looking approach. We shall consider some of these policy differences in more detail in the next three chapters.

NOTES

1. This expression was first coined by Sir Denis Robertson. See Robertson (1940).
2. For a discussion of the role of trade in the nineteenth century, see Kenwood and Lougheed (1971).
3. See Haberler (1959, p. 5).
4. The essence of this approach can be found in Prebisch (1964).
5. This had particularly strong implications for the relationship between factor prices and goods prices across different countries. We shall discuss this question of factor price equalisation in Chapter 8.
6. The analysis here is quite difficult since it requires an understanding of social cost-benefit analysis. In essence, however, the problem arises because of a failure of market prices to adequately reflect social costs and benefits. For an introduction to this theory, see Thirlwall (1983, ch. 8).
7. A review of these theories can be found in Evans (1976).
8. Balogh (1963, p. 123). Note that the transformation curve is another name for the production possibility frontier.
9. Prebisch also hypothesised that primary prices would fall more during a cyclical downswing, such as the 1930s, than industrial prices, and by more than they rose during the upswing. It is not very clear, however, how this 'ratchet' effect comes about. For a critical evaluation of the Prebisch thesis, see Flanders (1964); and for some background on Englels' law, see Samuelson (1980, p. 198).
10. These issues are surveyed in greater depth in Wilson (1983).
11. See the International Monetary Fund (1981).
12. A leading exponent of this view is Bela Balassa. See Balassa (1977) and Little (1982).

FURTHER READING

A classic survey of the early literature on trade and development can be found in Meier (1968). A good supplement to this, including plenty of historical examples, is contained in the review article by Diaz Alejandro

(1972). For more recent contributions, see Thirlwall (1983) and Balassa (1977). For those who wish to explore the original sentiments of the new trade theorists and early criticisms of them by trade economists, Prebisch (1964) and Flanders (1964) are recommended.

PART 2
Trade Policy

5 Protection

Having examined some of the theoretical arguments used to explain and justify a particular pattern of trade between nations, in Part 2 we switch our attention to trade policy. In particular we shall investigate the policy issues which lie behind the formation of international cartels, international commodity agreements and integration movements. But before looking at these specific policy problems, we begin in this chapter with a general analysis of the theory and practice of protection, including a discussion of tariff and non-tariff barriers to trade.

5.1 TARIFFS

Protection usually refers to an advantage given to domestic producers in competition with imports in the home market, although a broader interpretation might also embrace export promotion. We shall consider a number of different forms of protection in this chapter, beginning with the most popular—the tariff.

A tariff is essentially a tax on commodity imports designed principally to change the relative prices of commodities and thereby alter the pattern of international trade, although it may also be levied as a revenue-raising exercise. It is most commonly applied on an *ad valorem* basis, i.e. as a percentage of value indicated by the foreign price, but sometimes it takes the form of a specific amount per unit, such as $1 per ton. The former method is generally favoured since it has a built-in allowance for inflation in world prices.

An important distinction also needs to be made between the nominal tariff rate and what is known as the effective rate of protection given to domestic producers. An example will bring out the difference clearly.

If the UK imposes a 20 per cent tariff on imports of wine, while the tariff on clothing is only 10 per cent, at first sight it might seem that wine producers are benefiting from higher protection than clothing manufacturers. In fact this need not be the case, since the tariff on the final goods ignores any tariffs domestic producers of these goods must pay on inputs bought from abroad. For example, if 50 per cent of costs in both industries consist of imported materials and the tariff on grapes was 40 per cent while zero on cloth, the wine industry would find that its 20 per cent protection from imports of wine would be entirely used to pay for the 40 per cent increase in the cost of grapes, leaving it with an effective protection of zero. The clothing industry, on the other hand, with its relatively low nominal 10 per cent protection, receives higher effective protection.

The key to effective protection is, therefore, the extent to which tariffs affect the value that domestic producers add to imported inputs, and in general the rate of effective protection can be defined as the proportionate increase in value added in an industry made possible as a result of the whole structure of protection, covering both the outputs of the industry and its inputs. The basic formula for measuring it is:[1]

$$te = \frac{(t1 - wt2)}{1 - w}$$

where te is the rate of effective protection, t1 is the tariff rate on the output, t2 is the tariff rate on the input, and w is the proportion of the total price (value-added) accounted for by the inputs. In the wine case effective protection is zero, i.e.:

$$te = \frac{[0.2 - (0.5 \times 0.4)]}{1 - 0.5} = 0$$

While in the clothing case it is 20 per cent, i.e.:

$$te = \frac{[0.1 - 0.5\,(0)]}{1 - 0.5} = 20 \text{ per cent}$$

In practice there are substantial differences between nominal and effective rates both in developed countries (DCs) and less developed countries (LDCs), mainly because countries escalate their tariff structures so as to levy higher nominal rates on final goods imported than on imports of intermediate goods. Tariffs on raw materials are therefore low or zero, while manufactured goods attract the highest rates. This raises the effective protection to domestic manufacturing producers and makes it especially difficult for LDCs to diversify away from traditional primary exports and compete in manufactured goods in developed country markets. For some evidence on the discrepancy between nominal and effective tariffs, see Balassa (1965, 1971), and for the impact on LDCs, see Johnson (1966).

As far as the effects of a tariff are concerned, in general one would expect it to shift demand away from foreign goods, thereby lowering imports, and to attract resources to the protected sector.

Figure 5.1 illustrates the effects of a nominal *ad valorem* tariff on wine imports into the UK. Pw represents the world price of wine, ss' and dd' indicate domestic output and UK demand at

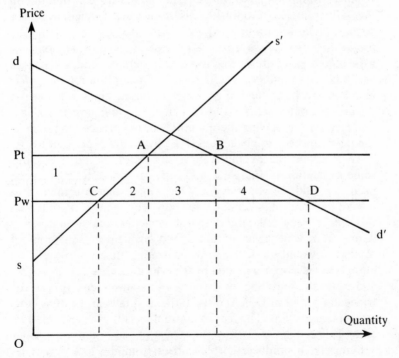

Figure 5.1: The effects of a tariff on wine imports into the UK

various prices respectively, under the assumptions that the UK is a
net importer of wine and a price-taker in the international wine
market. The latter is justified in so far as the UK is a small
producer of wine on the world market so that the tariff has no
discernible effect on the world price. Our analysis is also one of
partial equilibrium since it focuses exclusively on the wine market
and ignores any repercussions on other markets. We shall return
to these issues below.

In the absence of the tariff the world price of wine is given by
OPw, with domestic producers supplying PwC and imports CD
purchased in the world market. The UK now imposes a tariff on
wine imports at the rate per unit of PtPw (giving a nominal tariff
rate of PtPw/PwO). Since the world price is unaffected, the new
domestic price after payment of the tariff rises to Pt, assuming that
some imports are still purchased. The tariff will have implications
for consumers, producers and the government.

The *consumption effect* refers to the fall in wine consumption in
the UK from PwD to PtB. This is because foreign wine has
become relatively more expensive in the UK market. The
production effect arises from the protection given to the domestic
wine industry, resulting in an increase in output from PwC to PtA
and a fall in imports from CD to AB. Finally, the *revenue effect*
results from the change in government tax receipts from zero in
the absence of the tariff to the area labelled 3 in Figure 5.1. This is
obtained by multiplying the quantities of imports coming in after
the tariff has been implemented (AB) by the tariff per unit PtPw.

To ascertain the overall welfare effects of the tariff requires
some evaluation of the gains and losses to domestic consumers,
producers and the government. One way to measure them is to
invoke the concept of economic surplus. For some background on
this, see Lipsey (1983). For consumers the total welfare they
derive from wine consumption would be measured in terms of
what they would be prepared to pay rather than forgo the good
entirely. This is approximated by the area under the demand curve
and above the price line. In Figure 5.1 this consumer surplus is the
triangular area PwdD before the tariff, and falls to the area PtdB
after its imposition. The loss to consumers is thus represented by
areas 1 + 2 + 3 + 4.

Similarly, a producer surplus arises from the fact that some
factors of production earn more than the opportunity costs of their

services. In Figure 5.1 this is represented by the area between the supply curve and below the price line. Before the tariff it is given by sCPw, and after the tariff, it rises to sAPt. Hence, the producer surplus has risen by the amount shown by area 1.

As far as the change in government revenue is concerned, it is generally assumed that the increase in revenue resulting from the tariff (area 3) is redistributed back to consumers, and is therefore treated as an addition to consumer surplus.

What can one say, therefore, about the overall effects of the tariff? Consumers lose an amount of surplus equivalent to areas 1 + 2 + 3 + 4, producers gain by the amount of area 1, and government revenue grows to the extent of area 3. The net loss in welfare to the UK is thus given by areas 2 and 4. Area 2 represents the extra cost of obtaining wine from domestic sources rather than from abroad and is sometimes referred to as the 'deadweight production loss'. The term 'deadweight' indicates that neither domestic producers nor the government gain from the inefficiencies involved. In similar fashion, 4 is referred to as the 'deadweight consumption loss' resulting from the tariff forcing consumers to lower their consumption of wine. It is 'deadweight' in the sense that what consumers lose, nobody else gains.

Since our analysis ignores any repercussions the tariff might have on other markets or on the balance of payments, assumes the UK is a price-taker in the international wine market, and abstracts away from any distortions in the economy other than those arising from the tariff itself; it should be viewed only as a rough indicator of the positive and normative implications of a tariff. We shall look at the balance of payments aspects of tariffs in Chapter 12 and relax the price-taking assumption in section 5.3 when we consider the case of the optimal tariff.

In addition, one has to be careful about the association of economic surplus with welfare since it assumes that a dollar loss to a consumer (whether rich or poor) is equivalent to a dollar gained by a producer or the government. In economic jargon this amounts to a constant marginal utility of income. If, however, in your opinion a dollar lost by a consumer is worth *more* than the dollar gained by the other two parties, then you would not want to accept 2 plus 4 as an indication of the net welfare loss arising from the imposition of the tariff. You could, if you wish, go a stage further and weight each dollar of effect on the parties concerned (with perhaps lower weights for the government and domestic producers) and recalculate the net effect of the tariff.[2]

None the less, it is on this basis that economists generally conclude that a tariff reduces net national welfare. Empirical studies trying to estimate the magnitude of these gains and losses have generally concluded that the costs are quite small as a percentage of GNP, amounting to about 1 per cent, but in absolute terms the effects could be quite significant, especially for a country like the UK which is highly dependent on international trade. There is also some evidence that these studies tend to underestimate the costs involved. For example, there would be administrative costs involved in the levying of the tariff. For a discussion of the problems connected with the estimation of these costs, see Leamer and Stern (1970). A good review of statistical work in this area is also provided by Stern (1971).

Before we turn our attention to non-tariff barriers to trade, it needs to be pointed out that there is an alternative way of showing the effects of a tariff on a particular country such as the UK, by using the production possibility frontier and community indifference curves discussed in Chapter 3. The details of this analysis are presented in Appendix 5.1.

5.2 NON-TARIFF BARRIERS

Although tariffs remain a popular barrier to international trade in both developed and developing countries alike, there are a number of alternative ways of restricting unwanted imports into a country, or providing help to exporters. Indeed, as we shall see in section 5.3, there has been a clear tendency since the second world war to substitute these non-tariff barriers for tariffs as pressures for the removal of the latter gained momentum through such organisations as The General Agreement on Tariffs and Trade, otherwise known as GATT.

The most explicit forms of protection in this category are export subsidies, export taxes, quotas and exchange controls. An export subsidy represents a payment to exporters by the government. The production and consumption effects are similar to those of an import tariff in so far as it increases the output and price of the subsidised good in the domestic economy and reduces its domestic consumption, but whereas a tariff increases government revenue, the subsidy increases government spending. Export taxes involve the placing of a duty on exports as the mirror image of the import tariff. Instead of putting a tax on wine imports, the UK would simply tax clothing exports in order to divert them to the domestic market. The consequences would be a fall in the domestic price of clothing and a redistribution from producers to consumers (including the government). As with the import tariff, there would be an overall welfare loss (measured by economic surplus) to the UK since the export tax would hurt producers more than it helps consumers or raises government revenue.[3]

A second method of providing protection to an import-competing industry is by imposing an import quota, i.e. a quantitative restriction on the amount that can be imported: so many bottles or dollars worth of wine. In an extreme situation the quota could be set at zero, thus ensuring a total ban on the product. Usually, however, the government would issue licences (less than the quantity people would choose to import) and the effects would be similar to a tariff in so far as the domestic price of wine rises in the UK.[4]

The appeal of the quota lies in its administrative flexibility and its ability to substitute for a tariff. It is especially popular in LDCs where it provides the government with a quick and selective way of curbing unwanted imports in line with its development priorities. In more recent years the threat of a quota or tariff has often been sufficient to force manufacturers to accept 'voluntary' quotas on their exports. Japanese producers for example, have agreed to limit their car exports to the UK as a result of such a threat.

Although in principle the welfare effects of a quota are similar to an equivalent tariff, in practice economists tend to regard the tariff as preferable on the grounds that it will introduce fewer distortions into the economy. The problem arises because the import licences have to be distributed in some way. Unless they are auctioned off at competitive prices, in which case the redistributive effects are identical to the tariff, there are bound to be problems of one form or another. In fact governments usually distribute the licences in a more *ad hoc* fashion, either on a first-come-first-served basis, or so as to maintain market shares between firms as before the quota. An example here might be the US government's issue of licences for oil imports between 1959 and 1973. This generally gives rise to corruption or other inefficiencies no matter how conscientious the authorities try to be. A good survey of the magnitude of these distortions found in a number of LDCs based on the work of Bhagwati and Krueger in the 1970s is contained in McKinnon (1979).

Export duties and quotas suffer from the limitation that they are not usually designed to control invisible transactions and capital movements.[5] Foreign exchange controls, on the other hand, are administrative restrictions on *any* transactions involving foreign exchange. In effect the importer must obtain permission to buy foreign exchange to pay for the imports. In this way the government can allocate exchange in line with its balance of payments priorities. For example, an LDC might only distribute licences if the imports are seen as necessary within the development context. Exchange for luxury consumption items might be refused, and preference given to essential machines or raw materials. It is also common for such countries to operate a system of multiple foreign exchange rates with low rates for some transactions and higher rates for others. In this case the rationing is carried out by way of price.

These controls are attractive primarily because of their administrative flexibility and their potentially wide coverage, but they also suffer from the same drawbacks as quotas in as much as they are open to abuse. We shall have something more to say about exchange controls when we examine the workings of the foreign exchange market in Chapter 14.

The measures of protection we have discussed so far are usually quite explicit and identifiable, but there are a number of more subtle ways by which a country, consciously or unconsciously, can obtain a trading advantage. These include state trading practices, differences in taxation systems, and differences in trading standards.

State trading practices refer to the allocation of certain importing rights to state entrepreneurs. This is seen most clearly in socialist or communist countries where the state is an important regulator of exports and imports; but it is a practice not exclusive to such regimes. Servicemen stationed abroad, for instance, are often provided for from the home economy rather than from local services which might be cheaper. This is merely an institutionalised version of such slogans as 'Buy British', or 'Buy American'. Other examples might include the proviso that the police force or other government agencies buy their equipment from domestic suppliers.

Even if there were no other barriers to trade, there would still be inefficiencies in trading practices as long as countries operate different taxation systems and customs valuation procedures. For example, a high excise tax on wine consumption in the UK (even if levied on both domestic and foreign wine) could distort consumption patterns and trade. Similarly, one country may value imports for tax purposes at world prices while another may use the wholesale prices of competing goods within the domestic economy. Taken individually these differences may not amount to much, but within the context of integration movements where other forms of protection are gradually lowered, they are taken quite seriously. We shall return to these harmonisation problems in Chapter 7.

Finally, there are differences in trading standards to consider. These are restrictive practices exercised by a civil service in line with national standards relating to traded items. For example, countries may impose certain safety regulations on electrical or other goods, or control chemical strengths or food hygiene standards. In some cases these procedures arise quite naturally from national practices, but they are sometimes used as a deliberate attempt to discriminate against imports.

5.3 THE CASE FOR PROTECTION

Most economists, it seems, since Adam Smith have regarded protectionist measures with suspicion, usually because other methods are available to achieve the same results but without the distortions and inefficiencies which tend to accompany protection. It is not simply a case of free trade versus protection, since few people would in practice advocate unadulterated free trade policies in the context of modern government decision-making. Yet it remains hard to convince mainstream economists that tariffs and other barriers to trade are justified. In this section we shall examine a number of arguments presented in support of protection, beginning with two which have become grudgingly accepted within trade theory as defensible in some circumstances—the optimal tariff and the case of the infant industry.

The optimal tariff situation arises where a country can exert some degree of buying power (monopsony) or selling power (monopoly) in world markets. Individual firms within the economy may still be competitive, but the economy as a whole can improve its terms of trade as a result of the tariff. This is tantamount to dropping the small country assumption used in section 5.1. In other words, the optimal tariff for a small country would be zero.

To see how a country could benefit from such a tariff, imagine the UK levies a tariff on wine imports and is a 'large' country in international trade. The tariff would reduce the quantity of exports the UK placed on the world market and also the imports it purchased from abroad. These reductions would, in turn, tend to raise wine export prices (since world supply would fall significantly) and lower import prices (as a result of the contraction in domestic consumption). Both of these changes will improve the terms of trade (the ratio of export to import prices) and welfare will be higher in the UK in the sense that it can now buy more imports with a given quantity of exports. The result is still an unambiguous fall in real consumption for the world as a whole, but as long as the tariff is not set so high as to be prohibitive to importers, appropriate compensation is available to make all consumers better-off, and other countries don't retaliate; an 'optimum' tariff can be derived to enable the country to reach the highest community indifference curve.[6]

Retaliation, however, is quite likely and may ultimately lower the welfare of one or more countries, despite the fact that at each step in the retaliatory process, the country imposing the tariff gains compared with the previous step. It is not possible to say what the final outcome will be, except that the total value of trade will have decreased and it is likely that the country imposing the optimal tariff will be worse-off at the end of the day.

The infant industry argument is applied wherever an industry is believed to have a potential comparative advantage but for some reason or other is unable to compete internationally in the short run. Protection is justified in these circumstances to 'nurture' the infant through a 'gestation' period while it takes advantage of economies of scale and the benefits of 'learning by doing'. After this point protection is supposed to be removed. Much emphasis is placed on the expected linkages and spin-offs that the protected industry will generate for the economy as a whole, especially for an LDC striving to compete in manufactured goods with DCs. In this context, some economists have even talked about an infant-government effect, based upon the extra revenue accruing to the government from the protection, which might be used to provide social infrastructure such as roads, education, etc. This argument is again usually reserved for LDCs where the supply of finance for these projects from other sources might be severely limited.

Although the infant industry case for protection has become accepted within trade theory, and it is an important feature in policy-making in LDCs, there remains considerable scepticism about its practical validity. It is not enough to argue that a potential larger scale of output could reduce costs, but it must be shown that protection could ultimately be withdrawn and that the market is sufficiently large to provide the scale to enable costs to fall and the industry to compete successfully abroad. The fact that consumers pay more in the short run also needs to be offset against any expected future gains.

There is some justification for the view that the infant-industry argument has in the past been used too readily to justify support for inefficient industries which manifestly fail to 'grow up' and fulfil their parents' expectations about long-run comparative advantage. They might be acceptable as part of a long-run plan to restructure the economy, but this is not what the infant-industry analysis is all about, and there might well be more efficient ways of achieving the same results, such as through the use of subsidies.

The infant industry case has tended to become subsumed within the more general area of second best, pioneered by Lipsey and Lancaster (1956). This provides a basis for interventionist policies, including protection, if it can be shown that there are important distortions in the economy which drive a wedge between private costs and benefits and social costs and benefits. With these distortions present the economy is no longer regarded as 'first best' but as 'second best'. For example, if the manufacturers of a product which generates pollution, such as petrol, do not take into account the costs to society of their activities, then a discrepancy may arise between the private costs affecting producers and the social costs facing the community as a whole. The government might then be justified in intervening to correct the distortion, possibly by taxing the manufacturers of petrol. First-best policies would then be appropriate in situations where the distortions could be neutralised or eliminated without creating further distortions in the economy. In practice, however, policy intervention usually does introduce distortions and such policies are therefore described as 'second-best'.

In the infant industry case it might be argued that there are potential new skills to be acquired by workers in the import-competing industry, such as clothing in the UK, which will benefit persons other than those directly employed in that industry. Hence the social benefits of clothing production exceed the private benefits accruing to clothing workers and intervention is justified to equate private and social benefits. In this case the output of clothing is less than is socially desirable and protection could be used on second-best grounds to increase output.

The problem with protection, however, is that it is usually possible to envisage alternative policies which eliminate the original distortion but with less harmful side-effects. In the clothing case, for example, a subsidy encourages the training of skilled labour without driving a wedge between the international price of clothing and its domestic price. UK consumers are still able to purchase clothing at the world price. Another second-best policy might be to subsidise production directly, but the disadvantage of this is that it gives firms no incentive to offer labour-training. This would still, however, be preferable to the tariff.

A second example might be where a government wishes to reduce the consumption of imported cars because they are considered non-essential to development. A tax on car consumption would still leave producers to face world competition at world prices, but a tariff would increase the domestic price to producers as well as to consumers and would encourage resources to move from exports to the production of these 'luxury' items.

The arguments we have looked at so far are generally accepted as valid under some circumstances within trade theory. There are, however, other arguments for protection, often with a strong non-economic basis, which are regarded with much less enthusiasm by trade economists. The most popular come under the headings of self-sufficiency, unfair competition, income redistribution and employment creation.

The self-sufficiency case refers to the fact that all countries in reality protect certain types of domestic production even if the goods could be obtained at a lower cost from the international market. Typically, these 'key' industries include armaments, military equipment and even agriculture, which might be construed as being vulnerable during a war.

The use of protection against 'unfair' competition also encompasses a heavy non-economic component. Sometimes it refers explicitly to the belief that labour in other countries is being exploited in the sense of being paid less than a 'fair' wage, which might be reflected in cheap imports. More generally it might refer to disguised subsidisation by foreign governments to keep prices down.

There are two separate issues at stake here: first, whether factor payments are too low in terms of some judgement about income distribution, which is ultimately a normative question; and secondly, whether countries are deliberately lowering their costs artificially. In the first case one should seriously consider whether a particular protective measure such as a tariff is really going to be as effective as some more direct action such as a boycott or other trade sanction. In the second case, where a clear example of unfair help can be identified, some retaliatory action might be justified, but too often such action is used against genuine comparative advantage. The discriminatory practices by many DCs against the exports of the newly industrialised developing countries could well fall into this latter category.

In a similar vein, protection is often defended in terms of retaliation against foreign firms 'dumping' their goods in the export market at a lower price than they are charging in another (usually the home) market. Sometimes this represents the expression of monopoly power by these firms through price discrimination, i.e. they can increase their total profits by selling at different prices in different markets. On other occasions it is part of a marketing strategy to capture foreign markets, after which point prices are raised to the competitive level.

Economic theory is ambiguous on the question of dumping. The International Anti-Dumping Code of 1967 allows a retaliatory tariff to eliminate price discrimination, but ironically, it is consumers in the importing country who are made worse-off by having to pay the higher price. It is, therefore, domestic competing firms who stand to benefit and who lobby most forcefully against dumping. None the less, if the tariff persuades the dumper to lower prices (exclusive of the tariff itself), the importing country could benefit along the lines of the optimum tariff argument, and a retaliatory tariff is justified as a departure from free trade to remove a distortion specific to international trade.

Our analysis thus far has tended to overlook the repercussions that protection might have on income distribution within an economy, but a further justification for protectionist measures arises out of the Stolper–Samuelson theorem.[7] This shows that under certain conditions a tariff can benefit a factor used intensively in an import-competing industry at the expense of the other factor. If wine is particularly labour-intensive in the UK, then a tariff on imports may be seen as desirable because it benefits workers, albeit at the expense of other factors of production such as capital. We shall return to the effects of trade on income distribution and factor prices in Chapter 8.

Finally, there is the important question of the effects of protection on employment. It is very tempting for a country suffering from excess capacity or structural unemployment (possibly in declining industries) to adopt protection to improve the balance of payments and save jobs or create new ones in import-competing industries. The inefficiencies introduced by these policies may be regarded as less harmful than the under-utilisation of resources and unemployment, especially if it allows time for structural adjustment and the reallocation of factors.

An argument along these lines was used by Keynes to justify British tariffs in the 1930s. Although he did not advocate it as a general case for protection, he saw moderate tariffs as the only viable way of stimulating recovery without substantially reducing foreign competition, given that simultaneous expansion by all countries was not likely and devaluation had been ruled out. Keynes' views on protection are discussed in Harrod (1952, p. 424).

Although protection can improve the balance of payments and increase employment, it may be self-defeating for the country concerned if it encourages retaliation or reduces the incomes of its competitors to such an extent that they in turn reduce their demand for the protected country's exports. We shall examine these repercussions more fully in Chapter 12, but once again, protection is often seen as at least a second-best response. If the problem is an adverse balance of payments, then devaluation of the currency might be a more appropriate solution, and if there is excess capacity, then first-best policies might focus on curing the allocative inefficiencies directly. For example, retraining and adjustment assistance to help those whose jobs or investments have been displaced by import competition, especially if the adjustments required are the result of permanent structural deficiencies, rather than the temporary result of a cyclical downturn in demand.

5.4 COMMERCIAL POLICY SINCE 1945

The attitude of governments since the second world war presents a paradox in commercial policy: protectionist measures are seen as detrimental to international trade as a whole, but 'unilateral disarmament' is risky for an individual country if other countries do not follow suit. Perhaps this explains why DCs have generally pursued multilateral negotiations to reduce protection yet are reluctant to take individual action to remove barriers, especially if domestic pressures to mitigate the impact of foreign competition are vociferous.

The commitment towards freer trade after 1945 was reflected in the establishment of The General Agreement on Tariffs and Trade (GATT) as a framework of rules for international commercial policy and a forum for settling disputes between member countries. Its guiding principles of non-discrimination and reciprocity of treatment signalled a genuine desire to abandon the 'beggar thy neighbour' policies characteristic of the inter-war years, and to move quickly towards the removal of barriers to trade. We shall examine the post-war international trading system, including GATT, in Part 5 of this book, and we confine ourselves here to a summary of the major developments in commercial policy during this period.

Under the auspices of GATT in Geneva in 1947 significant cuts were achieved in nominal tariff rates over a broad area, but after this immediate post-war flourish little further progress was made until the Kennedy Round, completed in 1967. At this meeting the major industrial countries agreed to an across-the-board cut in nominal tariff rates of 50 per cent, although the final result of the negotiations was a weighted average tariff cut of about 35 per cent.[8] This has been followed up in more recent years by the Tokyo Round from 1973 to 1979, including an agreement to reduce nominal tariffs on average by one-third over an eight-year period.

Despite the very real success achieved by GATT in reducing nominal tariff rates, two important problems remain. First, as we saw in section 5.1, nominal tariffs are not the same as effective protection, and the practice of levying higher tariffs on goods the more final their stage of production means that effective protection remains high. Secondly, although countries were willing to reduce tariffs as part of an international agreement, they often simultaneously substituted other non-tariff barriers of the kind described in section 5.2. Indeed, some of these measures, including quotas, were allowed under GATT rules if a country could make a case for the protection of domestic agriculture, or if an important home industry was seriously threatened. Most countries have used these escape clauses to justify protectionist measures. A good illustration of this with respect to the USA is presented in Johnson (1974).

Some attempt to deal with these problems was made at the Tokyo Round where agreement was reached on codes governing non-tariff barriers. These were designed to expose the more deceptive forms of non-tariff barriers including state trading, differences in taxation practices, and differences in trading standards. Until there is a genuine commitment to remove these barriers as well as the more explicit forms of protection, then protection will continue to be an important feature of the international trading system.

A final note is needed here with respect to LDCs. These countries remained largely on the sidelines of these multilateral negotiations. Indeed they established their own forum within the United Nations in 1964 largely because they felt that the post-war international trading system had been created primarily for the benefit of the richer developed countries and that a different set of trading rules ought to apply to them. We shall consider these institutional developments in more depth in Chapter 17, together with the special tariff concessions obtained by LDCs in the 1970s. As far as protectionist policy in general is concerned, many LDCs became heavily protectionist in the 1960s, using the whole range of policies discussed in this chapter. In the 1970s, however, a feeling of disillusionment set in about these policies, and many LDCs began to dismantle some of their protectionist armour as part of a more outward-looking stance, especially in the so-called newly industrialising countries of Asia and Latin America.[9] Protection remains, however, an important feature of developing country commercial policy.

APPENDIX 5.1

The welfare effects of a tariff using the production possibility frontier and community indifference curves

An alternative way of showing the effects of a tariff on UK wine imports is to invoke the analysis used in Chapter 3 based upon the production possibility frontier (PPF) and community indifference curves. Points P and C in Figure 5.2 indicate the free trade production and consumption positions prior to the imposition of the tariff. After the tariff has been applied, the domestic price of wine in terms of clothing (Pt) rises above the world price Pw thus making the domestic price line flatter (since it now costs more clothing to buy a unit of wine). The *production effect* is implied by a movement from P to P' as producers shift resources out of clothing and into wine until the marginal costs of each are brought into line with the tariff-based price ratio. The *consumption effect* is represented by the movement from C to C' as consumers adjust their consumption in response to the new domestic prices. In the process, domestic consumption of wine falls and wine imports have declined from M to M'.

The decline in overall welfare is indicated by the movement from C on indifference curve CIC2 to C' on indifference curve CIC1, resulting from the increase in the domestic production of wine and the fall in imports. Even though the government receives revenue from the tariff (assumed to be passed on to consumers) there is still a decline in real consumption, since the domestic price of wine has risen above the world price.

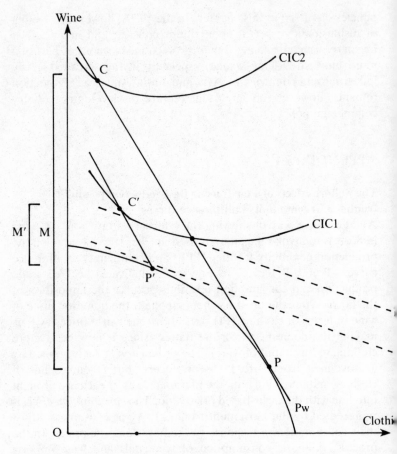

Figure 5.2: The effects of a tariff using the production possibility frontier and community indifference curves

NOTES

1. In practice the formula becomes more complex if there are many inputs involved. See Caves and Jones (1981, p. 228).
2. For a critical evaluation of the concept of economic surplus, see Mishan (1968).
3. For further details on export taxes and subsidies, see Williamson (1983, pp. 89–91).
4. See Caves and Jones (1981, pp 246–8).

5. Invisibles include income from services such as shipping and tourism. These items are discussed more fully in Chapter 12.
6. For more details, see Caves and Jones (1981, pp. 212–13).
7. See Stolper and Samuelson (1941).
8. A good analysis of the Kennedy Round can be found in Evans (1971). An important assessment of its quantitative implications is also available in Cline *et al.* (1978).
9. For a discussion of this change in outlook, see OECD (1979).

FURTHER READING

The most authoritative treatment of the theory of protection can be found in Corden (1971, 1974), although a simpler treatment is available in Caves and Jones (1981, chs 11–13). A non-technical analysis of the concept of effective protection was presented by Grubel (1971), and the infant-industry case is explored in Baldwin (1969). For surveys of developments in thinking on trade policy, see Stern (1971) and more recent papers on current issues in Amacher *et al* (1979). The National Bureau of Economic Research has also published a series of ten country studies and two summary volumes. The major conclusions are reproduced in McKinnon (1979). Papers on several aspects of trade liberalisation are contained in Baldwin and Richardson (1981), and a useful attempt to measure the effects of liberalisation in the post-war period can be found in Cline *et al* (1979).

6 Cartels and Commodity Agreements

6.1 INTERNATIONAL CARTELS

Cartels are essentially agreements by producers to restrict competition and raise price. International cartels, therefore, arise when producers (or governments) are located in different countries. This makes their control by monitoring agencies difficult since they usually fall under the jurisdiction of more than one country. Historically, cartels go back at least to the 1880s in tobacco, railway services and oil, and they proliferated during the depression of the 1930s, especially in primary products and steel.[1] Since the second world war, however, they have generally been illegal in the USA and UK, and restricted in Europe, although they are often sanctioned by governments. A good example is the International Air Transport Association (IATA), a cartel of major airlines established to set air fares and restrict competition.

Cartels are a manifestation of imperfect competition in as much as producers cooperate to exert their joint monopoly power, and their behaviour is typical of the market structure known as oligopoly where there are a relatively small number of producers who anticipate the decisions of their rivals. It is a characteristic of this type of market that firms tacitly collude to keep out potential competitors and to reduce the degree of competition between themselves. Although these firms do not formally agree on these policies, they carry them out *implicitly* because it is in their mutual interest to do so. For example, oligopolists tend to restrict their competition to a non-price basis, such as through advertising, rather than engage in cut-throat price wars. Cartels, however, generally involve more *explicit* collusion including formal contracts with penalties for non-compliance. Clearly the degree to which cooperation is substituted for competition can vary from a complete merger to much looser forms of agreement on particular aims, but the greater degree of formality involved in a cartel distinguishes it from less formal oligopoly collusion.

Cartels should also not be confused with international commodity agreements (to be discussed later in this chapter), although they share some common analysis. The cartel is basically a unilateral decision by producers to cooperate whilst a commodity agreement, in principle, includes consumers in the negotiations, although in practice consumers (as opposed to consuming governments) have little direct say in their operation.

Finally, although the major objective of a cartel is to raise price and restrict competition, it may have other goals as well. For example, to develop the industry in a broader sense; or, as in the case of the Organisation of Petroleum Exporting Countries (OPEC), to act as a distributor of international aid.

Although cartels are not new in international trade, traditional economic analysis has tended to emphasise their inherent instability, and relatively little space was devoted to a discussion of them in textbooks. All this changed, however, with the quadrupling of the price of oil in the early 1970s and the arrival of OPEC as an effective cartel in the oil market. Developed countries (DCs) were anxious to establish whether OPEC would be able to survive, and less developed countries (LDCs) were interested in the possibilities for replicating its example in other commodities exported in the main by poorer countries. Cartel theory has thus come back into fashion, and two questions in particular will dominate our discussion in this chapter. First, is oil unique as a commodity? And secondly, is OPEC unique as an organisation? We begin by looking at what current economic analysis has to say about cartels.

6.2 THE ECONOMIC ANALYSIS OF CARTELS

When producers combine together to restrict competition and raise price they are behaving in a manner analogous to a joint monopoly in economic theory. A pure monopolist is a single seller of a product which has no close substitute, and the extent to which a cartel can redistribute income in its favour will depend on its costs, the response of consumers as represented by the market demand curve, and the ability of the cartel to erect barriers to prevent the entry into the industry of potential rivals.

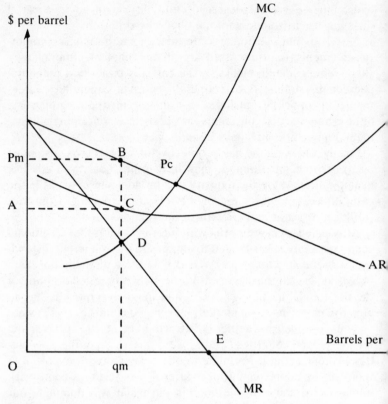

Figure 6.1: The cartel as a monopolist

Figure 6.1 depicts the situation of a cartel in the oil industry acting as a pure monopoly. AR represents the demand curve facing the cartel. Its downward slope indicates that the cartel can exert some monopoly power over price, i.e. be a price-maker in the oil market. The steeper its slope (the more price inelastic), the more the cartel can raise price ($/barrel) by restricting output (barrels/day). MR indicates how revenue from the sale of oil changes with output (marginal revenue). AC represents the average costs of the producers taken as a whole, and MC shows how these costs alter with output (marginal costs). Since we are assuming here that the cartel faces the same technological facts of life as producers operating under perfect competition, it is the price-making ability of the cartel which is its distinguishing feature and not the structure of costs.

Economic theory suggests that if the monopolist seeks to maximise profits, then output will be expanded up to the point where marginal revenue equals marginal cost, i.e. D in Figure 6.1. Beyond that point the cartel would be adding more to its costs than to its revenues. Equilibrium output in the short run will be qm, and at that point consumers will be willing to pay Pm from the demand curve. Monopoly profits will then be given by the difference between the revenue obtained OPmBqm and the cost outlay OACqm, and are represented by the rectangle APmBC. The implication is that price will be higher and output lower than would have occurred under perfect competition. The equivalent position for perfect competition would be point Pc, where marginal cost is equal to average revenue. The cartel has thus succeeded in transferring income from consumers of oil to itself by raising price above marginal cost and the net loss to the world as a whole is given by the area BPcD, based on the difference between what consumers would have paid under perfect competition and what they actually pay to the cartel.

Before examining the factors which will influence the strength or weakness of a cartel, some qualifications are in order. First, we have implied that the cartel wants to maximise profits. Certainly, profits are likely to be an important objective, but other objectives may also be sought. For example, if all oil is exported by the cartel then it may want to maximise export revenue rather than profits *per se*, in which case the equilibrium position in Figure 6.1 would be replaced by E where marginal revenue becomes zero. For more details on the application of price theory to cartel objectives, see Radetski (1976).

Secondly, we have assumed that the cartel is successful in maintaining barriers to entry in the long run, and hence Pm is the equilibrium price. Such a price, however, is generally not attainable because of the constraint imposed by potential rivals, i.e. if the cartel price exceeds the marginal costs of potential entrants into the market (the 'limit price'), then it will attract rivals. The cartel must usually, therefore, charge a price low enough to discourage entry and increase output beyond qm.

Finally, although we have shown how the cartel can transfer income to itself, we have not considered how this income is to be shared out amongst its members. One solution would be to allocate production on the basis of minimum costs and to pool the overall profits. However, high-cost producers may be reluctant to close down, and low-cost producers unwilling to share profits generated exclusively from their resource base. Another solution would be to limit output to qm and distribute market shares on the basis of quotas. The problem here is that it is always tempting for an individual member to exceed its quota as long as the other members don't do likewise. If too many members cheat, then cartel output would expand beyond qm, and price would fall.

In practice, therefore, most cartels operate on a price-fixing basis, i.e. instead of setting qm the cartel fixes Pm and consumers are left to determine qm. This nevertheless still necessitates a procedure for determining price differentials to allow for quality differences and variations in transport costs between the members and ensure all participants remain reasonably content. Usually one member of the cartel with the largest share of the market or the lowest costs will act as the price leader and other prices will be set in accordance with this marker price. As we shall see below, OPEC is a price-fixing cartel with Saudi Arabia acting as the price leader.

As well as applying standard price theory, economic analysis can also shed some light on cartel behaviour by focusing directly on the concept of elasticity. In particular, it is possible to derive a formula containing some of the major factors influencing the long run survival of a cartel, based upon the elasticity or responsiveness of demand for the cartels's *sales* (Ed*) to changes in the cartel price:[2]

$$Ed^* = \frac{Ed - Es^* (1 - x)}{x}$$

The more inelastic is Ed* (less than unity) the stronger the cartel's monopoly power, since it can raise price without losing sales in the same proportion. Within this formula Ed represents the elasticity of demand for the *product* sold by the cartel. The more inelastic this demand, the more the cartel can exploit consumers or manufacturers who purchase the commodity by pushing price above marginal cost. Es*, on the other hand, measures the elasticity of supply of non-cartel output. The more inelastic this response (perhaps because costs are high), the less the cartel has to worry about its price-raising activities encouraging an expansion of production by producers outside the cartel. Finally, x refers to the cartel's market share. The larger this share, the stronger the cartel is likely to be, since it can dominate the market and act as the sole supplier of the product.

It was precisely this sort of analysis which led economists before OPEC made its mark on the international scene to conclude, with some confidence and historical evidence, that cartels were inherently unstable and unlikely to succeed in the long run.[3] Ed was expected to become more elastic over time as the high cartel price encouraged consumers to reduce consumption and switch to cheaper substitutes. Similarly, Es* would tend to rise as the lucrative price acted as a signal to other producers to enter the market or expand output to satisfy the excess demand created by the cartel's restriction of output. Also, for a cartel to operate effectively, it requires a limited number of producers with a high market share. Unfortunately, for most commodities there are many producers, often widely separated geographically. Moreover, x would more than likely fall over time since, by definition, the cartel is restricting its own output in relation to its competitors.

Finally, although these conditions might be considered as prerequisites for the successful operation of a producer alliance, there are other factors which may threaten the organisational cohesion of the cartel. As we suggested earlier, there is always the temptation for an individual producer to cheat within a price-fixing cartel—to sell more at the going price, or to lower price bilaterally to increase sales to particular buyers. The cartel can only maintain its position in the market if its members stick to common policies, yet as we shall see when we examine the case of OPEC, the objectives of the individual members of the alliance may differ widely and lead to serious strains within the organisation. It is for all these reasons that cartels were believed to be inherently unstable in the long run.

6.3 THE UNIQUENESS OF OIL

Petroleum accounts for about a quarter of the value of all commodities exchanged in international markets, and it is by far the most important internationally-traded commodity measured by volume and monetary value.[4] In this sense oil is undoubtedly unique as a commodity. Moreover, if one examines the characteristics of oil in terms of the formula described in section 6.2 above, it becomes clear that oil is very well placed as a commodity suitable for cartelisation.

By far the greatest source of its strength is the sheer dependence of the world economy on it as a source of energy. As Table 6.1 shows, 44 per cent of world energy consumption is derived from liquid petroleum. Among OECD countries, Japan is highly dependent on oil imports, with European countries only slightly less dependent; only the USA and Canada are relatively self-sufficient. Oil is the principal energy source at present because it is cheap relative to other fuels and demand is highly inelastic, especially where diesel or petrol engines are used, since there are virtually no viable substitutes except conservation.

Table 6.1: Primary energy consumption derived from crude oil and natural gas liquids in 1980

	\% of primary energy consumption from:		
	Domestic energy resources	Imported oil	Total
USA	26	17	43
Western Europe	9	44	53
Japan	negligible	68	68
Canada	36	4	40
World	—	—	44

Sources: British Petroleum (1981), United States Department of Energy (1981).

None the less, there were signs by the late 1970s that the stagnation in energy demand is not solely due to the macroeconomic effects of world recession, but that high oil prices have also encouraged conservation and a switch to other sources of energy such as coal and solar energy.

The supply of oil by non-OPEC members is also very inelastic because of the concentration of low-cost oil resources in the Middle East, and the long time lag required before higher prices materialise in oil supply increases. Although non-OPEC production has been growing quite fast since 1974 (Britain, Norway and Mexico), most commentators feel that the more prolific fields have already been found and that OPEC will continue to dominate the market for many years to come. Nevertheless, the cost of energy from non-OPEC sources probably constitutes the single most important constraint (via the limit price) on OPEC.

If there is an Achilles' heel to the oil cartel, it lies in the large number of producers (13) involved, and the market share parameter x. As Table 6.2 indicates, OPEC accounts for about a half of total world production of oil (about 60 per cent of output excluding the USSR), although it fell in the 1970s as non-OPEC countries expanded their production. In this respect there are other commodities such as copper, cocoa and tea which have greater potential for producer market domination. OPEC's strength, therefore, lies not so much in its potential monopolisation of supply, as in the highly inelastic demand for oil and the relative difficulty of increasing supplies by non-OPEC members.

Table 6.2: OPEC's share of average daily oil production, 1940–80

	OPEC	World	OPEC share
	(millions of barrels per day)		%
1940	1.004	5.890	17.05
1950	3.432	10.419	32.94
1960	8.800	21.026	41.85
1970	23.408	43.210	54.17
1980	26.890	59.455	45.23

Sources: American Petroleum Institute (1971), Central Intelligence Agency (1979), United States Department of Energy (1981).

OPEC's success in the 1970s stimulated considerable interest in LDCs in the prospects for cartelisation of other commodities which are produced principally by poorer countries. Unfortunately, however, it seems that there are few commodities exported predominantly by LDCs which are feasible in terms of the formula we have applied to oil, even assuming that organisational problems could be solved. Compared with oil, most minerals are widely distributed or found mainly in DCs (such as uranium in the USA and diamonds in South Africa and the Soviet Union), and nearly all agricultural products can be cultivated in many different countries.

Radetski (1976), for example, found that only eight commodities (cocoa, coffee, tea, tin, bauxite, manganese, phosphate rock, copper) satisfied the necessary economic conditions for a successful cartel between LDCs. Other studies have come to similar conclusions: for example, Van Duyne (1975) and Mikdashi *et al.* (1974). It seems that most non-fuel minerals are relatively price-elastic in the long run since they have substitutes or can be recycled from scrap (such as copper). Even where foodstuffs are relatively concentrated in supply (such as bananas), it is generally fairly easy for consumers to substitute into other goods if prices are forced up. As Radetski also points out, the potential redistribution of income from the cartelisation of these commodities is small compared with oil. Even if the producers of all eight feasible commodities in her study had been as successful as OPEC in raising prices in 1973, they would only have achieved about two-thirds of the revenue obtained by the oil producers during the same period. Hence, although cartels currently exist for rubber, coffee, bauxite, copper and bananas, and there has been some success in phosphates and bauxite in the 1970s, these producers have generally failed to achieve supply-dominated markets.[5]

6.4 THE UNIQUENESS OF OPEC

OPEC officially came into being as a result of a conference held in Baghdad in September 1960 and currently includes 13 full members.[6] Contrary to popular belief, it is not an Arab organisation and its members vary considerably in population and land area, and are geographically dispersed over three continents and an island. Nor is it true that all member countries are wealthy. As Table 6.3 shows, some are really quite poor.

Prior to the foundation of OPEC, the international oil economy had been dominated by oligopolistic oil companies, which reached agreements amongst themselves under the umbrella of the International Corporate Cartel founded in 1914. By the 1950s this cartel consisted of the French Compagnie Française des Petroles and seven international corporations known collectively as 'the seven sisters'.[7] Producing countries had little say in the running of the oil market, but were generally content to receive a share of the profits per barrel as royalties. Indeed, the immediate reason for the formation of OPEC was the fall in royalties in the late 1950s due to a drop in oil prices.

Table 6.3: Selected statistics of OPEC members in 1980

	Reserves (barrels/ bn)	Population (m)	Land area (000 sq.m)	Per capita GNP ($)	Per capita oil wealth[2] ($'000)
UAE[1]	30.4	0.8	32	24,360	1216
Kuwait	64.9	3.0	8	18,390	692
Qatar	3.6	0.2	4	29,900	676
Saudi Arabia	165.0	8.1	873	9,500	652
Libya	23.0	2.6	680	6,960	283
Iraq	30.0	12.8	172	2,730	75
Gabon	0.5	0.6	103	5,250	27
Iran	67.5	36.9	636	2,170	58
Venezuela	17.8	12.7	352	3,370	45
Algeria	8.2	18.0	920	1,720	15
Nigeria	16.7	84.5	380	620	6
Ecuador	1.1	7.3	109	1,100	5
Indonesia	9.5	143.0	788	350	2
USA	—	—	—	10,719	5

Notes: [1] United Arab Emirates. [2] Oil reserves valued at $32 per barrel.
Sources: International Petroleum Encyclopaedia (1981), Central Intelligence Agency (1981), Council of Economic Advisers (1981).

Despite the window-dressing embodied in formal resolutions at OPEC meetings, the organisation was singularly impotent during the first decade of its existence. As Alnaswari (1974) has clearly shown, OPEC failed to exert its collective bargaining strength, and although it was successful in preventing a further erosion in royalties, it remained an instrument of moderation and on the sidelines of the international oil market.

By about 1970, however, the balance of power had begun to shift in OPEC's favour encouraged by oil shortages following the Arab oil embargo after the 1967 Arab-Israeli War and the closure of the Suez Canal, and success by Libya and Algeria in extracting unilateral concessions from the oil companies. This demonstrated that the 'Emperors did not have any clothes', and encouraged a bandwagon effect on other OPEC countries. Growing Arab political unity and success in isolating Israel from the rest of the international community also played a part. Striking evidence that OPEC had come of age followed the Egypt–Israel War of 1973 when an OPEC oil embargo, ostensibly to put pressure on the West, resulted in the quadrupling of the price of oil in three months.

After 1973 a process of nationalisation ensued in the oil-producing countries, with foreign companies providing capital and expertise under contract, and organising the transportation and distribution of oil to consuming countries. OPEC did not literally control prices, but it has undoubtedly become the dominant influence in world petroleum markets.

From the perspective of the 1980s, few would doubt that OPEC has been uniquely successful as an organisation, not only in effecting the most dramatic redistribution of income in history, but also in maintaining surprising cohesion, despite a relatively large number of members by cartel standards and considerable potential differences of interest between them. Some idea of the magnitude of the transfer from oil consumers to OPEC producers is provided by Table 6.4. What this shows is that between 1973 and 1974 prices quadrupled to a level of $11–$12 per barrel and remained fairly stable until the second 'oil shock' in 1979.

Table 6.4: The average posted price and annual percentage changes in crude oil prices 1970–80

	Average price[1] ($ per barrel)	% change from previous year
1970	1.80	0.0
1971	2.23	24.0
1972	2.48	11.1
1973	3.63	46.3
1974	11.45	215.7
1975	12.18	6.4
1976	12.13	−0.5
1977	12.40	1.0
1978	12.70	2.4
1979	17.26	35.6
1980	28.67	66.1

Note: [1]Posted price of Saudi light crude oil.
Source: Exxon Corporation (1980).

In the 1970s, OPEC exhibited a degree of cohesion that few thought possible, especially in view of the diversity of interests of its members. OPEC is a price-fixing and not a profit-sharing cartel, so market shares determine the distribution of benefits between the countries concerned from the exercise of monopoly power. The main determinant of market shares is the price differential among the various crude oils, and it is this problem of differentials which lies at the heart of the cartel's organisational problems. Since about 1970 the process of bargaining has revolved around the setting of the Saudi Arabian crude marker price at twice-yearly ministerial meetings; then the other countries set their prices to reflect quality differences and transport costs. OPEC, therefore, determines prices, but buyers determine the level of output and its distribution between the member countries. Over the years this problem of establishing price differentials has become more apparent, especially since 1976. In 1979, for example, a variation of up to 30.6 per cent of the basic export price of reference crude has been allowed. OPEC's cohesion as an organisation has also been weakened by the effects of world recession on oil prices and in particular the sale of North Sea oil below official OPEC prices. It is no coincidence that Nigeria, the cartel member most prone to break the rules, produces oil which competes directly with that produced by Britain.

OPEC also has to solve the long-run problem of choosing a rate of depletion for oil. OPEC countries which are relatively poor, such as Nigeria and Ecuador, are keen to sell as much oil as they can even if it means early depletion in order to generate funds for immediate development. Other producers such as Saudi Arabia would prefer to leave the oil in the ground longer and adopt a more evolutionary strategy towards economic development. Balancing these views has not been easy and much of the success of OPEC in the 1970s has been due to the conciliatory role of Saudi Arabia in keeping cases of 'cheating' to a minimum.

In this sense OPEC has been remarkably successful as an organisation and there is no strong evidence that it is about to break up. There is evidence, however, that tensions within the OPEC camp have been higher in recent years with the Iran–Iraq War and Iran selling oil below OPEC agreed prices. There is also evidence that some Gulf states have been selling oil to South Africa in defiance of an official embargo. These events have persuaded people such as Mattedeen (1983) that, although OPEC will continue to survive, it may be in the form of a looser oligopoly arrangement rather than a cohesive cartel.

If we accept that oil is unique as a commodity and OPEC has been uniquely successful as an organisation, how useful is cartel theory in explaining developments within the oil industry since 1970?

In so far as traditional cartel theory emphasises the instability of such formal cooperative ventures and the tendency for price to fall in the long run, its predictions have not been borne out in the case of oil, at least not in the first decade of effective cartel power. Similarly, it is perhaps naive to have expected OPEC to behave along the lines of a perfect textbook cartel given the complexity of the international oil market and its distinctive blend of competition and cooperation. After all, it consists of buyers and sellers of crude oil and refined products, as well as a whole network of service and distribution activities right down to the sale of petrol at the pumps. Thus, although OPEC is undoubtedly a dominant force in the process of oil-price determination, it does not literally control price. It is also worth pointing out that the price of oil has not, as many people seem to think, risen continuously since 1973. It fell in 1976 and has fallen since 1982.

In addition, the characterisation of OPEC as a cartel conflicts with the theory of depletable resources.[8] This theory, based on the work of Hotelling (1931), suggests that the holders of an exhaustible resource such as oil will optimise their wealth over time by extracting the resource at a rate in line with the path of real interest rates (nominal interest rates adjusted for price inflation), representing the opportunity cost of leaving it in the ground as a future investment. In other words, OPEC would attempt to determine the price of oil in such a way as to ration out supplies over time to avoid excessive depletion leaving a scarcity before a substitute is found, and to avoid slow usage which delays development in the short run. According to this view, therefore, one might expect the price of oil to rise gently over time. In addition, since oil is a non-renewable resource, this theory provides good grounds for expecting its price to be well above extraction costs, even in the absence of cartel monopoly power. Cartel theory, on the other hand, predicts the maximum use of monopoly power.

The theory of exhaustible resources is itself a considerable simplification of the situation, being based upon idealised conditions of either perfect competition or monopoly. Since the oil market contains a mixture of monopoly power and competition it is not generally possible to derive the optimal price trajectory.[9]

What this theory does, however, is to emphasise the importance of intertemporal considerations in cartel policy formulation and provides a justification for those views in OPEC which fall short of the full exercise of monopoly power in the short run. Cartel theory, on the other hand, is useful for explaining the uniqueness of both oil and OPEC, and the ability of the cartel to keep price well above marginal costs and redistribute resources in its favour. It also reminds us how vulnerable OPEC is to changes in economic or political circumstances.

Thus, neither cartel theory nor the theory of depletable resources can fully explain developments in the oil market in the 1970s and 1980s. Certainly, one should not be misled into believing that the only factor which determines the price of oil is the exercise of monopoly power by OPEC. In view of the complexity of the international oil economy, it is not surprising that such a simple story would be incomplete.[10]

6.5 THE ECONOMIC ANALYSIS OF INTERNATIONAL COMMODITY AGREEMENTS

In Chapter 4 we examined the case presented by LDCs for remedial policy action to tackle the problem of export instability arising from primary-product price fluctuations. Although there is still considerable debate about the validity of this case, the balance of opinion seems to have shifted some way towards the LDC's point of view, and in this section we assess the role that international commodity agreements might play in ameliorating the undesirable consequences of export price fluctuations.

Although we shall primarily be concerned here with international policies to counter export instability, there are certain domestic measures which the countries concerned could adopt. For example, if fluctuations in export receipts are seen to constitute the problem, then the government could hold extra reserves of foreign exchange to act as a cushion against swings in such receipts. Similarly, if the problem relates primarily to the uncertainty generated by fluctuations in the price of a particular commodity, then a marketing board could be set up with instructions to purchase the entire output and pay producers a stable, though not necessarily fixed, price. The board would then sell the output on the world market and any profits it makes in one year could be held in reserve for bad years. In this way it acts as a buffer between the world price and the price paid to domestic producers.

The call for international action, however, is not weakened by these policy options in so far as the country concerned is obliged to bear the full brunt of the adjustment process, and there could well be opportunity costs involved. For example, the funds tied up in foreign exchange reserves or in the marketing board could well have alternative uses—possibly to finance development projects. In this sense, international commodity agreements (ICAs) are seen as complements to, rather than substitutes for, domestic action.

Export restrictions, buffer stocks and multilateral contracts are all ways in which commodity markets can be manipulated by international agreement to achieve certain objectives. Their two basic goals are to stabilise prices within predetermined boundaries and/or to raise prices above the levels which would occur in the absence of the agreement. In the latter case the ICA is providing a form of disguised aid in transferring purchasing power from one country to another. Although these objectives are conceptually separate, in practice most ICAs have not been pure stabilisation schemes but have also been designed to redistribute 'aid through trade'. We shall examine these issues more fully in Chapter 17, and the implications of alternative schemes below, but first it is necessary to outline the mechanisms involved in them and the conditions under which they might be expected to work.

Export restriction schemes are designed to stabilise incomes by means of national quotas set in relation to expected demand. Figure 6.2 describes the operation of such a scheme. AB is a curve containing points at which earnings are constant no matter where you are on it. The curves ss and dd are the initial supply and demand curves intersecting at equilibrium p1q1, with export earnings given by the area Op1Eq1.

Imagine that a temporary decline in demand shifts dd to dd'. In the absence of intervention, price would fall to p2 and output to q2. However, the export restriction policy would reduce supply by artificially withholding the commodity. For example, in order to maintain the original level of earnings, supply would have to be reduced to q3 so that price rises to p3. The reverse action could have been taken if demand had increased. If, on the other hand,

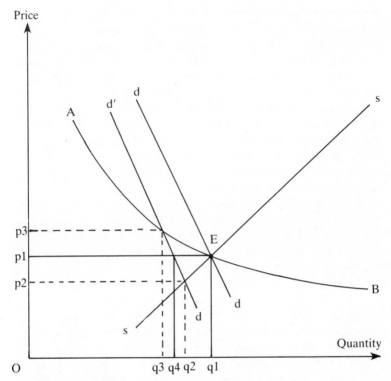

Figure 6.2: The operation of an export restriction scheme

the objective had also been to raise income, then supply would have been forced back beyond q3 and price pushed above p3. A good example of such a scheme is the International Coffee Agreement which operated almost continuously after 1962 to halt the long run decline in coffee prices.

In practice there are many problems associated with the operation of such a scheme. It is difficult to police an arrangement which offers incentives for producers to defect to avoid the necessary cutbacks, or to cheat by selling more at the high price. Moreover, there is always the danger that raising price will reduce earnings in the long run if demand becomes more elastic and new producers are attracted to the market by the prospect of high earnings.

Buffer stocks operate through an agency buying up the stock of a commodity when its price is lower than an agreed floor, and selling it when its price exceeds a ceiling. Again, the objective could be simply price stabilisation around a competitive price, or to raise price in order to redistribute income away from consumers to producers. An example of a pure price- stabilisation buffer is the International Tin Agreement which operated more or less without interruption from 1956. In terms of Figure 6.2, if p1 is the price to be maintained, then the fall in demand to dd' would signal the authorities to purchase q1q4. Conversely, the buffer would sell if the demand curve shifted to the right-hand side. Equivalent policy action could be derived from supply shifts, or a combination of supply and demand movements.

The success of a buffer stock depends critically on the foresight of its managers in ensuring that the price range it intends to defend is realistic in terms of long run supply and demand conditions. In particular, it needs sufficient financial reserves to be able to buy the commodity if price falls persistently; and enough stocks of the commodity so as not to run out if price rises. The commodity itself must be storeable, fairly homogeneous and have low storage costs to qualify. The authorities must also resist the temptation to maintain price at such a level that it encourages overproduction by producers and substitution by consumers. This is particularly risky where the long run elasticity of demand is expected to be much higher than in the short run. Finally, buffer stocks are prone to speculative pressures, especially when private traders believe that its stocks are too low for it to be able to hold its maximum price. Speculators could then make a killing by buying at the current low price and selling when price rises above the ceiling. If they are wrong then they only lose the margin between the buffer's buying and selling price.

Finally, there are multilateral contracts to consider. These contracts represent a direct bargain between buyers and sellers to exchange an agreed quantity within a stipulated price range. The sellers agree to a maximum price and the buyers to a minimum price. Once again the goal could be to stabilise price within the agreed range, or to provide 'disguised aid' to the producing countries. An example here might be the Commonwealth Sugar Agreement between the UK and her former colonies operating after the second world war.

There are two important drawbacks to the price intervention

schemes we have discussed so far. First, it is possible that in attempting to stabilise price the ICA may simultaneously destabilise income; and secondly, the common practice of raising price as well as stabilising it involves the mixing of efficiency with redistribution.

As far as the first problem is concerned, research has been undertaken in recent years to ascertain the conditions under which price stabilisation also stabilises income. The findings of this research are too complex to report here, but in general the more the instability in price originates from the supply side of the market, as opposed to the demand side, the less likely it is that price stabilisation will also stabilise income.[11] In terms of the second problem, we shall be looking at the international relations issues associated with the mixing of trade and aid in Chapter 17, but the existence of these problems has encouraged economists to look at alternative schemes based upon price or income *compensation*.

A good example of a price compensation scheme was suggested by Meade (1964). If the price of a given commodity fell, then the two countries concerned would agree on a sliding-scale of compensation paid by the importer to the exporter, possibly related to deviations of price from an agreed 'normal' price. Such a scheme would have the advantage of separating market efficiency from the question of income distribution, since the market is left alone, and the lack of full compensation would still encourage producers to shift resources out of the commodity if price fell over the long run. Moreover, if perpetual compensation seemed to be occurring, the scheme would be supplemented by a supply-restriction scheme.

An income-compensation arrangement, on the other hand, would take into account both price and quantity changes, and the compensation would depend upon deviations from some 'normal' income range. Examples of such schemes currently operating are the International Monetary Fund's Compensatory Financing Facility and the Stabex arrangements of the EEC. For a good review of the compensatory financing scheme operated by the IMF, see Green (1980).

So far we have taken it for granted that stabilisation schemes, if operated correctly, can bring important benefits to both producers and consumers; but the distributive effects of price-stabilisation schemes turn out to be rather complex to unravel.

A rigorous analysis of the impact of alternative stabilisation schemes under alternative assumptions is contained in Newberry and Stiglitz (1981), but some general points can be made here. If, for example, we take the case of a buffer stock and assume operating costs are low and the managers guess future price trends correctly, then the benefits of stabilisation arise essentially from the matching of supply and demand over time, although there may also be benefits from the reduction in uncertainty. The distribution of these gains between exporting and importing countries, however, depends critically on the source of the instability. What research has shown is that exporters tend to gain in revenue terms and importers to lose in expenditure terms, if instability originates primarily from the supply side. The reverse is true if instability is mainly demand-determined. Unfortunately, however, the gains from higher average incomes are liable to be offset by the increased risks associated with wider fluctuations in these incomes over time.[12]

It is, therefore, very difficult to come to any strong conclusions about the benefits of stabilisation schemes without looking more closely at the relevant empirical information about the commodity or commodities concerned. Nevertheless, there seems to be some support for the view that price-stabilisation schemes can, *in principle*, provide positive net benefits, especially for LDCs. A leading exponent of this view is Behrman. For further details, see Behrman (1979). The practice, however, may be a quite different matter, to which we now turn.

6.6 INTERNATIONAL COMMODITY AGREEMENTS IN PRACTICE

Many attempts have been made to control international commodity markets during the twentieth century, with the intention of both stabilising and raising price.[13] Conferences were held in 1902 for both coffee and sugar but concerted action was considered to be both unnecessary and impractical. After the first world war, influenced by the dislocation of the international economy and the growth of government intervention into areas hitherto considered taboo, further attempts at cooperation were made, but they were generally dominated by producers and lacked any coherent organisation. The depression of the 1930s ensured the collapse of any existing schemes, but the severe problems of excess capacity it engendered stimulated interest in multilateral negotiations under the supervision of the League of Nations. For the first time consumer interests played an important part, but there seemed to be little enthusiasm for the type of market intervention which would have been required.

In 1943, however, a United Nations conference on food and agriculture began an examination of international commodity problems which was to culminate in an international trade organisation at the Havana Conference of 1947. At this conference a code of behaviour was agreed to provide a more orderly means of settling disputes between consumers and producers, and especially to avoid unilateral supply restrictions.

Since 1945 there have been a number of ICAs, primarily in wheat, tin, coffee and cocoa, many of which were buffer stock arrangements, but few managed to survive for long periods. Buffer stocks, in particular, were prone to collapse in the face of severe disruptions in the market. A notable exception has been the International Tin Agreement.

It appears, therefore, that past efforts at price stabilisation have not generally been very successful, especially in the longer run. Part of the problem may be due to the fact that, whilst in the first two decades after the second world war the main goal of ICAs was seen in terms of price stabilisation, in subsequent years the balance shifted towards the goal of *raising* price to maintain or increase the purchasing power of imports. In this connection, the United Nations Conference on Trade and Development (UNCTAD) has played a major role in promoting ICAs, primarily to benefit poorer countries. Indeed, in 1976 it achieved agreement in principle to establish an Integrated Programme for Commodities as part of North–South negotiations over a new international economic order, including the setting up of a common fund to finance a number of buffer stocks. The programme was intended to cover ten core commodities, and a number of others to be settled by negotiation. Since 1976 the scheme has operated in a limited way, but there is considerable opposition to its full implementation by some DCs, particularly the USA, and the negotiations are currently deadlocked.

Despite the lack of success displayed by ICAs in the past, there is still considerable support for these schemes, and a feeling by many economists that there could be real gains from an integrated programme of the sort suggested by UNCTAD, especially if DCs were willing to adopt a more conciliatory attitude. We shall return to these issues again in Chapter 17.

NOTES

1. See Stocking and Watkins (1946).
2. The derivation of this formula is discussed in Radetski (1976).
3. For the history of producer alliances, see Rowe (1965).
4. See Danielson (1982).
5. For the bauxite case, see Bergson (1976).
6. The founder members were Saudi Arabia, Iran, Kuwait, Iraq and Venezuela. Qatar (1961), Libya (1962), Indonesia (1962), The United Arab Emirates (1967), Algeria (1969), Nigeria (1971), Ecuador (1973), and Gabon (1975) subsequently joined the organisation.
7. Exxon, Mobil, Texaco, Socal, Gulf, Shell and British Petroleum.
8. In the long run all resources are depletable, but most, in practice, are not classed as such. For example, coal is expected to last for over 500 years; oil, on the other hand, may only last a few decades.
9. See Danielson (1982, ch. 2).
10. Another explanation for oil prices, which suggests that producers have reached a target income and prefer to leave the oil in the ground, even if its price continues to rise, has received much less support. See Ulph (1984).
11. For further details on this research, see Ezriel *et al* (1977).
12. See also Ezriel *et al* (1977).
13. See Behrman (1979) and Rowe (1965).

FURTHER READING

A good introduction to cartel theory can be found in Radetski (1976), which also assesses the prospects for establishing cartels between LDCs. The evolution of OPEC is discussed in Alnaswari (1974) and, more recently, in Mattedeen (1983). An excellent analysis of the relevance of economic theory to the international oil market, including cartel theory and the theory of depletable resources, is contained in Danielson (1982). A much shorter summary of the economist's attempt to explain oil prices, pitched at an elementary level, is presented by Ulph (1984). A useful review of the theory and practice of ICAs is Behrman (1979). The specific issues raised by price-stabilisation schemes are discussed in Ezriel (1977) and in much more detail by Newberry and Stiglitz (1981). Finally, the compensatory financing scheme operated by the IMF is assessed in Green (1980).

7 The Economics of Integration

7.1 ECONOMIC INTEGRATION

An alternative to liberalising trade by removing tariffs and other barriers is for a group of countries to evolve closer links by reducing trade restrictions amongst themselves, whilst leaving them intact against the rest of the world. In other words, to pursue economic integration, but at the same time to practise discrimination against 'outsiders'.

There are many possible forms of integration depending on the closeness of the ties adopted, ranging from the simple removal of tariff barriers to the more utopian elimination of all impediments to trade. In practice, economists distinguish between four stages of integration, ranging from preference areas to full economic union.

The preference area is a relatively loose arrangement by which certain countries are allowed preferential access to the domestic market of another country. A good example is the system of Commonwealth Preference concluded between Great Britain and her colonial associates in 1932, which involved the lowering of tariff rates on goods which the countries concerned imported from each other.

A closer form of integration is achieved when countries set up a free trade area, since this obliges them to abolish tariffs between themselves although they retain their individual tariffs against the rest of the world. In fact, free trade areas tend to be only partial in the commodities covered by the tariff reductions, and in the extent to which tariffs are cut. Examples of such arrangements in the period after the second world war include the European Free Trade Association (EFTA) and the Latin American Free Trade Association (LAFTA).

An altogether more formal commitment towards integration is established when countries agree to form a customs union since not only does it involve the removal of tariff barriers between member countries, but also the setting-up of a common external tariff structure against the rest of the world. This was the intention of the European Economic Community (EEC) when the Treaty of Rome was signed in 1957. The EEC is now recognised as a complete customs union and has moved some way towards the further stage of integration known as a common market. This implies not only the free movement of all goods and services within the customs union, but also permits the free movement of factors of production, such as labour and capital. In fact the EEC is often referred to as 'the Common Market'.

The final stage of integration, known as full economic union or complete integration, is a little ambiguous. Short of being a single unit, the union is committed to a substantial degree of pooling of national policies, primarily in monetary and fiscal matters, and the surrendering of decisions over these matters to a central authority. Belgium, Luxembourg and the Netherlands achieved this with the formation of Benelux, agreed in principle before the end of the second world war and set up in 1948. The union abolished internal tariffs and adopted a common external tariff. The aim of the union, which was reiterated in 1960, was the eventual merging of the fiscal and monetary systems of the members and the free mobility of capital and labour. In 1958 Benelux joined the EEC. The EEC eventually seeks the objective of full union. How far countries are prepared to concede sovereignty on these issues defines the extent of the union.

Although in this chapter we shall concentrate on the theory of customs unions, the analysis is also relevant to other forms of integration, including free trade areas and common markets. In section 7.2 we use this theory to assess the implications of forming closer economic ties between nations, and in section 7.3 we examine the practical experience of integration movements both in developed countries (DCs) and lesser developed countries (LDCs).[1]

7.2 CUSTOMS UNION THEORY

When countries get together to form a customs union they will be changing the pattern of tariffs between themselves, and between the union and the rest of the world. Consequently, there will be repercussions on trade volumes, prices and economic welfare. Prior to the work of Jacob Viner (1950), it was generally supposed that the removal of tariff barriers within the union would raise welfare because it implied a movement towards freer trade. However, since the formation of the union also involves the erection of a common external barrier trade will also be distorted, as goods entering a member country will pay different duties depending on their country of origin. Whether the customs union, on balance, will increase or decrease welfare for its members, therefore, depends on the net effect of what Viner called 'trade-creation' and 'trade-diversion'.

To take a simple example first, imagine there are three countries: the UK, France, and the rest of the world. Column (1) in Table 7.1 shows the hypothetical costs of producing wine in all three countries, and column (2) their selling prices in the UK market, which is protected by a 100 per cent tariff. In this situation, the UK would not import wine, since the tariff makes it more expensive to import it from both France and the rest of the world.

Let the UK and France now form a union with a 100 per cent common external tariff. The data in column (3) indicate that trade has been created, since the UK is now able to import wine at a lower cost from France, and is better-off by £20 per unit (i.e. £100 – £80). Sales from the rest of the world are irrelevant, since they were zero to the UK before the union was formed, and are unable to compete with French exports once the union has been established.

Table 7.1: The formation of a customs union between the UK and France

	(1) Production price (£ per unit)	(2) Tariff price (UK tariff = 100%)	(3) Union price (external tariff = 100%)	(4) Tariff price (UK tariff = 50%)	(5) Union price (external tariff = 50%)
UK	100	100	100	100	100
France	80	160	80	120	80
Rest of world	60	120	120	90	90

If, however, the initial tariff in the UK had been 50 per cent before the formation of the union, then column (4) implies that the UK would have been importing wine from the rest of the world since, even with the UK tariff, it would have been cheaper at £90 per unit than either domestic wine or wine from France. Hence, the effect of the formation of the union between France and the UK with a common external tariff of 50 per cent would, as column (5) shows, be to divert imports from the rest of the world to French sources.

Thus, the first case is one of trade-creation, as production is transferred from a high-cost producer within the union (the UK) to a lower-cost member of the union (France); and the second is a case of trade-diversion, when production is reallocated from a low-cost external source (the rest of the world) to a higher-cost member of the union (France). The benefits from trade-creation arise from the fact that the UK begins to import a product (wine) which it previously produced at home under protection; and the losses arise under trade-diversion from the fact that the UK is starting to import wine from a partner country when it previously imported it more cheaply from the rest of the world.

The concepts of trade-creation and trade-diversion can be further illustrated with the help of Figure 7.1. DD and SS represent the domestic supply and demand curves for wine in the UK. Given the world price OW, and the tariff levied on wine imports WH, some wine (OM) is produced inefficiently behind the tariff wall, and MN is imported. In this situation France cannot compete with the rest of the world, since her pre-tariff price of OF is higher than the rest of the world price OW. However, once the UK and France have formed the union and the tariff against France is replaced by the common tariff OH, all imports of wine now come from France.

Trade-creation still arises because the UK consumption of wine has increased to ON' as imports rise to M'N' and the UK's inefficient wine industry is partly competed down to OM'. The net welfare gain to the UK in terms of economic surplus is given by areas 2 and 4 in Figure 7.1, and represents the benefits to UK consumers of obtaining imports more cheaply from France. In other words, consumers gain 1 + 2 + 3 + 4, but 1 is a loss to domestic producers and 3 is lost revenue to the government.

In practice this net welfare gain could be measured quite easily if

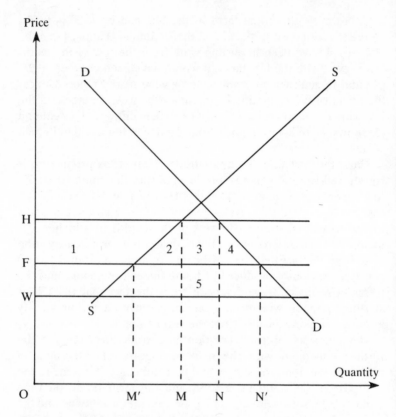

Figure 7.1: Trade-creation and trade-diversion

DD and SS are straight lines as equal to half of the tariff multiplied by the volume of trade created. Since we already know the tariff WH, and the increase in imports is given by M'N' minus MN, the product of these two multiplied by a half approximates the area 2 + 4.

Trade-diversion, on the other hand, is represented by the deadweight loss in area 5, reflecting the increased cost of getting MN of wine from the partner country rather than from the lower-cost rest of the world. This loss to the UK is due to the fact that wine is no longer supplied by the world's most efficient producer, but by the most efficient producer *within the customs union*. This in turn could be estimated as half the tariff multiplied by the volume of trade-diverted.

Thus whether the formation of the union has, on balance, increased or decreased welfare (as measured by economic surplus), depends on the relative magnitude of trade-creation and trade-diversion multiplied by the appropriate price differential in each case. This net welfare effect will be the difference between 2 + 4 and area 5 in Figure 7.1. Even though France is relatively inefficient compared with the rest of the world, the loss from switching to France as a source of supply could still be more than offset by the gains to UK consumers from relaxation of the restriction on consumer spending which the original tariff imposed.

We have, of course, continued to use the concept of economic surplus as a measure of welfare changes. As we discussed in Chapter 6, this assumes that equal weights are applied to the gains and losses of all parties concerned. If, on the other hand, wine were consumed predominantly by the poor and produced by the rich, we might conclude that the redistribution implied by area 1 (i.e. the net loss to domestic producers) is a net *improvement* in welfare. In other words, the gain by consumers is not to be offset by the loss to domestic producers.

Although the welfare effects of a customs union will depend upon particular circumstances, including the adding-up of the net effect of all the cases of trade-creation and trade-diversion arising from the formation of the union, there are a number of factors which could maximise trade-creation and minimise trade-diversion. To begin with, the more countries involved, the more likely the union will contain the most efficient producer of a product, and the less important will trade diversion be. In the extreme case of all countries joining, then the result would be tantamount to universal free trade. Secondly, the higher the initial tariffs before the union, the greater the liklihood of trade creation. Thirdly, the lower the common external tariff, the less the liklihood of trade diversion. Fourthly, the higher the price-elasticity of demand and supply in the home country, i.e. the flatter are DD and SS in Figure 7.1, the larger will be areas 2 and 4 representing the gains from the union.

Finally, and perhaps paradoxically, the countries concerned with the integration programme should be producing *similar* goods, but with large *potential* cost differences once the union has been formed. In other words it is not just a question of how many countries are involved, but also of whether they are potentially complementary. Trade-creation requires some overlap in production patterns, but significant reallocation possibilities within the union once protection has been lifted. This is one reason why LDCs specialising in one or two primary exports may have little to gain from closer economic ties with other LDCs, compared with the gains open to the industrially-diversified countries of Western Europe.

Useful though the preceding analysis is for examining the effects of economic integration, we need to complete our discussion by considering the simplifying assumptions upon which it rests, and raise one or two additional problems which are likely to arise when countries seek closer economic ties with each other.

Besides the problem of associating changes in welfare with changes in economic surplus, the major limitations of the Viner approach are its reliance on a partial equilibrium framework, and its failure to take into account the dynamic effects of customs union formation. As it stands, Figure 7.1 assumes that the supply of wine imported into the UK from the partner country and the rest of the world is perfectly elastic, i.e. it is available in unlimited quantities at prices OF and OW, respectively.[2] It is quite possible, however, that the formation of the union will alter the terms of trade for the countries concerned. With some knowledge of the relative elasticities it would be possible to make some judgement about the likely implications of the two countries joining the union but, unfortunately, the effects cannot be predicted accurately when one generalises to many countries and many commodities.

Our analysis also suffers from the drawback that it is essentially static. In fact, much of the debate over the benefits of integration relates to the potential *dynamic* gains from forming the union. These gains refer principally to the advantages of a larger market and the expected competitive 'shock' effects on domestic industry. The increase in the size of the market presents opportunities to exploit economies of large-scale production, and exposure to foreign competition might force domestic firms to defend their market position, thereby shaking out sheltered inefficient producers, as well as making oligopoly collusion harder to sustain. There might also be a bonus in the form of greater foreign investment if firms from abroad are attracted by the chance to become established inside the common external tariff structure. The

Japanese firm Nissan, for example, has shown increasing interest in setting up subsidiaries in the UK in recent years, possibly as a means of getting inside the EEC's common external tariff structure.

It would be hoped that these dynamic benefits would exceed any negative effects arising from the integration movement. For example, short-run adjustment costs brought about by disinvestment in industries harmed by trade-creation, i.e. in order to obtain the long-run benefits of trade-creation resources will need to be shifted out of import-competing industries which can no longer compete. Similarly, regional imbalances could arise from the pull of market-oriented industry towards the frontier and the markets of partner countries, or from the movement of factors of production to the more dynamic regions of the union.

Finally, there are some practical problems to be encountered when countries embark upon a process of greater integration. In the first instance, there will have to be some agreement on the structure of the common external tariff within a customs union, and on the mechanism for distributing the proceeds and financing common policies. This problem is made more difficult in as much as there is no unique way to classify goods and to measure and weight the individual tariff rates. Although the issue of the common external tariff doesn't arise within a free trade area, there is a separate problem here when goods imported from the rest of the world enter the free trade area via the country with the lowest external tariff, and are then transported to another member country with a higher external tariff. To minimise this practice, extensive documentation by so-called certificates or origin are necessary.

Further problems also arise once tariffs have been reduced if other domestic distortions persist, including subsidies, discriminatory freight rates and differences in internal taxation policies between member countries. These are especially acute if the countries involved are committed to full factor mobility and the coordination of macroeconomic policies. We shall refer to some of these problems in section 7.3 below, but a good example was associated with the formation of Benelux. Although barriers to capital and labour mobility were removed, Dutch capital tended to remain in Holland and Belgian workers stayed in Belgium, despite the fact that the returns to capital and labour were demonstrably higher in the other country. Private inertia thus prevented factor mobility.

One final problem relates to transport costs. One of the advantages of the EEC compared with EFTA was the existence of shared common boundaries and, therefore, relatively low costs of transport between member countries. In other integration movements such as LAFTA, however, countries which were contiguous geographically, such as Argentina and Chile, were not close economically. Clearly, the cost of transporting goods between member countries is likely to play an important role in the success of the integration movement.

7.3 INTEGRATION MOVEMENTS IN PRACTICE

Since 1945 there have been a number of integration movements, involving both developed and developing countries.[3] In this section we trace the development of some of the more important of these movements and review the evidence concerning their benefits and costs.

As far as DCs are concerned, the two best-known examples are The European Free Trade Association (EFTA) and The European Economic Community (EEC).

EFTA was founded in 1958 between Great Britain, Austria, Denmark, Finland, Iceland, Norway, Portugal, Sweden and Switzerland. Despite the diversity of its membership and their geographical spread, it was quite successful in expanding internal trade in manufactured goods. Trade-diversion, however, was probably also quite high compared with the EEC, since the heterogeneity of EFTA's membership meant more opportunities merely to switch the sources of imports to EFTA members, rather than to switch from domestic production to imports. In other words, these goods would probably have been imported in any case, only their sources were changed. At the current time EFTA continues to function, despite the loss of Great Britain and Denmark to the EEC in 1973, and it has established virtual free trade in industrial goods with the latter organisation.

The EEC was created by the Treaty of Rome in 1957. Its initial members, Belgium, France, West Germany, Italy, Luxembourg and the Netherlands, agreed to form a customs union in industrial goods with a common external tariff set (with some exceptions) by averaging the tariff rates of the individual members. This was completed ahead of schedule by 1968. Denmark, Britain and the Republic of Ireland joined in 1973, Greece acceded in 1981, and Portugal and Spain are negotiating entry terms at the present time.

The Community also has association agreements with a number of former colonies, and has *ad hoc* agreements with other individual countries, including EFTA. The first category established under the Lomé Agreement of 1975 involves preferential access for certain products as well as aid and price support programmes; and the second allows preferential access for countries such as Algeria, Israel and Turkey without reciprocity; and free trade in industrial products with EFTA. The EEC also operates a common agricultural policy and has agreed upon the principle of free mobility of labour within the Community and a coordinated anti-monopoly policy. Ambitious plans for full integration, including monetary union (to be discussed in Chapter 15), are underway, but progress in this area has been relatively slow.

It has generally been accepted that the EEC has been the most successful of all the post-war integration movements from the viewpoint of its members, especially in the first decade of its existence when it has been estimated that inter-EEC trade in manufactures grew by about 50 per cent more than would otherwise have occurred.[4] Although the expansion of trade between the original members slowed down significantly in the 1970s, trade involving the new members increased sharply. Unfortunately, this has been overshadowed by stagflation, disputes about payments into the EEC budget, and wrangles over the Common Agricultural Policy. In the 1980s, therefore, although still committed to monetary union, the EEC has lost much of its original momentum, and there must be some doubt about its future progress.

There is also ample evidence to suggest that the trade-creating effects of the EEC have outweighted trade-diversion, especially when dynamic gains are taken into account. For a review of the evidence in this area, see El Agraa (1980). Kreinin (1974), for example, estimated that by 1969, trade-diversion amounted to $1.1 billion and trade-creation to 8.4 billion. Other estimates have come to similar conclusions.

The trade-diverting effects, however, have been significant in agriculture, particularly after the UK became a full member in 1973. The EEC Association is also overwhelmingly trade-diverting at the expense of Latin America, Asia and the Middle East. It seems, therefore, that the substantial gains in trade in manufactures within the EEC have been at the expense of outsiders such as the USA and Japan, the British Commonwealth and producers of tropical products, excluding some former colonies. There is also some evidence that regional disparities within the Community have been exacerbated as production has been redirected closer to market outlets. Regions which have suffered relatively are southern Italy, the south of France and south-east Germany.

As far as LDCs are concerned, closer integration is often justified, not so much in terms of trade-creation and dynamic gains, as in terms of its contribution to development planning. Countries who wish to achieve industrialisation may want to establish infant industries and the motive for joining an integration movement may be to obtain the benefits of a larger market to foster recently established manufacturing industries. Thus, although buying a product from a partner which has established an infant industry may involve trade-diversion, the longer run benefits from encouraging the location of industries where production costs are lowest, and allowing them to expand within the larger protected market may be seen as worthwhile. Using the UK/France analogy, the two countries would agree to set up a clothing industry in the UK and a wine industry in France.

Of the integration schemes between LDCs which have operated since 1945, three perhaps stand out: the Latin American Free Trade Association (LAFTA), the Central American Common Market (CACM), and the Association of South East Asian Nations.[5]

LAFTA was formed in 1960 between ten Latin American countries (Argentina, Bolivia, Brazil, Chile, Colombia, Ecuador, Mexico, Paraguay, Peru and Uruguay) with the intention of achieving free trade by 1980. Despite some success in the early years, and a reduction in tariffs, it came up against strong resistance from domestic producers threatened by imports from partner countries, and it has achieved little by way of increases in inter-union trade in manufactured goods (as opposed to primaries). Disputes over the distribution of the benefits of the

Association culminated in 1966 with the formation of a breakaway group—the Andean Group—comprising Bolivia, Colombia, Chile, Ecuador and Peru and subsequently Venezuela; but again, an initial increase in trade has been overshadowed by squabbles over the distribution of new investment and other political problems. In 1980 LAFTA was replaced by a less ambitious organisation known as the Latin American Integration Association, based upon preferential tariff concessions.

CACM was founded in 1960 around five small Central American Republics: Costa Rica, El Salvador, Guatemala, Nicaragua and Honduras (which withdrew in 1968). Although there have been problems over the distribution of import-substituting industries, there was some trade expansion in manufactures, and a recent study by Cline (1981) concluded that all benefited in the 1960s from the union. In the 1970s, however, political problems have stifled any further progress.

ASEAN consisted of a movement by some countries in Asia (Indonesia, Malaysia, the Philippines, Singapore and Thailand) in 1967 to promote regional cooperation. After a slow start, it resolved in the mid-1970s to move towards gradual economic integration. As a result, trade was liberated and import substitution encouraged but within the framework of a generally export-oriented development strategy. Although South East Asia is currently one of the most rapidly expanding areas of the world, trade between members in manufactures has so far been modest, and probably not a major reason for their success.

On the face of it the evidence seems to point to the conclusion that integration has generally been successful in DCs but much less so in LDCs. Pazos (1973) surveyed six integration movements in LDCs in the 1960s and concluded that there were gains to all member countries, especially within CACM, despite the uneven distribution of these benefits. Cline (1981), in a comparative survey of the impact of six integration movements on trade between themselves, concluded that in every case there was an increase in trade during the first decade, but subsequent progress was much slower, and in some cases was retrogressive (eg. CACM). The most successful were the EEC and LAFTA.

These surveys emphasise the importance of going beyond the analysis of the static gains from integration discussed in section 7.2. Empirical studies of the static gains generally suggest that trade-creation has predominated over trade-diversion in integration movements between DCs but that the magnitude of these gains is quite small as a proportion of national income. Moreover, for LDCs there are usually net losses arising from the substantial amount of trade-diversion typically encountered. Johnson (1962), for example, concluded that trade-creation predominated by as much as 4:1 in the case of the EEC, but the effects were minimal in terms of GNP.[6]

A final note is needed here with respect to the LDCs. Although we have generally been pessimistic in our appraisal of the performance of integration movements between these countries, the criteria for success in this case should not be seen purely in terms of trade-creation and trade-diversion. As we suggested earlier, the long run objective may be the establishment of viable manufacturing industries through a coordinated planning process. There are likely to be considerable difficulties encountered here, since these countries may have little influence over their terms of trade, and countries in close geographical proximity may be more potentially competitive than complementary in their economic structures. Add to this the inherent problems of setting up competitive manufacturing industries and differences of a political nature between members, and it becomes apparent how daunting a task they face. The main stumbling-block has usually been over the distribution of the gains from the new, protected, import-substituting industries, since a member gains when an industry is set up in its home market but loses when it is set up in a partner country (because it raises import costs). Perhaps LDCs should limit regional integration to more *ad hoc* cooperation over tariff reductions in particular products, and joint bargaining with DCs over the importation of foreign capital and technology.

NOTES

1. We do not explicitly consider the trading links between socialist and communist states in this book since a rather special type of analysis is needed. For a good treatment of the issues involved, see Holzman (1966).
2. Hence the price lines are drawn horizontally from the vertical axis.
3. One of the earliest examples of integration was the Zollverein, a

customs union established in 1834 between a number of German states prior to their political unification in the latter part of the nineteenth century.

4. See El Agraa (1980, Part 2).
5. For other less prominent examples of integration amongst LDCs, see Williamson (1983, pp. 296–302).
6. To see why this should be the case, assume that trade accounts for about 20 per cent of GNP and the trade being liberalised constitutes approximately half of total trade. If the tariff to be removed is 10 per cent on average and trade might be expected to expand by about half upon joining the union, then by applying the formula we discussed earlier for measuring the benefits of trade creation (ignoring trade-diversion), the potential benefit is somewhere in the region of 0.25 per cent of GNP. Even if we alter some of these assumptions, the final estimate would still turn out to be relatively small.

FURTHER READING

The pioneering work on customs union theory is Viner (1950). Johnson (1962) also provides a good but simpler treatment of the basic analysis. For a review of developments in the literature, see Lipsey (1970) and Krauss (1973). For a summary of the evolution of trading blocs after the second world war, including the ones we have referred to in the text, Williamson (1983) is to be recommended. The history and institutional development of the EEC can be found in Swann (1970), and a direct attempt to apply the theory of integration to this particular organisation is available in El Agraa (1980). Finally, for attempts to compare the effects of different integration movements, see Cline (1981) and Pazos (1973).

PART 3

International Factor Movements

8 Trade and Factor Mobility

In our discussion of the pure theory of trade in Part 1, we focused primarily on the international movement of goods and services and assumed, as did Ricardo, that factors were mobile domestically but immobile internationally. Yet even the most cursory glance at history shows that some of the more important changes in the international economy have been brought about by the international transfer of factors of production. Although the twentieth century has not witnessed the mass exodus of capital and labour from Europe to other parts of the world which took place in the nineteenth century, and the majority of people in the world today are still relatively immobile, the trend is still towards greater ease of movement. Examples of this since the second world war include the transfer of foreign aid to developing countries, the migration of labour from Southern to Western Europe, and the transfer of capital internationally by way of the multinational corporation.

In this part of the book we examine the role of factor movements in international trade, beginning in Chapter 8 with two important theoretical contributions in this area: the factor price equalisation theorem, and the Stolper–Samuelson theorem. We then survey the issues and evidence with regard to the international movement of capital and labour, including the so-called 'brain drain' and the debt-service problem facing many poorer countries. In the following two chapters we deal with two especially controversial topics concerning the international transfer of foreign aid and the movement of foreign direct investment tied up with the activities of multinational enterprises.

8.1 FACTOR PRICE EQUALISATION

The Heckscher–Ohlin model discussed in Chapter 3 predicted that countries would export commodities which were intensive in their most abundant factor, since one would expect these goods to be relatively cheap to produce prior to trade. An important corollary to this theorem was that trade would also produce a *tendency* towards the equalisation of factor prices across countries. Paul Samuelson (1948) then proved that, under certain conditions which we shall elaborate on below, trade in commodities could lead to *complete* factor price equalisation without there being any need for factor movements at all. Trade in goods would act as a complete substitute for trade in factors.

The explanation for this result rests on the logic of the Heckscher–Ohlin approach, the theory of perfect competition, and the principle of free trade. For example, if the UK were relatively labour-abundant compared with the USA, then the Heckscher–Ohlin theory would suggest that the UK might export labour-intensive clothing to the USA in return for capital-intensive food. By engaging in trade and exporting more cloth we would expect the demand for the abundant factor in the UK to rise and the importation of food to relieve domestic pressure on relatively scarce capital. Hence, the returns to the abundant factor (labour) will rise relative to the scarce factor (capital) in the UK. In this way, trade irons out international factor price differences between countries, even though they differ in factor endowments. *Total* endowments in the two countries have not changed, so only factor prices and quantities can adjust to product price changes brought about by trade. The role of perfect competition and free trade is to ensure that goods prices are equalised between countries when they are opened up to trade. All one then needs to do is to establish a link between equal goods prices and equal factor earnings by making appropriate assumptions about costs and technology in the countries concerned.[1]

In reality, factor price equalisation has not occurred, and considerable differences remain between factor rewards in different countries. It is probably true to say that the international returns to capital and skilled labour, which are relatively mobile, are more equal than the more immobile land and unskilled labour; and there is some evidence to suggest the opening-up of a country to trade does put pressure on domestic factor payments. For some evidence on this with regard to Brazil, see Balassa (1979). None the less wage rates in particular vary considerably across countries, especially when comparing developed countries (DCs) and lesser developed countries (LDCs). The reasons lie in the stringent assumptions which accompany the factor price equalisation theorem.

First, it is assumed that countries have identical production functions, that is to say, they share a common technology and do not differ in climatic or other influences on the relationship between inputs and outputs, except in so far as factor endowments differ. In fact there are significant differences between production functions internationally.[2] For example, factor proportions may vary between countries producing the same good. Wheat production in the USA might be relatively capital-intensive compared with cloth production, while the reverse might be true in the UK. This problem is known technically as factor intensity reversal[3] and that it occurs in the real world is beyond doubt. The question is how prevalent it is. The first empirical study on this topic by Minhas (1962) suggested that factor intensity reversal was indeed quite prevalent. However, Leontief (1964) found it to be a rare occurence once he had corrected an important source of bias in the Minhas study. This was subsequently confirmed by Ball (1966). There does not, therefore, seem to be much evidence that factor intensity reversals are so common as to cast serious doubt on the Heckscher–Ohlin framework but they might be more important in agriculture. For example, the production of rice tends to be highly capital-intensive in the USA while it is much more labour-intensive in the Far East.

Secondly, the analysis assumes perfect competition and free trade, including the absence of transport costs or other impediments to trade, such as tariffs. Note that costs are not taken to be equal across countries *prior* to trade, since this forms the basis for comparative advantage, but only that after trade has got underway such cost differences will be eliminated. Hence, in as much as perfect competition and free trade are absent, factor price equalisation will be incomplete since the link between factor prices and product prices is broken. Indeed, such factors as transport cost differentials and tariffs will serve to widen the range of goods that countries *actually* produce other than for genuine reasons of comparative advantage.

Problems also arise if a factor of production is highly specific to one activity or is immobile for geographical or social reasons. For example, if labour in the UK were specific to food production, then this will imply that comparative advantage was being determined by factors other than relative endowments, and this will lessen the concentration of production in the UK clothing industry, and factor price equalisation will be incomplete.

Finally, there are difficulties with the factor price equalisation theorem if the model is generalised to many countries, many commodities, and factor supplies are allowed to vary in response to different rewards across countries. In these cases it is not possible to make simple predictions, and factor price equalisation is less likely to occur. For example, if some factor mobility takes place in response to differences in earnings internationally (as one would expect), then although these movements themselves may actually help to equalise factor prices, it is not generally possible to predict the effects on the production possibility frontiers of the countries concerned.[4]

Despite these weaknesses, the Heckscher–Ohlin and factor price equalisation theorems remain valid in emphasising that differences in broad endowments between countries will have some influence on the pattern of production and trade, and that commodity trade can act as a partial substitute for international factor mobility. In this sense all we can expect is a *tendency* towards factor price equalisation, and for trade in goods to reduce price differences. The emphasis, therefore, shifts towards the dynamic effects that international factor movements themselves have upon production and trade. Before considering these effects, however, we need to examine another important theory concerned with the effects of trade on income distribution.

8.2 TRADE AND INCOME DISTRIBUTION

Since trade both alters commodity prices and involves the international transfer of factors of production, it is likely to have important repercussions on factor payments and income distribution. Yet, prior to the work of Stolper and Samuelson (1941), it had generally been assumed that free trade was advantageous to everyone.

The Stolper–Samuelson theorem was originally used to describe the impact of protection on a country with labour-intensive imports within the Heckscher–Ohlin framework. What it showed was that a tariff would increase the income of the factor used intensively in the production of the good that received protection, while it would lower the income of the other factor. If imports were intensive in their use of unskilled labour, unskilled labour in the USA would therefore benefit from protection. The intuitive reasoning behind this result is that the tariff would raise the price of the commodity concerned, and so also the wage rate of workers employed in the import-competing sector.

The more general conclusion from the Stolper–Samuelson theorem was that trade would increase the returns to the owners of the factor of production used intensively in the expanding industry and lower that of the factor used intensively in the contracting industry.[5]

In other words, if trade is opened up between the UK and the USA, with the former exporting labour-intensive clothing in return for food, the rise in the relative price of clothing in the UK resulting from the change in trade patterns would pull up wage rates and lead to a relative fall in the return on capital. Moreover, even if capital owners in the contracting UK food industry spend a high proportion of their incomes on food, and therefore stood to benefit from the cheaper food resulting from the change in the pattern of trade, their losses from the factor price change still outweigh this favourable change in product prices. Hence, consumption patterns influence only *how much* factors gain or lose under these circumstances.

The Stolper–Samuelson theorem thus tells us something about the likely impact of commodity trade (and protection) on factor income distribution at a high level of aggregation, but what about the effects of international flows of factors such as capital and labour on income distribution?

In general, neoclassical economic theory suggests that an inflow of one factor will lower the rewards accruing to that factor compared with the other factor of production. For example, if there is migration from the UK to the USA, then this would encourage downward pressure on US wage rates as the total stock of labour rises in that country, and the relative reward to the other (now relatively scarce) factor, such as capital, will increase. Similarly, if there were to be an influx of capital into the USA, the return to capital would fall relative to wage rates. This is one reason, perhaps, why workers tend to favour capital inflows but oppose immigration, and capitalists prefer the reverse.

Whilst this analysis may hold true in general, in practice there are many more factors to take into account when looking at the impact of international factor movements. This is the task of sections 8.3 and 8.4.

8.3 THE INTERNATIONAL MOVEMENT OF LABOUR

In the same way as gains from trade can be obtained when goods move from where their relative prices are low prior to trade to where they are higher, one would expect benefits to arise when factors move from one location to another in search of higher rewards. Indeed, as we suggested in section 8.2, if trade in commodities is unlikely to bring about complete factor price equalisation, then factor mobility itself may have important repercussions on both world efficiency and welfare if it serves to iron out international earnings differentials.

As far as labour mobility is concerned, it is probably true to say that something approaching an international labour market has developed in the twentieth century, but that it is still very imperfect and not always based upon a rational response to economic incentives. Much has been written about the spectacular migration movements from Europe to the USA and the other 'regions of recent settlement' between about 1840 and 1914, motivated by 'pull' factors such as the prospect of a better life and the 'push' of economic hardship and political persecution at home.[6] By contrast the process of migration in the twentieth century has been a much more muted affair.

This may partly be due to fewer attractive opportunities, but much of it can be explained by the erection of barriers to immigration from the 1920s onwards. Since 1945 migration has tended to follow fairly rigid patterns, often reflecting political ties rather than any economic rationale. It is no coincidence that most of the immigrants into Britain have come from Commonwealth countries in Asia and the Caribbean; while French immigrants have come predominantly from her ex-colonies in North Africa.

Perhaps one of the most significant developments in the

post-war period has been the rise of a European labour market based upon the movement of workers from Mediterranean countries to the more prosperous countries of Western Europe. Initially, these immigrants were predominantly Italian, but subsequently Greeks, Turks, Spaniards, Portuguese and more recently Yugoslavs have joined the trail.

Nevertheless, international labour markets remain fragmented and imperfect. The jobs of many of these migrants are casual or seasonal in nature, and the process has been somewhat curtailed by world recession in the 1970s and 1980s. Possibly the highest mobility has taken place amongst skilled personnel, including consultants and 'experts' attracted by the oil-rich countries of the Middle East.

But even if international labour mobility has been limited, to what extent does it confer benefits on both host countries and countries of origin?

As far as the host country is concerned, we have already suggested in section 8.2 that factor mobility would tend to benefit one factor at the expense of another, but there are also potential benefits for the economy as a whole if immigrants bring with them appropriate factor endowments. As Johnson (1967) has shown, when these immigrants arrive there should be an increase in income for the community as a whole. An example of a favourable transfer would be where young unskilled labour migrated to countries which are relatively under-populated, yet are land and natural resource-abundant, such as Canada and Australia. Similarly, beneficial effects could arise from the transfer of both skilled and unskilled labour to low-population, capital-rich countries, such as the oil exporters of the Middle East.

It has also been suggested that West Germany benefited after the second world war from an influx of refugees from East Germany, since this enabled wage rates to be kept down and profits to be increased; and that Israel's progress during the same period was helped by the migration of Jews back to the 'homeland'. In these two cases, however, the social characteristics of the migrants, including their attitudes to work, must also have played their part in explaining the dynamism of their contributions to growth, as well as the purely economic implications of the transfer.

In spite of these potential advantages from immigration, there is much resistance to the free movement of labour between countries. This may be due in part to opposition by labour unions who feel threatened by an influx of 'cheap' labour which may be more willing to compromise with employers in matters of industrial relations than indigenous labour. But the major reason probably relates to the social problems (both real and imaginary) which accompany mass immigration. It is not simply a question of increased numbers putting a strain on social overhead capital such as health and education services, but the consequences of a dualistic labour market and the problem of cultural assimilation. Typically, immigrants are given low-paid and unattractive jobs, and their economic as well as cultural differences tend to put them in a segregated environment. Classic cases of this include Asians employed on the public transport system in Britain, and Mexican and Puerto Rican immigrants engaged in 'dirty' jobs in the USA.

As far as the effects on the country of origin are concerned, the most tangible benefit to be obtained from the loss of labour is through remittances which migrants may send home from the foreign country. This has the effect of raising national income and improving the balance of payments. A good contemporary example here would be the income sent home by Greeks and Turks working in Europe. Unfortunately, however, the more permanently attached the migrants become to the host country, the smaller the remittances tend to become.

Another less tangible advantage could be the stimulus to introduce modern technology brought about by the contraction of the domestic labour supply resulting from the migration, since this might be expected to push up domestic wage rates and make capital relatively more attractive. In addition, there might possibly be an improvement in the terms of trade if migration leads to an expansion (and cheapening) of production abroad. After all, cheap food and raw materials were seen to be a beneficial side-effect of British migration to the rest of the world in the nineteenth and early twentieth centuries.

On the negative side, much depends on the opportunity costs of the migrants. Certainly the donor country loses the benefits of 'human capital' accumulated through education and training, and migrants are often the most talented and dynamic sections of the community; but in so far as their alternative occupation would be the dole queue, their loss is less painful.

Much of the debate over the so-called 'brain drain' also concerns the magnitude of the unpaid benefits which society loses from the transfer. These unpaid benefits, or 'externalities' in the economist's jargon, arise where the full benefits to society of a potential migrant are not necessarily reflected in the payments they currently receive. For example, a country may lose young managers whose charisma and social dynamism have the effect of making those who work with them work harder. The loss to the community, therefore, is not just their own lost output, but also the unpaid benefits which society as a whole has lost. For some further analysis on the 'brain drain', see Bhagwati (1976). Clearly such intangible side-effects are hard to evaluate, but they may be no less important as a result.

8.4 THE INTERNATIONAL MOVEMENT OF CAPITAL

Capital is transferred internationally through the process of foreign investment and is carried out by both public authorities and private firms and individuals. A distinction is usually made between short-term and long-term capital, and between portfolio and direct investment. Short term capital generally includes assets whose maturity date is less than a year; while long-term capital comprises assets whose maturity time may be considerably longer.

The distinction between portfolio and direct investment is less clear-cut but it relates principally to the question of control over the income which the asset is expected to yield. Basically, portfolio investment involves the purchase of an asset, such as a government bond, which entitles the purchaser to a portion of the income which the investment generates. Direct investment, on the other hand, involves the buyer directly in the activities which generate the income, for example when a multinational corporation sets up and runs a subsidiary in a foreign country.

Since we shall be dealing with short-term capital movements in Part 4, and the next chapter is devoted specifically to foreign direct investment, we shall confine ourselves here to a discussion of long-term portfolio investment.

Portfolio lending can take a number of forms, including private bank lending, lending by multilateral organisations such as the

World Bank, and dealings by foreigners in existing securities on a country's stock exchange. But historically the most significant form of long-term lending has been through the issue of bonds. In the nineteenth century, for example, a major source of international finance was the sterling bond, enabling countries such as Argentina and the USA to borrow long term from Britain in order to develop their natural resources. The eclipse of London as the premier financial centre of the world after the first world war was mirrored in the rise of New York as an important lending centre. The development of the New York bond market continued after the second world war but was cut short in 1963 when the US government levied a prohibitive tax on new security issues in response to the growing weakness of the American balance of payments. The result was the rapid development of the Eurodollar market in Europe, where bonds denominated in dollars were traded outside of the USA. In recent years, the Eurodollar market has become an important source of long-term lending.

So much for the institutional structure of long-term lending, but what are the benefits to lending and borrowing countries of this transfer of capital?

In principle foreign investment should benefit both lender and borrower and equalise the returns to capital internationally by transferring resources from countries which are rich in capital to those which are relatively capital-poor. By receiving a capital inflow the borrowing country is able to increase imports and run a current account deficit but still remain in overall balance, since it can finance these extra goods and services from the inflow on its capital account.[7] In this sense the transfer of resources allows the borrowing country to spend more than it currently produces. As a result, one would expect income, output and employment all to be higher than in the absence of the capital flow. Then subsequently when the debt has to be paid back (serviced), the borrowing country must generate a surplus on its current account, i.e. create more output than it is currently consuming in order to provide the funds to transfer back to the lender. The lender, on the other hand, should be able to gain as a result of the exercise from the extra income it receives by way of interest charges.

In this way both parties should be able to gain from the redistribution of capital from where returns are low to where they are relatively high. The borrowing country will be able to increase its output and hence its income over time as long as the activities into which the funds are put generate more than enough income to repay the debt. Alternatively, the borrowing country can raise current consumption above what it would have been, albeit at the expense of future consumption, since consumption will have to be curtailed in the future in order to pay back the debt.

Lenders, on the other hand, benefit when their flow of savings exceeds the profitable domestic investment opportunities open to them, or they wish to postpone consumption now in order to create extra consumption for the future. A good example of the mutual benefits of foreign investment is the decision by oil-exporting countries with small populations and surplus savings to lend to capital-poor LDCs, or to resource-rich primary producers with insufficient domestic savings.

So far we have viewed foreign investment in a very favourable light yet, as with the international labour market, capital lending does not always follow the lines predicted by economic rewards. In practice, lending patterns are more rigid and are influenced by institutional factors, including government controls. To see why governments impose restrictions on capital flows we need to consider some of the disadvantages which might arise from them.

Clearly a capital movement is likely to have 'perverse' effects if it moves from a capital-scarce country to a capital-abundant country. This might be motivated by a desire to evade taxes or because it is attracted by artificially high interest rates which seem to bear little relationship to the true returns on investment in the country concerned. Similarly, governments often introduce controls on capital movements if they feel that not to do so could leave them vulnerable to a currency crisis, or that there would be other adverse effects on the balance of payments. We shall discuss this aspect of capital controls more fully in Part 4, but it turns out, in practice, to be very difficult to control capital movements even when governments feel justified in doing so.

One final issue connected with capital movements concerns the debt owed by many LDCs, which has been increasing at an alarming rate in the last few years. During the 1960s the economies of many LDCs grew relatively fast and most external development finance was accounted for by private direct investment and official development assistance. Commercial bank lending, on the other hand, was relatively small. Since official finance was given on relatively easy terms and the returns to direct investment to the parent company tended to be related to the investment's performance, debts owed abroad did not generally cause problems. Interest rates, too, tended to be low in both nominal and real terms.

However, during the late 1960s and early 1970s international banks began increasingly to lend to LDCs, and when the first oil price shock occured in 1973, some LDCs began to rely more and more on funds from commercial banks to maintain their growth rates and to finance their current account balance of payments deficits. Unlike the funds obtained from multilateral agencies, such as the World Bank, and from enterprises engaged in direct investment, these commercial loans had very few strings attached to them and were not subject to stringent supervision. The banks for their part were prepared to lend to these countries, partly because they still appeared to have a large potential for growth, and partly because the banks were awash with funds in the form of recycled oil revenues from the richer OPEC countries. Moreover, although nominal interest rates rose, real interest rates stayed low or negative as world inflation continued to be high. Consequently, as Table 8.1 shows, the debt-service ratio, which measures the ratio of debt (interest plus amortization) to exports of goods and services, rose only moderately from about 9.5 per cent in 1974 to about 15.0 per cent in 1979.

Table 8.1 Debt indicators for developing countries 1974–83

	1974	1975	1976	1977	1978	1979	1980	1981	1982	1983
	($ US billions)									
Total debt[1]	141.0	168.6	203.8	249.8	311.7	368.8	424.8	482.6	538.0	595.8
Debt-service ratio (%)	9.5	11.1	10.9	12.1	15.4	15.0	13.6	16.6	19.9	20.7

Note: [1]Based on a sample of ninety developing countries. [2]Ratio of interest payments plus amortization to exports.
Source: World Bank (1984).

By 1979, however, there had been an important shift in the structure of foreign lending to LDCs. While the proportions of private direct investment and official finance in debt-financing had declined since 1974, the share of bank financing had doubled. This increased reliance on commercial bank lending together with a failure to adapt policies to changed circumstances, left many LDCs with serious difficulties after the second oil shock in 1979. The banks became less willing to lend for long periods and tighter economic policies in the developed industrial countries to counter the inflationary impact of higher oil prices pushed up real interest rates. The problem for non-oil-producing LDCs was also exacerbated by the appreciation of the US dollar in the 1980s, since much Third World debt is denominated in that currency.

The result, as table 8.1 indicates, was a sharp rise in total debt from all sources from 368.8 billion dollars in 1979 to 595.8 billion in 1983, with the five largest debtors (Mexico, Brazil, Argentina, South Korea, Yugoslavia) accounting for almost half of the total. The debt-service ratio also began to rise steeply after 1980, with figures in excess of 30 per cent for the largest borrowers.

Although the debt-service ratio does not distinguish between countries which have the capacity to grow and use investment funds productively and are financially stable, and those which have poor prospects and are experiencing high rates of inflation, making it difficult for them to maintain their service payments, it does highlight some of the risks associated with foreign borrowing and the need to ensure that loans are invested productively so that the necessary resources are subsequently made available to service the debt. In this respect, countries which are borrowing to tide them over in the face of temporary fluctuations in their export receipts are likely to be in a stronger position to repay than countries facing a long-term decline in their terms of trade.

By 1982, however, it had become clear that the process of continual borrowing to finance current account deficits caused by international recession and oil price rises and perpetuated by lax lending policies by the commercial banks and overambitious plans for growth in LDCs, especially in Latin America, had produced a situation of crisis proportions. We shall consider the implications of the debt crisis for North–South relations in Chapter 17, including the negotiations currently taking place under the auspices of the IMF, but whether LDCs can find some relief from their debt problems by attracting other sources of external finance will be an important consideration in our discussion of foreign aid and foreign direct investment in the next two chapters.

NOTES

1. For those who are familiar with the microeconomic theory of production, this is achieved by assuming identical production functions in the two countries and constant returns to scale. There will then be a unique point of equilibrium on the isoquant map, and given perfect competition, prices will be determined by costs. Since production functions are identical in the two countries, the relationship between factor earnings and production costs will also be the same.
2. For example, see Arrow *et al.* (1961).
3. There is also the possibility of 'factor demand reversal' if high demand for the product leads to a high demand for the factor used intensively in its production. This subsequently can lead to a rise in the factor's price, in spite of its abundance in physical terms. In this case, demand conditions have led to a reversal of the trade pattern to be expected from cost considerations alone.
4. For more details on this difficult area, see Jones (1979).
5. An exception to this is where a factor is completely immobile and is employed in the production of a commodity for which the country has a comparative disadvantage. In this case it will be impossible for that factor to gain employment in the expanding industry and it will be worse-off as a result.
6. See, for example, Thomas (1972).
7. The distinction between current and capital account on the balance of payments will be discussed more fully in Chapter 11.

FURTHER READING

For a more detailed analysis of factor price equalisation and the Stolper–Samuelson theorem, see Caves and Jones (1981). The international movement of capital and labour is discussed in Kindleberger and Lindert (1978).

Two recent accounts of the debt problem are available in Brau *et al.* (1983) and McKenzie and Thomas (1984).

9 Foreign Direct Investment

9.1 FOREIGN DIRECT INVESTMENT AND THE MULTINATIONAL CORPORATION

One of the most controversial issues in international economics during the last decade concerns the activities of multinational corporations (MNs) engaged in the process of direct investment. The distinctive feature of foreign direct investment (as opposed to portfolio investment which we discussed in Chapter 8) is that the owners of the assets have *direct* control over the activities in the foreign country which generate the income flow. It therefore involves not merely the transfer of capital abroad, but also the transfer of management and 'know-how' which comes about when a company registered in one country decides to set up a subsidiary abroad. The process of foreign direct investment is therefore closely bound up with the expansion of MNs after the second world war, dominated in the 1950s and 1960s by American-based enterprises, but matched in more recent years by companies registered in Europe and Japan.

The multinational corporation is not an easy phenomenon to describe, but a good approximation was presented by Dunning (1971) when he defined it as 'any enterprise which owns and controls income-generating assets in more than one country'. This definition emphasises that it is control and not merely ownership which distinguishes this form of foreign investment from other forms, and that MN activity involves a multi-plant production process, with a parent firm establishing subsidiaries in foreign countries. In addition, unlike portfolio investment, direct foreign investment tends to be highly industry-specific in as much as capital flows not just from country A to country B, but usually from industry x in A to industry x in B.

As well as being closely associated with the process of foreign direct investment, MNs also share a number of characteristics which distinguish them from large domestic enterprises. As Table 9.1 demonstrates, MNs are very big and often boast gross sales in excess of the GNPs of some smaller countries. For example, in 1976 Exxon and General Motors had higher gross sales than the GNP of Austria, Turkey and Yugoslavia. They also tend to exhibit a high degree of central control on the part of the parent company based in the USA, France, Germany, Britain or Japan, and are highly integrated outfits.

Table 9.1 The ranking of countries and multinational corporations by size of annual products in 1976

		Product ($ billion[1])			Product ($ billion[1])
1.	USA	1695	16.	East Germany	76
2.	USSR	718	17.	Sweden	74
3.	Japan	514	18.	Iran	69
4.	West Germany	462	19.	Belgium	69
5.	France	356	20.	Mexico	66
6.	China	307	21.	Switzerland	58
7.	UK	234	22.	Czechoslovakia	57
8.	Italy	183	23.	Exxon	49
9.	Canada	183	24.	General Motors	47
10.	Brazil	143	25.	Austria	42
11.	Spain	107	26.	Turkey	41
12.	Poland	99	27.	Argentina	41
13.	Australia	97	28.	Denmark	39
14.	Netherlands	92	29.	Yugoslavia	38
15.	India	88	30.	Royal Dutch Shell	36

Note: [1]GNP for countries and gross sales for corporations.
Sources: World Bank (1978), United Nations (1978).

MNs also typically operate as large sellers in oligopolistic markets and produce a range of differentiated products, rather than in markets closer to the economist's model of perfect competition. As Table 9.1 suggests, MNs are most prominent in products such as oil, motor cars, consumer durables and pharmaceuticals, rather than in textiles or cereals. Finally, they are also likely to have a wide access to sources of information by virtue of the scale of their international operations, and their ability to gain practical production experience on the spot.

These characteristics of size, market imperfections and access to information might, however, be construed as only of *relative* importance when comparing a MN with a large domestic firm, but two further differences are perhaps more fundamental.

The first concerns the motivation of the MN. As well as operating in many different countries, the decision-making process in these concerns is bound to take on a global perspective. It is how all the production pieces fit together which becomes important and not necessarily how well one particular unit is performing in any one country. If, for example, we assume that the MN sets out to maximise post-tax profits, then this world-wide perspective could well have important welfare consequences for the individual countries concerned as resources are shifted about between different production centres in the pursuit of overall profitability.

The second refers to the question of who controls the MN. As with any large modern enterprise, it is the managers who generally run the firm and exercise control over its operations, while in principle, ownership lies in the hands of the shareholders. Complications arise with the MN when these shares are floated in more than one country and the activities of the firm are subject to the legal jurisdiction of more than one authority. As a result, the government in the home country will have certain powers over the parent company, and foreign governments will attempt to regulate the activities of the subsidiaries operating within their territories; but there will be no overall responsibility to any *one* authority. As we shall see in section 9.3 below, these features of a global perspective and amorphous control will raise important questions about the benefits and costs of MN activities.

9.2 THE THEORY OF DIRECT INVESTMENT

Although the MN is an international phenomenon, the theory of direct investment probably has more to do with industrial economics than with international trade. This is because the emphasis in economic theory has been directed towards explaining why a MN would prefer to set up a subsidiary abroad, rather than producing the product at home in a familiar environment and exporting it, licensing a foreign firm to undertake production abroad, or using the portfolio market to buy foreign securities in search of a profit.

The answer seems to lie in the make-up and motivation of the modern large oligopolistic company. In this sense the theory of perfectly competitive markets must be abandoned in favour of theory dealing more explicitly with oligopoly behaviour. These firms seem to enjoy special advantages which enable them to benefit from market imperfections in foreign countries to the detriment of local competition. These special advantages or 'intangible assets' include trademarks, patents, managerial skills and economies of large-scale production. What they do is to provide the MN with something distinctive to sell abroad by setting up a subsidiary and penetrating local markets.

Typically, this process involves backward vertical integration to gain access to raw materials or important inputs, rather than the simple sale or distribution of a product manufactured at home in the foreign market, since it is usually easier to adapt the product to local demand on the spot. There is also a link here with the product-cycle theory of Vernon (1966) discussed in Chapter 3. According to this theory, the basis of comparative advantage in the production of a modern consumer durable is often related to innovation. This enables a firm to capture the domestic market and export until rivals overcome any patents or other barriers to entry and compete away the innovating firm's monopoly profits. The MN responds to this erosion of its comparative advantage by moving the location of production abroad in order to seek out remaining market imperfections.

The theory of direct investment also highlights the importance of the oligopolistic environment in which a MN operates. The features of oligopoly markets are the existence of monopoly profits, the ability of producers to differentiate between brands of a product, and the presence of rivalry in the market. These features lie at the heart of the 'intangible assets' which the MN seeks to exploit. In this sense the investment transfer is only an incidental part of the decision by the oligopolist to exploit the advantages which give it such a distinctive range of products. For example, the decision to set up a foreign subsidiary may be motivated not by a desire to make a profit *per se*, but in order to pre-empt a similar move by a rival. This 'defensive' type of behaviour is especially prevalent where a MN depends heavily upon an essential input or natural resource.

It is now clear why the MN is not content simply to export goods produced at home, to license foreign firms to undertake production, or to engage in portfolio investment. Exporting or licensing is only sensible if the firm is not big enough to benefit from large-scale production abroad, and portfolio investment is not really an alternative where the motive is not a profit *per se*, but to improve the firm's market position in the long run at the expense of its competitors. Setting up a subsidiary also has the advantage that trade secrets are not lost to foreigners and the firm abroad may be able to sell within a protected market.

9.3 THE WELFARE CONSEQUENCES OF MULTINATIONALS

Few topics can have generated so much controversy in the last decade or so as the debate over the costs and benefits of MN activities, whether from the point of view of donor countries, or from that of the hosts.[1] In this section we consider some of the more important arguments put forward both for and against MNs, and in section 9.4 we review the evidence, both with respect to developed countries (DCs) and lesser developed countries (LDCs).

From the perspective of host countries, our analysis of factor movements in Chapter 8 led us to expect gains when resources are reallocated from countries where they are relatively abundant to where they are relatively scarce. In so far as factor flows substitute for factor price equalisation brought about by commodity trade, there should also be an improvement in allocative efficiency resulting from the ironing-out of international market imperfections. Similarly, the transfer should, in principle, augment resources in the host country and increase the value of net world output to be distributed in factor payments.

The way in which these extra resources manifest themselves will vary from country to country, but in general one might expect an increase in local savings, an increase in taxes or other revenues accruing to the government, and possibly an increase in foreign exchange if the MN exports its products abroad. In addition, employment could well rise and there might even be less tangible spin-offs to the local economy in the form of competitive 'shock-effects' stimulating indigenous firms to improve efficiency, and gains arising from the training of local staff.

These are the conventional benefits which foreign direct investment is supposed to bestow on host countries, but perhaps the most attractive feature of the MN, especially to LDCs, is that it brings with it many of the skills most scarce in the host country already wrapped up in a single package. The MN arrives with skilled management and technology, well-tried production processes based upon economies of scale, and possibly even more important, ready-made marketing outlets for established brands. These are often the very skills and resources which the country concerned would find hard to create locally, or to purchase piecemeal on the international market.

Yet despite these potential benefits, there remains considerable hostility towards MNs. This generally arises from a belief that the contribution which the MN can make might well be quite small in practice, or outweighed by other costs associated with the foreign firm's activities.

In the first place, MNs are often not as cosmopolitan as they seem to be. Most have a central base in one particular country, usually in a major city such as New York, irrespective of whether it is the most appropriate centre for financial reserves or decision-making; and staff appointments in the subsidiaries may be heavily weighted in favour of home nationals even though local staff may be better equipped to do the job. Similarly, oligopolistic rivalries between MNs may mitigate against short-run efficiency considerations, especially when natural resources are at stake, and market inperfections could be increased rather than decreased if barriers to entry are erected to keep out rival firms. The competitive shock-effects are also likely to be muted if the foreign company simply buys up local firms and secures for itself a stronger monopoly position in the domestic market. Only, therefore, if the MN sets up a new subsidiary to compete with existing oligopolies will it have improved the competitive situation. The extent to which the MN improves allocative efficiency, therefore, requires closer examination than the general theory of factor mobility would suggest.

The strongest scepticism about the benefits of a MN, however, relates to its effects on host country resources. Although one would expect a MN to augment local savings, government revenues and foreign exchange earnings, this need not always be the case; for example, where production involves luxury items for a local élite, or is geared towards the creation of a mass domestic market (through advertising). The stimulus to domestic consumption may in these cases militate against increasing national savings ratios. Examples of mass market products are Coca Cola and powdered baby food.

The foreign exchange gain may also be small if a large percentage of the income generated locally is repatriated in the form of interest, dividends and profits; or if the firm's import bill is particularly large. Finally, the government may find that, on balance, the revenues it receives from the MN are offset by generous concessions it may have made to attract the firm in the first place. This is particularly likely if the firm is practising transfer pricing.

Transfer pricing is the means by which a MN can reduce its tax bill by artificially increasing the prices of its inputs imported from one of its other plants.[2] Since these inputs are unlikely to pass through any conventional markets, but rather represent internal accounting prices set by the firm itself, a MN can declare low profits in a country where taxes are relatively high (such as in the UK), and high profits (by reducing input prices) where taxes are relatively low (such as in Bermuda). This is a direct manifestation of the global behaviour of these firms which we referred to in section 9.1 above.

The problem from the viewpoint of the host government is not just that the MN may be able to conceal its true profitability from tax officials, but that the information may simply not be available upon which to make tax calculations in the absence of any obvious market prices for the relevant inputs. To repeat the standard cliché in this respect, what is the true price of a Volkswagen door? Unfortunately the stakes are high, since an excessive tax burden may well drive the MN away, while an over-generous policy can seriously eat away the share of the net value of output accruing to the host country and the benefits to the trade balance. In practice, a daunting task faces tax officials in poor countries where administrative resources may be limited, to get this balance right.

Although the financial balance sheet for the host country is going to be an important indicator of the benefits it obtains from the presence of the MN, it is by no means the whole story. The host government also needs to look closely at the impact of the foreign firm on employment, and how it fits in with the government's broader economic strategy. If the MN is highly capital-intensive, carries out most of its research and development in the parent country, and drives out local competition, then the benefits in terms of employment-creation may be very small indeed.

Similarly, LDCs often complain that MNs bring with them technology inappropriate to local needs and that they accentuate dualisms in their economy. These dualisms might take the form of regional enclaves of modern industrial production developing at the expense of more backward sectors, such as agriculture. This in turn can lead to a cumulative disparity between the sectors concerned, especially where the modern sector becomes associated with the urban centres, and the traditional sector with the rural areas. The problem of people migrating from the rural to the urban sector, attracted by higher expected earnings in the cities, has become a serious problem in many LDCs. See, for example, Todaro (1982, ch. 14).

A second dualism may occur in the labour market. Unfortunately, the MN can't win in this respect, since if it pays local labour too little in relation to its contribution to output (marginal product) it is accused of exploitation, and if it pays higher wages than local firms it is accused of accentuating the gap in earnings between its own labour force and the rest of the labour market!

Thus far our analysis has been presented very much from the perspective of the economist, but much of the opposition to MNs centres on the political repercussions they might have on host countries.

One common fear is that the ownership of strategic resources or industries will fall into the hands of foreigners, or that part of the nation's capital stock will be taken over by neo-colonials. This may reinforce feelings of dependency and vulnerability if it appears that important decisions about trade and technology are being determined by forces outside the control of the particular country concerned. A government may feel at the mercy of MNs which have the power to initiate foreign currency crises by altering the composition of their currency portfolios, or which can close down plants almost at will. These sentiments are most vociferous in

LDCs, but not exclusively so. Many French and Belgians in the 1960s and 1970s felt a certain loss of national identity in the face of the influx of American MNs into Europe. The mere presence of large numbers of foreign technocrats led to fears of a dilution of national culture and language.[3]

But perhaps the strongest emotions are aroused when MNs are accused of overt political interference in the affairs of the host country. Much has been written about the supposed attempts of MNs to influence political decisions on their own behalf, or in the interests of their home government. Perhaps the most famous case was when the giant American firm ITT was implicated in a plot to overthrow the Chilean President Salvador Allende in 1973. A more recent example was that of Stanley Adams, an employee of the giant pharmaceutical company Hoffmann–Laroche who, it is claimed, was persecuted by his former employer after exposing its illegal trading activities to the European Commission.[4] There has also been some concern in the last few years about the practice of pharmaceutical companies selling drugs to the Third World which are banned in the industrial developed countries. Needless to say, these aspects of the MNs' activities will continue to attract attention in the future.

The amount which has been written about the effects of MNs on *donor* countries may seem insignificant compared with that relating to host countries, but there are, none the less, some important issues at stake.

In theory, donor countries lose foreign exchange when the initial resources are transferred abroad, but they may gain eventually when factor payments are repatriated back to the parent company. Home governments also expect to benefit from tax revenues once these earnings are declared in the home country. In addition, there might be a complementary rise in the donor country's export receipts connected with the provision of equipment and other inputs to the subsidiary, although these receipts would have to be offset against the exports which would have gone directly from the parent company instead of from the subsidiary abroad.

Research in this area seems to suggest that in the absence of foreign direct investment going to LDCs, donor country exports would indeed have been higher, but in the case of the investment going to another DC, the relevant exports would probably have been supplied instead by a local firm. For some evidence on this relating to the USA, see Hafbauer and Adler (1968); and for the British case, Reddaway *et al.* (1967).

Nevertheless, these studies are unlikely to allay fears by workers in donor countries that MNs export jobs. This is, after all, what one would expect from our discussion of the distributional effects of factor movements in section 8.2, where we suggested that a loss of capital would tend to lower wage rates relative to the return on capital in the donor country. This follows from the fact that if a country loses capital, less remains to be combined with labour. Hence, one would expect the marginal contribution of capital (marginal product) to rise and that of labour to fall. If factor prices are flexible then this would be reflected in a rise in the rewards to capital and a fall in wages. Whether labour loses overall, however, depends on the extent to which direct investment stimulates employment by increasing exports. It is not at all clear that labour has in fact become worse-off. For a review of these issues, see Bergsten *et al.* (1978).

It is also not entirely clear that the home country always gains from the taxation practices of MNs. Since the convention is that the host country taxes first, and these payments are then offset against tax liabilities in the donor country once profits have been repatriated, it is quite possible for the home government's share of the fruits of foreign direct investment to be quite small. In fact, the USA administration became so concerned about the effects on the balance of payments of direct investment going abroad and dividends being remitted by foreign MNs that it imposed mandatory controls in 1968.

9.4 APPRAISAL

Needless to say, the debate over the distribution of benefits and costs from MN activities will continue, and one must be careful not to generalise too readily from particular cases. Yet it is hard not to associate the rapid expansion of MN activities in Europe after the second world war with the impressive growth performance of these countries over the same period. A particularly interesting account of the growth of MNs in Europe during this period is contained in Tugenhat (1973).

The picture is far less clear, however, when it comes to the effects of MNs on LDCs. In the first place it is important to bear in mind that MNs have shown relatively little interest in LDCs to date, unless they possess essential raw materials needed by the MN, a pool of cheap but *skilled* labour, or they have a large domestic market in terms of purchasing power. In fact, according to Dunning and Stopford (1983), the share of foreign direct investment accruing to LDCs fell from 32 per cent in 1960 to 31 per cent in 1971 and 27 per cent in 1980.

The distribution of foreign direct investment accruing to LDCs is also biased towards those countries which exhibit the characteristics listed above, which are stable politically, and which are not overly hostile to the presence of MNs. Favoured countries in this respect include Brazil, Mexico, Hong Kong, the Philippines, Singapore and South Korea. It is perhaps ironic that Brazil, with its large domestic market, is more successful in attracting MNs than Egypt with its poorer consumers and less skilled labour force, even though the terms Brazil lays down for foreign companies are much tougher.

Furthermore, many economists concerned with development problems have concluded that, on balance, the benefits from the presence of MNs in LDCs in the past have been rather heavily weighted in favour of the MNs. Although it is difficult to put this into quantitative terms, the suspicion is that government tax concessions have been too generous, and that the operations of the MNs have in many instances clashed with the broader development objectives of the host country.

More recently, however, some LDC governments have come to the conclusion that a warmer welcome, together with a carefully thought-out package of conditions, can bring benefits to both parties. These conditions may vary from guarantees that a minimum amount of local personnel be employed, to more stringent conditions requiring the gradual transfer of ownership and control of the enterprise to the host country.[5] Moreover, the balance of bargaining power is not always tipped in favour of the foreign firm, since the MN itself may be quite vulnerable if the motive for being in the country concerned is defensive in the sense of seeking out an essential resource, or it stands to lose heavily from the loss of sunk capital if it decides to leave, or is sent packing.

NOTES

1. Any given country can, of course, be both a donor and a recipient of foreign direct investment. This is likely in so far as it is the prospects in industry x which may interest the MN rather than the characteristics of the country as a whole. For some evidence of this, see Graham (1978).
2. For more details on transfer pricing, see Lall (1973).
3. This is reminiscent of Galbraith's 'New Industrial State'. See Galbraith (1967).
4. The case of Stanley Adams is reviewed in the *Financial Guardian* (1984).
5. For the sort of conditions which LDCs might impose on MNs who wish to establish a foreign subsidiary, see Meier (1984, ch. V). Penrose (1976) also suggests that LDCs would do better to have some, but not all, of the equity of MNs operating within their territories. To have all of it would be expensive and it might be better to concentrate their efforts on obtaining *de facto* control over these enterprises through management participation, effective access to information, etc.

FURTHER READING

For the basic economic analysis of MNs, see Caves (1971) and Dunning (1971). More recent contributions are summarised in Hood and Young (1979) and Baldwin and Richardson (1981). The costs and benefits of MNs with respect to LDCs are well discussed in Streeten (1973) and Lall (1974). A more recent evaluation is contained in The United Nations (1978). The impact of MNs on Europe after the second world war is discussed in a lively and entertaining fashion by Tugenhat (1973); and Vernon (1971) provides some evidence on American multinationals abroad. The case against MNs is put very forcefully by Barnet and Miller (1974).

10 Foreign Aid

10.1 THE INTERNATIONAL TRANSFER OF AID

The success of the Marshall Plan in speeding the economic recovery of war-torn Europe after 1945 gave rise to a certain degree of optimism that similar flows of capital and other resources from developed countries (DCs) could be directed towards helping the poorer countries of the world. It is probably fair to say that in spite of this euphoria, and the concerted efforts of international organisations such as the United Nations to maintain the flow of aid, a growing scepticism set in after about 1960 about the usefulness of such transfers. It is the purpose of this chapter to try to shed some light on the reasons for this 'aid weariness' by considering both the motives for giving aid and its effects on recipient countries. But first, however, we need to consider the magnitude of aid flows after the second world war and some of the problems which surround its measurement.

Aid constitutes, in essence, a concessionary transfer of resources, with the key word being 'concessionary'.[1] In any given year a country will experience a net inflow of financial resources, including commercial transfers of private investment, export credits and bank loans; and concessionary transfers of grants, loans and technical assistance. The latter items could come either direct from aid-giving countries, or by means of multilateral agencies, such as the World Bank. The concessionary element which distinguishes the second set of items from the first arises from the fact that, in one way or another, the receiving country is getting the resources on better terms than it could have obtained commercially. As we shall see in section 10.2, this concessionary element may not turn out to be very significant; but as long as it is positive, it counts as foreign aid.

Column 1 in Table 10.1 shows the magnitude of the total net

flow of financial resources (TNFFR) from the 17 developed country members of the OECD development assistance committee (DAC) to lesser developed countries (LDCs) in 1980 as a percentage of their GNPs. The 'net' refers to the fact that some resources may have moved in the opposite direction in the form of interest and amortisation payments due on past debts. Column 2, however, focuses on the narrower concept of foreign aid or official development assistance which supposedly only consists of concessionary transfers from DAC countries.

Table 10.1: The total net flow of financial resources and official development assistance from DAC countries, 1980

	Total net flow of financial resources as a % of GNP*[1]	Net flow of official development assistance from DAC countries as a % of GNP[2]
Australia	0.63	0.47
Austria	0.32	0.22
Belgium	2.43	0.48
Canada	1.12	0.42
Denmark	1.22	0.72
Finland	0.40	—
France	1.77	0.62
Germany	1.28	0.43
Italy	1.01	0.15
Japan	0.65	0.32
Netherlands	1.46	0.99
New Zealand	0.48	0.27
Norway	1.49	0.82
Sweden	1.51	0.76
Switzerland	2.60	0.24
UK	2.43	0.34
USA	0.53	0.27
Total DAC countries	1.04	0.37

Note: *Excluding grants by voluntary agencies
Sources: [1]OECD (1981). [2]World Bank (1981, Annex, Table 16).

By comparing columns 1 and 2 it becomes apparent that, whilst many DAC countries have achieved the United Nations' target of 1 per cent for TNFFR, since this figure includes commercial lending, most DAC countries have failed to achieve the second UN target of 0.7 per cent of GNP as official development assistance. The most generous aid-givers in this respect appear to Denmark, the Netherlands, Norway and Sweden.

One cannot help but conclude from these figures that aid flows have been remarkably small when compared with the rhetoric which often surrounds discussions of aid budgets in the donor countries and, as Table 10.2 shows, the picture seems to have worsened rather than improved since 1960. Compared to a figure of 0.51 per cent for total official development assistance from DAC countries in 1960, the figures in later years have stabilised around 0.35 per cent of GNP. Moreover, one of the sharpest drops is recorded for the USA, although in absolute terms it remains the largest donor.

Table 10.2: The net flow of official development assistance from DAC countries as a percentage of GNP for selected years

	Net flow of official development assistance as % GNP				
	1960	1970	1976	1978	1980
Australia	0.37	0.59	0.41	0.54	0.47
Austria	—	0.07	0.12	0.29	0.22
Belgium	0.88	0.46	0.51	0.55	0.48
Canada	0.19	0.41	0.39	0.52	0.42
Denmark	0.09	0.38	0.56	0.75	0.72
France	1.35	0.66	0.62	0.57	0.62
Germany	0.31	0.32	0.36	0.37	0.43
Italy	0.22	0.16	0.13	0.14	0.15
Japan	0.24	0.23	0.20	0.23	0.32
Netherlands	0.31	0.61	0.83	0.82	0.99
New Zealand	—	0.23	0.41	0.34	0.27
Norway	0.11	0.32	0.70	0.90	0.82
Sweden	0.05	0.38	0.82	0.90	0.76
Switzerland	0.04	0.15	0.19	0.20	0.24
UK	0.56	0.41	0.40	0.48	0.34
USA	0.53	0.32	0.26	0.27	0.27
Total DAC	0.51	0.34	0.33	0.35	0.37

Source: World Bank (1981, Annex, Table 16).

These figures from DAC countries also contrast sharply with the quantity of aid distributed by some of the richer OPEC countries such as Qatar, the United Arab Emirates and Kuwait. As Table 10.3 indicates, official development assistance by OPEC countries as a whole as a percentage of GNP in 1980 was above the UN target of 0.7 per cent. There is a qualification to this, however, since OPEC aid tends to be rather narrowly distributed, with over half remaining within the Middle East and about 70 per cent given to Arab countries.

Table 10.3: Major donors and recipients of OPEC aid

Major donors (1980)	Official development assistance as a % of total OPEC aid[1]	% GNP[2]
Qatar	4.3	4.50
UAE	15.2	3.96
Kuwait	16.9	3.87
Saudi Arabia	43.3	2.60
Iraq	12.2	2.19
Total	91.9	3.42
Total OPEC	100	1.36
Major recipients (1978)	% of total OPEC aid[3]	
*Egypt	20.1	
*Syria	13.4	
*Jordan	9.5	
India	7.3	
*Yemen	4.9	
Lebanon	4.8	
*Mauretania	4.3	
Total	64.3	

Note: * Arab countries.
Sources: [1,2]World Bank (1981), [3]Overseas Development Council (1980, Table E-20).

International capital (both concessionary and non-concessionary) can be transferred either bilaterally from donor to recipient, or through multilateral agencies such as the World Bank.[2] Table 10.4 provides a breakdown of the sources of the TNFFR in 1980.

Two important facts stand out with respect to the origins of these capital flows. First, the relatively high proportion of commercial bank lending which reflected, in the main, surplus OPEC petrodollars accumulated during the 1970s and deposited in western banks; and secondly the growing importance of multilateral agencies in aid distribution and in particular the World Bank.

The International Bank for Reconstruction and Development (IBRD), to give it its proper title, was created at the Bretton

Table 10.4: The total net flow of resources to developing countries, 1980

	$ billion	% total receipts
A. Official development assistance	33.46	37.62
Bilateral	25.75	28.95
DAC[1]	17.64	19.83
OPEC	6.11	6.87
CMEA[2]	1.80	2.02
Other	0.20	0.22
Multilateral	7.71	8.67
World Bank	0.12	0.13
IDA	1.54	1.73
IFC	—	
Arab/OPEC Funds	0.26	0.29
Other	5.79	6.51
B. Non-concessionary flows	55.49	62.38
Bilateral	50.69	56.99
Private	41.89	47.09
Official DAC	4.70	5.28
OPEC	1.00	1.12
Other Countries	3.10	3.49
CMEA	—	—
Multilateral	4.80	5.40
World Bank	3.17	3.56
IFC	0.30	0.34
Arab/OPEC Funds	0.14	0.16
Other	1.19	1.34
C. Total receipts	88.95	

Notes: [1]Development assistance countries. [2]Committee of Mutual Economic Aid.
Source: OECD (1981).

Woods Conference of 1944 (to be discussed in Chapter 16) to provide long-term finance in the years immediately following the second world war in the absence of an effective private capital market. In the event, however, it turned out to be grossly inadequate for the task and was quickly overshadowed by the bilateral transfer of aid from the USA to Europe as part of the Marshall Plan. As a result, the IBRD was transformed into a development agency for the Third World.

Although the World Bank channels funds to LDCs for development purposes, it is primarily a commercial organisation which, by virtue of its size and prestige is able to raise money on favourable terms from the capital market and is hence able to lend to poorer countries on concessionary terms and make a profit.

Since 1960 it has been joined by two affiliates—the International Development Association (IDA), and the International Finance Corporation (IFC). The former is the 'soft loan' agency lending at very low interest rates with long repayment periods to the poorest countries, and the latter concentrates on encouraging private enterprise in LDCs through equity investment.

Traditionally, the policy of the World Bank was to lend primarily for particular projects rather than for programmes of development, to restrict its lending to the foreign exchange costs involved, and to give priority to infrastructure projects. In the 1970s, however, some important changes were made with respect to lending procedures, coinciding with the appointment of Robert McNamara to the Presidency of the Bank. First, it began to supplement its project lending with 'structural adjustment lending' designed to support countries encountering balance of payments difficulties, on condition that the country concerned was prepared to accept a package of policy measures suggested by the Bank. This new policy represented an encroachment on the traditional domain of the International Monetary Fund (see Chapter 16), but unlike the latter institution, the main objective of the Bank is to encourage longer term structural changes which would lead to an expansion of exports and a contraction of imports, rather than simply to finance essentially short-term balance of payments difficulties.

Secondly, in recent years the Bank has also become more flexible in terms of the foreign exchange rule and it is now prepared to cover more than the foreign exchange costs of projects. There was never any real logic in restricting its lending to imported inputs, except as a means of rationing out scarce funds.

Finally, and perhaps most important of all, the emphasis in lending policy has tended to move away from infrastructure projects towards tourism and rural-based projects, as well as towards helping the poorest sectors of the community in both rural and urban areas. This reflected a more general change in attitude by development economists in the 1970s away from policies which focused rather narrowly on industrial growth through highly capital-intensive projects based in the urban sector, and towards rural-based, labour-intensive projects catering for the basic needs of the majority of the population.[3] The Bank still, however, lends overwhelmingly for projects rather than for programmes.

10.2 THE MEASUREMENT OF AID

Aid is distinguished from total capital flows in general by virtue of its concessionary status, and in our analysis of the data in section 10.1 we attempted to separate out the concessionary component of the TNFFR transferred to LDCs by identifying aid with official development assistance. Unfortunately, however, not all concessionary flows are equally concessionary, and economists have attempted to measure the concessionary element contained in 'nominal' official flows by standardising them in terms of their 'grant equivalent'. Since a grant is the closest one can get to 'pure' aid, the procedure adopted is to measure all nominal aid flows in terms of their grant equivalent. For example, a loan has to be repaid with interest so it cannot constitute pure aid, but it may, none the less, contain a concessionary element.

The practice of measuring the grant equivalent of official aid flows is complicated by the fact that the borrowing and repaying of loans takes time and a suitable comparison has to be made between the terms of the loan offered to the LDC and the alternatives available commercially. In essence what happens is that the repayments due are discounted at the market rate of interest and are deducted from the nominal flow. In this way the market rate of interest represents the opportunity cost of the funds available from the private capital market. As long as the rate of interest to be paid by the LDC is lower than the market rate, the grant equivalent will be positive. The 'aid' component is also increased if the borrower is allowed a long 'grace period' before the first repayment becomes due, and the time over which repayment is to be made is extended.[4]

Seen in this light, the figures in Tables 10.1 to 10.4 overstate the true value of the aid being given, especially as most nominal flows take the form of loans rather than outright grants. In fact, calculations that have been made suggest that the grant equivalent of the TNFFR in 1980 was about 45 per cent of the nominal amount. As one might expect, the grant equivalent of official development assistance is higher, at around 80 per cent (with OPEC at 90 per cent), and flows from multilateral agencies in aggregate amount to about 50 per cent.[5]

This is not the whole story, however, since it is common practice for aid-givers to insist that some of the finance given is spent on goods from the donor country, and sometimes on specific goods as well. This practice of 'aid-tying' means that the benefits to LDCs are overstated in so far as the prices charged for the goods are higher than the country would have paid if it were free to purchase them in the world market, or they are unsuitable for the production process concerned. The aid component is also reduced if the loan has to be repaid in a scarce foreign currency. For some evidence on the magnitude of aid-tying, see Bhagwati and Eckhaus (1970).

Although in the last resort it is a matter of opinion as to whether the amount of aid given to LDCs is 'sufficient', the point remains that the 'true' value of such aid flows is often considerably less than the official figures would suggest. An example here might help to put matters in perspective. If we were to represent the gross earnings of the UK in 1980 by £100m then approximately 34p found its way abroad in *nominal* official development assistance. India, the UK's largest recipient of aid, would have received about 13p per head of population. Moreover, this is before any adjustments are made to isolate the grant equivalent, or to allow for the fact that the UK gains from an increase in export receipts in the process. Hopkin *et al.* (1970) calculated that the immediate 'true' foreign exchange cost of £100 worth of bilateral aid in the 1960s was about £37.

Perhaps an explanation for these figures can be found by looking at the motives for giving aid and its effects on recipient countries.

10.3 THE AID DEBATE

There have been many attempts to identify the motives for giving aid, a task which is not made easier by the failure of donors to publish the criteria upon which they base their aid policies. Economists, in particular, have been keen to see if there is any relationship between the distribution of aid and criteria such as 'need' or 'economic potential'. Studies by Davenport (1970) and Henderson (1971), however, found no significant relationship between factors such as income per head, 'poverty', unemployment, balance of payments difficulties and the receipt of aid. Similarly, those countries which might be thought to benefit most from the extra resources in terms of some economic criterion such as 'growth potential' or 'absorptive capacity', do not seem to receive a disproportionate amount of aid. Yet the distribution of aid per head of population is extremely unequal, with some countries receiving less than $1 per head, and others receiving over $100.

Most aid, it seems, is given for political reasons in as much as any shifts in the distribution of aid tend to reflect changes in the political interests of donor countries, including the USA and the Soviet Union. This process has its origins in the cold war psychology after the second world war when the reconstruction of Europe was seen by the western powers as a means of containing the spread of communism, and ideologically uncommitted LDCs were regarded as potential allies by both sides of the Iron Curtain.

In this sense, aid was regarded as a means of maintaining the allegiance of a Third World country rather than in promoting economic development as such, although some aid administrators may have believed that economic development could be a means to that political end if it brought about social and political values and institutions which were in line with the model of democracy they had in mind. It may also be that one of the reasons for the disenchantment with the effects of aid by both the USA and the Soviet Union in the 1960s was that the political benefits it induced did not increase in proportion with the quantity of aid given. Countries could be 'bought but not rented', and a relatively small amount of aid could achieve the same degree of political allegience as a much larger quantity.

The most consistent explanation for the pattern of aid, therefore, seems to be found by looking at the political interests of the donor countries and how these interests have changed over time. This is true, it appears, not only for the USA and the Soviet Union, but also for countries such as Britain and France where much of their aid budgets is accounted for by their ex-colonies. Only countries such as Sweden, West Germany and possibly Japan are relatively neutral in this respect. As one economist has put it: 'It would seem advantageous to be a small island of ex-colonial status in a politically sensitive area of the world.'[6]

A further motive for giving aid was re-emphasised by the Brandt Report (1980) on North–South relations. An important theme here was that the transfer of resources to the Third World should be viewed in its global context rather than in terms of narrow political self-interest, since it is in the interests of all rich countries to stimulate growth and development in the Third World, if only because it would lead to an expansion of international trade to the mutual advantage of all countries. It is somewhat ironic that in the 1980s, when many of the governments in the West were publically applauding the sentiments of the Brandt Commission, they were simultaneously reducing their aid budgets.

So much for the motives for giving aid, but what about its effects?

At least part of the reason for the general decline in the quantity of aid given as a proportion of GNP lies in the belief that aid has not been very effective in achieving the economic ends it was designed to meet. In spite of attempts by economists such as Bhagwati and Eckhaus (1970), Chenery and Carter (1973) and Papanek (1973) to find a positive correlation between aid and growth, and their references to apparent success stories such as Greece, Israel, Korea and Taiwan, there remains a strong air of disillusionment in some development circles.

A prominent sceptic in the aid debate is Peter Bauer, who has consistently argued that the contribution of aid to long-run development is at best marginal, and may even reduce it.[7] Bauer draws upon case studies to show that aid often reinforces political rivalries or creates tribal or other group conflicts by virtue of its ability to confer political patronage on those who distribute it. An example here might be the plight of the Ugandan Asians under Idi Amin in the 1970s. Aid also, he suggests, often substitutes for domestic resources rather than increasing them and can militate against self-help by fostering a dependency psychology. Matters are made worse when the aid fails to get through to those it was intended to help or is spent on wasteful and over-ambitious projects.

Attention has also been focused in recent years on the damaging effects which food aid can have upon the economies of poorer countries. It may seem a good idea for surplus American wheat and EEC dairy products to be distributed to the Third World, but the effects can often be counterproductive if dumped in these countries in unpredictable quantities without regard to local harvests. One result may be to encourage farmers to neglect local food production and turn instead to other crops with more regular outlets.[8]

Although most economists would probably accept that aid has not been as effective as they would have liked, or that it does not always trickle down to the poorest sections of the community, few, I suspect, would follow Bauer's argument through to its logical conclusion and actually reduce the quantity of aid given to LDCs. According to economists such as Meier (1984) and Thirlwall (1983), it is the inefficient management of aid which is at fault rather than the principle of aid itself. Once inefficiency and corruption are accepted as an inevitable part of the development process, the emphasis switches towards improving both the quality and the quantity of aid flows, including a reduction in the 'tied' component, and greater supervision over its distribution. It is also not always appropriate to measure the contribution of aid purely in terms of the financial returns to resources invested, since there are many projects, especially those connected with infrastructure and 'social overhead capital', which generate a low monetary return but are successful in the wider development context. There is also little evidence that LDCs are worse-off with aid, especially in view of the relatively small amounts actually given.

NOTES

1. We are referring here to 'open' aid which is explicitly given by donor countries and is published in their official aid figures, and not to 'disguised' aid transferred through trade. An example of the latter is when an international commodity agreement (discussed in Chapter 6) raises the price of a commodity above its competitive level in order to redistribute resources in its favour. We shall look at the relative merits of these two types of aid in Chapter 17.
2. Other multilateral agencies include regional development banks, the International Fund for Agriculture, the Islamic Fund for Economic Development, the Kuwait Fund and the Arab Fund.
3. For further information on this change of attitude, see Todaro (1982, ch. 6).
4. For example, if the interest rate charged on a 20 year loan were 2 per cent and the grace period before the first repayment were set at 10 years, then given a commercial discount rate of 7 per cent, the grant equivalent of the loan would work out at approximately 46 per cent. For details of the formula used and some illustrative calculations, see Thirlwall (1983, pp. 319–25).

5. See Thirlwall (1983, p. 325).
6. *Ibid.*, p. 327.
7. See, for example, Bauer (1971), and Bauer and Yamey (1981).
8. See, for example, *The Guardian* (1984).

FURTHER READING

The aid question is well presented in the specialist development texts by Todaro (1982) and Thirlwall (1983), and extracts from some of the more important writings in this area are reproduced in Meier (1984) and Bhagwati and Eckaus (1970). Bauer's views on the contribution of aid can be found in Bauer (1971) and Bauer and Yamey (1981).

PART 4
The Balance Of Payments

11 The Balance of Payments Accounts

The first three parts of this book have been primarily, though not exclusively, concerned with the pure theory of trade, employing an essentially microeconomic framework and focusing upon the impact of trade on resource allocation and distribution. Our main interest has, therefore, been with 'real' variables and relative prices rather than with monetary values measured in pounds or dollars. In Parts 4 and 5, however, our attention shifts to international monetary theory, in which values are measured explicitly in currency units, including the general price level, financial assets and exchange rates between different currencies. This will enable us to study important macroeconomic problems such as inflation and unemployment within the context of international trade.

In this part of the book we investigate the balance of payments (BOP) and the foreign exchange market, beginning in Chapter 11 with a description of the BOP as an accounting system and a discussion of the meaning of 'disequilibrium' in the BOP. An important objective here will be to explain the apparent paradox that 'the BOP always balances', and yet 'the BOP may be in disequilibrium'. In Chapter 12 we switch our attention to 'traditional' BOP policies, and contrast these in Chapter 13 with more recent contributions to the literature, including the monetarist and structuralist approaches to the BOP. Finally, in Chapter 14 we look specifically at the foreign exchange market and the debate over fixed versus flexible exchange rates.

11.1 THE BALANCE OF PAYMENTS ACCOUNTS

The BOP may be defined as a record of all the transactions between the residents of one country and the rest of the world over a given time period, usually a year.[1] Although, as we shall see, the way in which the accounts are compiled and presented differs between countries, and also for a given country over time, it is still possible to identify the principle 'ingredients' of a typical BOP sheet, and to explain some of the more important structural relationships between its various components. This is done in Table 11.1 which is based loosely on the UK accounts for 1968. A more detailed account for 1980 is presented in Appendix 11.1.

Table 11.1: *The basic ingredients of a balance of payments account*

		(£ million)
1.	Merchandise exports	+6 273
2.	Merchandise imports	−6 916
3.	visible trade balance	−643
4.	Government services/unilateral transfers, net	−466
5.	Private services/unilateral transfers, net	+818
6.	current account balance	−291
7.	Official long-term capital, net	+33
8.	Privte long-term capital, net	−160
9.	Short-term capital, net	−627
10.	Balancing item	−365
11.	Official settlements balance	+1 410
12.	capital account balance	+291

The first thing to notice about Table 11.1 is that all the items are recorded as credits (+) or debits (−), depending upon whether they signify a receipt from the rest of the world by UK residents or a payment by UK residents to the rest of the world. So when the UK exports goods and services to another country, exporters receive an inflow of purchasing power which is duly recorded as a credit. Imports, on the other hand, represent payments to foreigners for goods and services consumed by UK residents and are entered as debit items. In addition, where transactions are a two-way affair, they are often registered in 'net' terms. For example, the net flow of official long-term capital in column 7 records the inflow of capital into the UK minus the outflow. Things are also complicated, however, by the way in which capital items are treated, and by the principle of double-entry book-keeping.

To take capital items first, the confusion arises basically because the export of capital, such as when a UK resident buys a foreign bond, is in fact treated as a *debit* because it involves the sending of liquid purchasing power abroad. In this sense it is the foreigner who is benefiting initially from the capital export. Perhaps it is easier to think of the capital export as equivalent to importing a foreign security which gives us the right to a future income stream when the asset matures. On the other hand, when we sell an asset to foreigners we are borrowing liquid purchasing power. An import of capital is thus equivalent to an export of a good or a service. One must be careful, therefore, when interpreting the capital items in Table 11.1 to remember that it is a (−) which indicates an increase in assets and a decrease in liabilities (capital exports), and a (+) which signifies a decrease in assets and an increase in liabilities (capital imports).

The double-entry book-keeping principle requires all items to appear twice in the accounts—once as a credit and once as a debit. This is so as to ensure that the accounts balance in a book-keeping sense. An example might help to clarify the position. Imagine that the UK exports some cars to Japan. This will be recorded as a credit in column 1 of Table 11.1 since it involves a payment to UK residents. However, a debit must also be entered somewhere in the accounts to record the means of payment. For instance, if the Japanese importer pays for the cars in foreign exchange i.e. pounds sterling, this will be entered in the UK accounts as a fall in foreign holdings of the pound. If, on the other hand, payment is made in another currency such as the US dollar, then the means of payment will appear as an increase in UK holdings of foreign exchange

Having cleared up one or two methodological problems, we are now in a position to examine the structure of a 'typical' BOP account.

The first distinction is between *current account* transactions, represented in Table 11.1 by columns 1–6, and capital account transactions denoted by columns 7–12. The current account is designed to show all those items which relate to currently-produced goods and services. In other words, they give rise to a flow of income within the 'current' time period, conventionally defined as 1 year. The export of cars from the UK, therefore, would be recorded as a current account transaction because it generates income which would be included in the national income accounts for that year.[2] *Capital account* transactions, on the other hand, are concerned with changes in a country's stock of assets and, therefore, with financial claims which affect *future* income. In this sense, selling a UK bond to a foreigner is tantamount to selling a promise to repay a sum of money in the future.

The current account is itself decomposed into 'visibles' and 'invisibles'. Visibles, represented in Table 11.1 by columns 1 and 2, refer to merchandise exports and imports which could be said to pass 'visibly' through customs barriers. Sometimes the net balance of visible exports and imports is referred to as 'the balance of trade'.

Invisibles, on the other hand, (columns 4 and 5) include non-factor services such as freight and insurance costs and tourism, factor payments from abroad and 'unilateral transfers'. Factor payments are net inflows of interest, profits and dividends from abroad. Unilateral transfers cover such things as remittances by migrant workers to their 'home' country, income received from relatives living abroad and government grants. The term 'unilateral' expresses the fact that they confer purchasing power without a *quid pro quo*, i.e. are one-way transfers. When a migrant worker in West Germany sends part of his wage packet home to his family in Turkey he does not expect to receive anything in return.[3] In Table 11.1 we have adopted the common convention of separating private and government invisibles.

To complete the current account, the final balance of credits and debits is totted up in column 6 to produce the *current account balance*. If this turns out to be negative it is described as a deficit on current account, and if it is positive, it is a surplus on current account. It will *not* balance out exactly to zero except as a statistical freak.

Capital account transactions are generally much more heterogeneous than those on current account and they can be represented in many different ways. Generally, a distinction is made between assets with different maturity dates; between private and official investment (excluding the official settlements balance); and between portfolio and direct investment (which we discussed in Chapter 8).

As far as maturity dates are concerned, in Table 11.1 we have classified investment flows into short-term and long-term. Short-term here implies a maturity period of less than 12 months, with a further sub-division into short-term liquid assets such as bank deposits used to finance trade which mature in under 90 days, and short-term non-liquid assets such as export credits which take more than 90 days to mature. Long-term capital flows, on the other hand, are where the maturity period exceeds 12 months. The distinction between these time periods can be useful, but is essentially arbitrary. In fact the tendency nowadays is for all these capital items to be listed separately and the labelling to be left to the reader.

Finally, there is the official settlements balance in column 11 and the balancing item in column 10 to consider before reading the *capital account balance* in column 12 which, like the current account, will either be a surplus or a deficit.

The official settlements balance (OSB) registers changes in the UK's holdings of gold and convertible currency and its net position with the International Monetary Fund. It therefore provides an indication of the Government's dealings in the foreign exchange market.

The balancing item records any errors and omissions arising from the statistical compilation of the accounts, such as the failure to include the value of some of the transactions which have given rise to changes in foreign exchange reserves, which have themselves been recorded. Usually these errors occur on the capital account, but they will also appear in the current account if, for example, smuggling and other illicit transactions are prevalent.

Having looked at the current account and capital account in isolation, we need to complete our discussion of the structure of the BOP by emphasising three important relationships between its various components. To begin with, it is worth pointing out again that a positive effect on the BOP can be achieved either by exporting goods and services, *or* by borrowing from abroad. Secondly, although capital exports may be recorded as an outflow on capital account in the short run, the fruits of this lending may return in the future in the form of factor payments and be registered as a credit item under invisibles. This after all is an important motive for sending capital abroad in the first place. Finally, and probably most important of all, although we have said that there will always be either a surplus or a deficit on the current and capital accounts taken separately, the two accounts when added together *must* balance out.[4] In other words, if you were to add the current account balance in Table 11.1 (−291) to the capital account balance (+291), the result will always be zero. This is the sense in which the balance of payments always balances.

When you think about it, the reason is obvious: all current account transactions must have been financed from somewhere else in the system. Thus, if the UK is running a current account deficit with the rest of the world, then it would not have been possible for it to have imported more than it had exported, unless some payment had been made for the extra imports, registered under the capital account. Somewhere in the capital account a financial adjustment would have taken place to have enabled the extra imports to be purchased. Perhaps the adjustment took place through the sale of assets to foreigners or through private or government borrowing from abroad. Or perhaps it was financed by a fall in foreign exchange reserves. Whatever the means of financing, it remains the case that in an *ex-post* accounting sense, the BOP always balances.

11.2 THE BALANCE OF WHICH PAYMENTS?

If the BOP always balances, then what do we mean when we say that the BOP is in disequilibrium? To answer this question requires, first, an assessment of the economy's external position in the context of its performance as a whole. For example, one might be wary of concluding that a hefty surplus on the current account indicated a healthy external position if at the same time 20 per cent of the labour force were involuntarily unemployed!

The second task is to identify disequilibrium in terms of those 'unplanned' adjustments which took place in the BOP in order to offset other items which were adverse. For example, a country on a fixed exchange rate might have experienced an unplanned depletion of its foreign exchange reserves in order to finance a current account deficit.

Unfortunately, it is not a straighforward matter to identify those items in the accounts which are planned and motivated primarily by commercial considerations—known technically as 'autonomous' transactions[5]—and those which 'correct' the others—known as 'accommodating transactions'.

In practice what happens is that a line is drawn horizontally somewhere in the accounts leaving some items 'above the line' and the rest 'below the line'. Because of the principle of balance embodied in the accounts, this means that any overall credit or debit *above* the line will be offset by an equal and opposite imbalance *below* the line. In other words, once the line has been drawn, one is implicitly saying that the source of the disequilibrium lies in the autonomous items left above the line and the magnitude of this disequilibrium is associated with the unplanned accommodating adjustments which have taken place below the line in order to bring the accounts as a whole into balance.

Since countries differ in their trading structures, and classify autonomous and accommodating transactions differently (thus drawing the line in a different place), there is no universal measure of disequilibrium in the BOP. Instead, there are a number of alternative balances which are used to present the picture in different ways. In this sense, there is no single statistic to be taken from a BOP sheet to define unambiguously the 'health' of the country's external position. This does not mean, however, that one cannot make some sensible comments about a country's payments position by looking at the accounts from different angles.

The first balance one might consider is the *current account balance*. The line would be drawn after all current transactions, leaving all capital movements below the line. This might be useful to show whether the country is adding to, or subtracting from, its net foreign wealth, since a country which has a current account surplus must, by definition, be lending to the rest of the world and adding to its stock of wealth. A deficit, on the other hand, would indicate a net inflow of foreign funds. However, to focus on the current account in isolation would be quite misleading since it implies that all capital transactions are accommodating. In fact some will be autonomous, including long-term private investment. It is quite possible, therefore, that these autonomous capital movements could compensate for the deficit on current account and that the overall picture would look much healthier in so far as no unplanned adjustment would have been necessary.

A second method of presenting the accounts, which was used by the UK before 1970, is called the *basic balance*. This puts all long-term capital movements above the line, since they can generally be considered to be autonomous, but leaves all short-term capital items below the line, including the official settlements balance.[6] The items left below the line were termed 'monetary movements' and served to indicate the magnitude of the deficit or surplus. No attempt was made to distinguish between short-term capital transactions which might be autonomous and those expected to be accommodating. In effect, they were all seen to be accommodating and in principle controllable by the banks. The rationale behind this procedure was to focus attention on the relatively stable, long-term trends in the BOP and to abstract away from more volatile short-term capital movements.

In the 1960s and early 1970s, when most of the important trading nations were committed to maintaining a fixed exchange rate, two further balances were popular: the *net liquidity balance* (NLB), and the *official settlements balance* (OSB), sometimes referred to as the *overall balance*. Both were designed to shed light on the potential problems facing the monetary authorities when defending their currencies, especially where foreign exchange crises were common.

The NLB put private, short-term, non-liquid capital above the line on the grounds that it was generally used to finance trade, and left below the line all short-term liquid capital, as well as official settlements. The transactions left below the line were intended, therefore, to indicate the magnitude of the task facing the monetary officials if they wanted to maintain the value of their currency.

The difficulties involved in separating out autonomous and accommodating short-term capital movements encouraged governments to go one stage further and to publish the OSB. Private short-term liquid capital was now moved above the line, leaving only official settlements below. This identified official action as the only accommodating action and was standard practice in the USA after the mid-1960s, and in the UK after 1970.

In the context of fixed exchange rates, where countries were obliged to buy and sell foreign exchange to maintain par values for their currencies, it was relatively easy to identify disequilbrium in the BOP with changes in reserves, and the OSB system worked quite well. However, by 1973, when the major trading countries were allowing their currencies to float to a much greater degree, the link between the OSB and disequilibrium was broken. In theory, if the exchange rate is allowed to float freely no accommodating transactions are necessary and the OSB would be zero. In practice, all countries engaged in 'dirty' floating and intervened to 'manage' their currencies within certain limits, in which case the options available to the authorities when dealing with BOP problems was much wider than simply running down or building up reserves.

Other problems had also arisen which made the sharp division between private and official capital flows too rigid. For example, OPEC holdings of US treasury bills were recorded as accommodating transactions, whereas in fact they were bought for commercial reasons. Similarly, it was not always the case that an increase in liquid liabilities and a deficit on the NLB or OSB was a problem even if reserves were low. In fact, during periods of trade expansion this was quite likely and beneficial. Both the UK before 1914 and the USA after 1958 lent long-term to the rest of the world and allowed liquid liabilities to rise faster than the absolute value of their reserves, but their deficits on NLB and OSB were essential if the international economy was to be provided with sufficient liquidity to grow. It had become apparent that it was not possible in practice to distinguish between short-term capital movements which could be influenced by policy, and those which were speculative or volatile and could not.

As a result of these changes, the NLB and the OSB have been significantly demoted in the official publications of BOP data. The current convention is to move away from 'balances' which are often wrongly associated with welfare changes, with debits representing losses and credits gains. Instead, the emphasis has switched towards presenting all transactions in as much detail as possible and leaving the reader to work out the balances as required. This is clearly shown in the full table for the UK presented in Appendix 11.1

11.3 THE UK BALANCE OF PAYMENTS

To illustrate the essentially arbitrary nature of 'disequilibrium' in the BOP, Table 11.2 shows some of the balances we discussed in the previous section for the UK economy over the years 1958, 1968 and 1977. These years have been deliberately chosen to emphasise some of the points made in section 11.2.

Table 11.2: The UK balance of payments 1958, 1968, 1977

		(£ million)	
	1958	1968	1977
1. Visible trade balance	29	−643	−2 239
2. Current account balance	344	−291	−224
3. Basic balance	148	−418	2 484
4. Balancing item	67	−114	3 179
5. Basic balance and balancing item	215	−532	5 663
6. Total currency flow*	290	−1 410	7 361
7. Official settlements balance	−290	1 410	−7 361

Note: * The algebraic sum of the current account balance and the total of
          investment and other capital flows plus the balancing item (and EEA
          losses on forwards), representing the balance of autonomous official and
          all private transactions.
Source: Central Statistical Office (1981).

If we look first at the data for 1958, then one would generally conclude that there was no 'fundamental disequilibrium'[7] on the UK balance of payments, since long-term (autonomous) capital outflows were covered by a current account surplus (row 2) and short-term capital inflows. The total currency flow (row 6), representing the net balance of autonomous official and all private transactions was, therefore, positive at £290 million. This enabled the government to improve its reserves to liabilities position to the tune of −£290 million represented by the −£290 million under the OSB in row 7. (Remember that a (−) sign here indicates an accumulation of reserves and a fall in liabilities.)

By 1968, however, the picture had changed dramatically, and few would dispute that the BOP was in a state of 'fundamental disequilibrium'. The current account was in deficit and was aggravated by a net outflow of both short- and long-term capital. Hence, considerable official finance was required to accommodate a negative total currency flow, including loans from the International Monetary Fund. The positive sign in row 7 now indicates a fall in reserves an an inflow of funds from abroad. The seriousness of the problem had been recognised by the government and remedial action was taken, including a heavy devaluation of sterling in 1967.

The two cases above were relatively easy to diagnose, but the picture in 1977 is much more ambiguous. The basic balance and total currency flow are positive, which might be taken as indicative of a healthy position. However, if one looks a little closer at the reasons behind this, the situation becomes less clear. To start with, the visible balance is strongly negative and was only kept from being reflected in a more serious deficit on current account by an inflow of factor payments associated with the exploitation of North Sea oil. In fact, in the 1980s the current account has continued to be in surplus overall, but only because North Sea oil revenues (due to run out in the 1990s) are masking a serious and unprecedented deficit in manufactured goods.

Secondly, the capital account position is also a little misleading in so far as the inflow of short-term capital represents OPEC oil revenues deposited in short-term UK banks and is likely to be quite sensitive to fluctuations in international interest rates. Finally, the importance of viewing a country's external position in line with what is happening to the economy as a whole is highlighted by the fact that much of the 'improvement' in the UK current account reflects the dampening effects that recession has upon imports. Statements about external equilibrium cannot, therefore, be divorced from the corollary that the economy was operating at substantially less than full employment. We shall return to these issues when we look at the UK BOP again in Chapter 13.

APPENDIX 11.1

UK Balance of payments in 1980

	Current account (£ million)
Credits	
Exports (fob)	47 389
Services:	
General government	397
Private sector and public corporations	
Sea transport	3 816
Civil aviation	2 210
Travel	2 965

Financial services	1 595
Other services	4 826

Interest, profits and dividends:

General government	943
Private sector and public corporations	7 261

Transfers:

General government	958
Private sector	793

Total invisibles	25 764
Total credits	73 153

Debits

Imports (fob)	46 211

Services:

General government	1 188
Private sector and public corporations	
Sea Transport	3 681
Civil aviation	1 815
Travel	2 757
Other services	2 180

Interest, profits and dividends:

General government	1 598
Private sector and public corporations	6 644

Transfers:

General government	2 790
Private sector	1 083

Total invisibles	23 736
Total debits	69 947

Balances

Visible balance	+1 178

Services:
General government	−791
Private sector and public corporations	
Sea transport	+135
Civil aviation	+395
Travel	+208
Financial services	+1 595
Other services	+2 646

Interest, profits and dividends:
General government	−655
Private sector and public corporations	+617

Transfers:
General government	−1 832
Private sector	−290

Invisible balance	+2 028

of which private sector and public corporations: services and IPD	+5 596

Current balance	+3 206

Capital account
(£ million)

Investment and other Capital Transations

Overseas investment in UK:
Direct	+2 094
By oil companies	+1 714
Portfolio:	+841
of which, British government stock	+568

Miscellaneous investment   —
Total overseas investment in UK   +4 649

UK private investment overseas:
  Direct   −2 569
  Investment by oil companies and
    miscellaneous investment   −1 364
  Portfolio   −2 958
  Total UK private investment overseas   −6 891

Official long-term capital   −125

Import credit   −238
Export credit   −907

Foreign currency borrowing or lending abroad by
  UK banks   +2 024

Exchange reserves in sterling:
  British government stocks   +930
  Banking and money market liabilities, etc.   +316

Other external banking and money market
  liabilities in sterling   +2 569

External sterling lending by UK banks   −2 462

Other external borrowing or lending:
  UK public sector   −165
  UK private sector   −938

Other transactions   −237

Total investment and other transactions   −1 475

Allocation of SDRs   +180

Gold subscription to IMF   —

Official Financing

Net transactions with overseas monetary
　　authorities   −140

Foreign currency borrowing, net   −941

Official reserves (drawing on +/ additions
　to −)   −291

Total official financing   −1 372

Balancing item   −539

Source: Central Statistical Office (1981).

NOTES

1. Although quarterly figures are often available and monthly figures for some of the items involved.
2. Conventionally, exports are recorded free on board (fob) and exclude costs of transportation beyond the point of export; while imports are measured with the cost of international insurance and freight (cif) included. If this were not done, then double counting would result when imports and exports were aggregated.
3. The entry for unilateral transfers is in fact a fiction to keep the double-entry accounting system in balance, since the outflow of money is matched by an inflow of 'value' only the sense that it is an inflow of 'gratitude'. For example, if the export of cars from the UK to Japan were a gift, then the credit on the export side would be matched by a debit on unilateral transfers.
4. Any statistical errors would, of course, have been taken care of by the balancing item in row 10.
5. They are 'autonomous' in the sense that they are not intended to affect the BOP or the foreign exchange rate.
6. In practice the balancing item was also put above the line to represent gaps in trade or long-term investment data.
7. This term was invented by the International Monetary Fund, but it was never clearly defined. It was intended to cover a situation where a country was running a persistent current account deficit which could only be corrected by heavy sacrifices in terms of domestic goals, or by abandoning its commitments to the international community.

FURTHER READING

For further details on the construction and interpretation of the BOP accounts, see Cohen (1969). The accounts for most countries are reproduced in the International Monetary Fund's International Financial Statistics. The UK BOP is discussed in Prest *et al.* (1982), and raw data can be found in Annual Central Statistical Office UK balance of payments (pink) books. Regular analyses are also available in the March, June, September, and December issues of *Economic Trends*. For a discussion of the USA BOP, including the changes in procedure described in section 11.3, see Stern (1977).

12 Traditional Balance of Payments Policies

12.1 THE BALANCE OF PAYMENTS AS A POLICY PROBLEM

In Chapter 11 we considered the balance of payments (BOP) as an accounting framework, and discussed the various meanings attached to the notion of 'disequilibrium' in the BOP. In this chapter we look at a number of traditional policy options available to a government which believes that remedial action is warranted. The label 'traditional' is applied because these policies were derived from a synthesis of BOP theory during the 1950s and 1960s within the context of essentially fixed exchange rates and limited capital mobility. By the 1970s, however, it was obvious that things had changed, especially after the major industrial countries adopted managed floating in 1973, and the orthodox approach came increasingly into question. We shall review some of these later developments in Chapter 13, including those associated with the revival of monetarism. Before analysing these policy options, however, we need to consider the sense in which the BOP is viewed as a policy problem.

As we saw in Chapter 11, the BOP only balances in an accounting sense, and the real problem is to identify the sources of disequilibrium which necessitate accommodating action, depending upon where in the accounts the line is drawn. Some disturbances or 'shocks' to the BOP are likely to be viewed by the authorities as essentially of a short-term nature, arising perhaps from seasonal fluctuations in output or industrial disputes; while others will reflect cyclical variations in supply or demand within the international economy. In both these cases the government may be content to 'ride out the storm' and take no significant corrective action.[1] If, on the other hand, these disturbances are seen to be more long-term and indicative of more fundamental

169

changes in the structure of the economy or of its international trading position, then appropriate policy action may be required. In our policy discussion below we shall be dealing with the latter situation and policies designed to correct a fundamental or persistent BOP problem.

The BOP is regarded as a policy problem not only because some forms of disequilibrium will reflect long-term structural imbalances in the economy, but also because automatic adjustment mechanisms are seen as either insufficient to restore equilibrium, or undesirable in their consequences. For example, a country operating under a gold standard (to be discussed more fully in Chapter 16) might find that the outflow of gold used to finance a payments deficit automatically contracts the domestic money supply, which in turn reduces the aggregate price level and restores BOP equilibrium by making exports cheaper and imports more expensive. If this adjustment is inefficient, the government might step in to reinforce the process by contracting prices and incomes directly. If, on the other hand, it finds the deflationary consequences of the gold standard mechanism too bitter a pill to swallow politically, it could intervene to solve the problem in a less uncomfortable way, possibly by abandoning its commitment to the fixed exchange rate. Other examples of automatic adjustment mechanisms will be given during the course of our discussion of BOP policies.

The BOP is thus regarded as a policy problem because governments generally wish to reinforce automatic adjustment mechanisms which are insufficient to restore equilibrium on their own, or to override them if their consequences are seen as undesirable.

For the remainder of this chapter we shall look at the various ways in which the BOP can be brought back into 'balance'.[2] In section 12.2 we take a number of policy options on a one-by-one basis, and in section 12.3 we place them within a more explicit general equilibrium framework, where the aim will be to achieve simultaneous internal and external balance and to assign various policies to achieve these two ends.

12.2 BALANCE OF PAYMENTS POLICIES

There are a number of policy options available to a government wishing to influence its BOP, directed at both the current account and the capital account. We shall consider them under three headings: (I) expenditure-changing, (II) expenditure-switching and (III) direct controls. In addition, we shall assume that the exchange rate is initially fixed and that the country concerned is running a persistent deficit on current account. A surplus can, of course, be equally problematic if, for example, it generates inflationary pressure, but it is usually the case that a deficit is more difficult to eliminate and thus constitutes more of a problem in practice. In most cases the policies to cure a surplus are simply the reverse of those we shall discuss in connection with a deficit.

Expenditure-changing policies are designed to alter the level of spending in the economy.[3] For example, to cure a deficit the economy would be deflated so as to cut spending on imports, whilst leaving exports intact. This approach is based upon a Keynesian income adjustment mechanism which is opened up to international trade.[4] Exports are viewed as 'injections' into the circular flow of income as income is received from abroad, while imports constitute a 'leakage'. The extent of the leakage effect depends upon the marginal propensity to import which measures the change in imports resulting from a given change in income.

Figure 12.1 shows how imports might be expected to vary with national income. A rise in income from Y0 to Y1 brings about an increase in imports from M0 to M1, and the ratio of these two changes (equivalent to the slope of the import function) defines the marginal propensity to import. One would expect a direct relationship between imports and income or expenditure, since any expansion of domestic activity would tend to suck in imports of raw materials for industry, and consumers are likely to spend a proportion of their extra incomes on imported goods.

So if the government wishes to cure a deficit it would employ fiscal and monetary policies to contract domestic activity in order to reduce spending on imports. This could be done by lowering government spending, raising taxes, reducing the domestic money supply, raising interest rates, or any combination of these. National income will fall as a result through the Keynesian multiplier process and the trade balance should improve, depending upon the strength of the marginal propensity to import. In general the higher this propensity the more effective the expenditure changing policy will be.

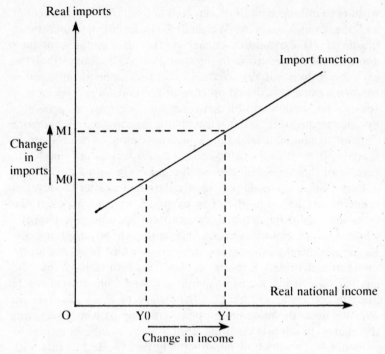

Figure 12.1: The marginal propensity to import

Two interesting conclusions follow from this analysis. The first is
that an export-led 'boom' would have more favourable effects on
the economy than a policy of domestic contraction to cure a
deficit, as long as the economy is not at full capacity. This is
because in the former case the expansion of national income
resulting from the increase in exports will be more than enough to
counter the rise in imports induced by the income increase, and so
the trade balance will improve. With a domestic contraction,
however, although the trade balance improves when imports are
forced down, national income itself has fallen. Unfortunately,
however, it is not usually possible for the government to engineer
an increase in exports since they tend to be determined by factors
outside the control of the exporting country, such as the growth of
foreign income.

A second conclusion is that although an increase in exports is
equivalent to an increase in domestic spending, in so far as it

stimulates national income through the multiplier, the export-led expansion would improve the balance of trade at the same time, while the domestic expansion would make it worse. This is because in the former case the rise in exports is sufficient to outweigh an increase in imports which the extra income generates. In the latter case, however, domestic spending will draw in imports without affecting exports, and so lead to a deterioration in the balance of trade.

Before leaving expenditure changing policies we need to consider the 'absorption' approach which also emphasises the importance of reducing domestic expenditure when correcting a deficit. This approach, which was invented by Alexander (1952), starts from the national income accounts by stating a truism that output or income (Y) is equal to consumption (C) plus domestic investment (I) plus government spending (G) plus the difference between exports (X) and imports (M):

$$Y = C + I + G \quad + X - M$$

If we now let A stand for total domestic expenditure (C + I + G) or total domestic 'absorption', and B for the trade balance (X − M), we can rewrite our truism as:

$$Y = A + B$$

Of if we subtract A from both sides:

$$Y - A = B$$

That is to say, the trade balance is the difference between domestic income or production and domestic spending or absorption. So, if total domestic absorption exceeds total domestic output, by definition, the country must be running a current account deficit and be absorbing more than it is actually producing and importing the difference. Hence, to cure a deficit requires *either* an increase in Y *or* a reduction in A. Since it is usually difficult to expand output in the short run, the brunt of the adjustment will tend to fall on A through expenditure-reducing policies.

The income adjustment model we have been using is a very simple one, based only on one country and some quite restrictive assumptions, including fixed exchange rates and an economy which is operating at less than full employment. None the less, it is possible to make this model more complex within the general equilibrium framework we shall be discussing in section 12.3, and it serves to capture the basic principles involved in income adjustment and the way in which expenditure-changing policies work.

The analysis can easily be expanded to incorporate more than one country. This is important since one country's exports will be another country's imports. Hence, if the UK were to adopt expenditure-reducing policies to help solve its payments deficit, this would contract incomes in the rest of the world which in turn *could* reduce the demand for UK exports as the rest of the world's imports fall.

Expenditure-switching policies are not intended to alter the magnitude of spending in the deficit country but to *switch* this spending away from imports to import substitutes produced locally, and to switch spending by foreigners towards the deficit country's exports. This can be achieved by imposing tariffs on imports or subsidising exports to alter relative prices in the manner described in Chapter 5; but the main policy application of this analysis is devaluation of the currency.[5] The question is whether devaluation can set in motion expenditure-switching effects which lead to an improvement in the trade balance.

The analysis which sought to answer this question has become known as the 'elasticities approach', and owes much to the early work of Machlup (1939). Instead of assuming relative prices constant and varying income as under the multiplier analysis we discussed above, the elasticities approach asks what happens when relative prices (of currencies) change, and income is held constant.

The term 'elasticities' was coined because the answer to this question depends to a large extent on the elasticities of demand and supply for imports and exports. The conditions under which devaluation would improve the balance of trade were formally represented in a famous formula named after the economists who derived it, known as Marshall and Learner. The full formula which contains a number of different cases is too complex to reproduce here, but the condition from this formula which has become best known (and is often called *the* Marshall–Learner condition) is that devaluation will improve the balance of trade only if the sum of the elasticity of demand for the country's exports plus the elasticity of demand for its imports exceeds unity.

The reasoning behind this condition concerns the relationship between changes in the foreign exchange market brought about by the devaluation, and changes in exports and imports. Devaluation raises the price of foreign currency and therefore makes imports look more expensive in the home market, unless foreign suppliers choose to drop their prices to compensate. Similarly, export prices will be cheaper in terms of foreign currency, and one might expect exporters to pass this on in lower selling prices abroad. The outcome, therefore, depends critically on the response of imports and exports to the price changes brought about by the devaluation. If, for example, buyers' habits are rigidly fixed when prices change, as is likely in the case of oil and tobacco imports, the devaluation will not succeed. Only if the demand for imports and exports is responsive (elastic) will the rise in import prices choke off imports and the fall in export prices stimulate a sufficient increase in export demand to enable devaluation to work.

The Marshall–Learner condition should only be interpreted as a *rough* guide to the likely effects of a devaluation since it is based upon a model incorporating some strong assumptions, and requires empirical estimates of the relevant elasticities which in practice can only be approximate.

An important theoretical qualification to the elasticities approach came from the absorption approach which we discussed above. Indeed, the absorption approach was designed specifically to investigate how devaluation affected both the balance of trade and national income. What the absorption approach suggested was that devaluation could only improve the trade balance if it either increased real output Y, or it cut real expenditure/absorption A. In conventional elasticity analysis it was taken for granted that devaluation would improve the trade balance even if the economy were at full employment. The absorption approach, however, makes it clear that it will only do so if total absorption is *reduced*. In other words, if the economy is at full employment, then devaluation must be accompanied by policies to reduce absorption in order to leave room for the necessary reallocation of resources to increase exports and decrease imports. This is why devaluation policies are typically accompanied by deflationary monetary and fiscal policies. In practice, therefore, the absorption and elasticities approaches need to be combined to explain the full repercussions of devaluation. For an attempt to do this, see Tsiang (1961).

On the practical question of the measurement of the elasticities, early estimates for the 1930s and 1940s were surprisingly low. This gave rise to 'elasticity pessimism', and the belief that devaluation would often worsen the balance of trade. In the 1960s, however, this gave way to greater 'elasticity optimism' and the view that devaluation could work, especially for the major industrial countries such as the USA, Canada, Japan and France, although the picture was less clear for Great Britain.[6] This reversal of attitude was partly due to a change of circumstances, with the later years being much less hampered by trade restrictions which had made it difficult for trade flows to respond to price changes. Similarly, the larger proportion of manufactured goods traded in the 1960s also increased the sensitivity of exports and imports to price changes.

In addition, econometric techniques had improved which made the elasticity estimates less 'biased'. A good example here relates to the so-called 'J' curve. Because trade contracts tend to be signed in advance of delivery, devaluation has no immediate effect on the *volume* of trade. But since exports are typically invoiced in the country's own currency and imports in foreign currency, the initial effect of devaluation is to worsen the trade balance, because the home value of exports falls while the foreign price of imports remains unchanged. As Figure 12.2 shows, the trade balance initially worsens and the Marshall–Learner condition is satisfied only after a time period has elapsed. By allowing, therefore, for time lags in the import and export equations, the estimates obtained of the relevant elasticities become more realistic approximations of their 'true' values. For further details on this, see Orcutt (1950) and Leamer and Stern (1970).

The consensus, therefore, was that devaluation could improve the trade balance and that the larger the elasticities the more likely it was to be successful. Only monetarists remained more sceptical than this and we shall consider their views on this matter in Chapter 13.

If governments are pessimistic about the efficiency of relative price or income adjustment, and are unhappy about the political repercussions of deflationary expenditure changing policies, or the 'loss of face' involved in a devaluation, then they might turn instead to direct controls to solve their BOP problems. We have already discussed some of these controls in Chapter 5, including tariffs and quotas, but there is one form of direct control which is

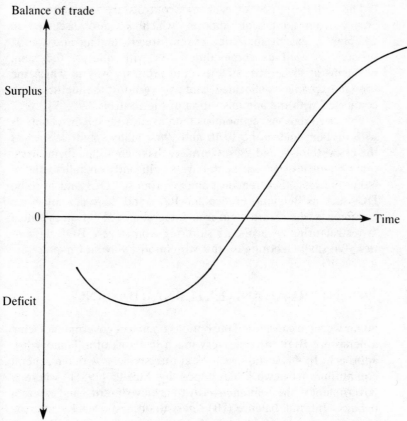

Figure 12.2: The 'J' curve effect

particularly popular in the BOP context—foreign exchange controls.

Exchange controls are restrictions on the transfer of one currency into another, whether the motive is to buy foreign goods and services, to travel abroad, or to engage in foreign lending. Most countries have some form of exchange control, usually on capital transactions, but occasionally they spill over into foreign travel, as in the UK in the late 1960s and in France in 1983. LDCs are also fond of employing multiple exchange controls (discussed in Chapter 5) to ration foreign exchange towards imports which are considered essential in their development programmes, and to discriminate against 'luxury' imports.

The welfare effects of exchange controls are similar to those arising from quotas on imports, which we also discussed in Chapter 5, except that they cover foreign lending and tourist services as well as commodities. As with quotas, the main problems arise because of the often arbitrary way in which the foreign exchange is allocated, and as a result of the inefficiencies connected with the administration of the controls.

For these reasons, economists tend to regard exchange controls with disdain, and in the 1970s and 1980s many countries such as the USA, the UK and West Germany, have abolished them, while other countries such as Japan have significantly liberalised them. None the less, they remain popular in most LDCs and in some DCs such as Belgium, France and Italy, and there are still some economists who regard them as an integral part of a strategy aimed at restructuring an economy suffering from severe BOP difficulties. We shall elaborate on this structuralist view in Chapter 13.

12.3 INTERNAL AND EXTERNAL BALANCE

So far we have considered the options open to a government facing a persistent BOP problem very much in terms of a 'laundry list' approach. In this section we look at these policies within a general equilibrium framework developed by Meade (1951), where a government wishes *simultaneously* to achieve internal and external balance. Internal balance (IB) refers to domestic macroeconomic objectives which we shall take for expositional simplicity to mean full employment and zero price inflation.[7] External balance (EB) in this context refers to BOP equilibrium, and in the absence of international capital mobility this comes down to a current account balance.

As in many areas of economics, the simultaneous achievement of IB and EB is likely to involve a trade-off between the two. Table 12.1 shows some possibilities. For example, in case A the economy is suffering from both recession and a deficit on the BOP. Hence, an expansionary policy is desired to increase employment and achieve IB, but this will tend to make the BOP worse by increasing imports. Similarly in case C a contractionary policy is appropriate to cure inflation, but this pushes the BOP out of balance by generating an even larger surplus. Only in cases B and D, therefore, will the policy for IB *also* improve EB.

Table 12.1: The conflict between internal and external balance

Case		Policy for internal balance	Effect on external balance
A	Recession deficit	expand	worse
B	Recession surplus	expand	improves
C	Inflation surplus	contract	worse
D	Inflation deficit	contract	improves

A further conclusion from Meade's analysis is that for the achievement of both IB and EB it will usually be the case that *two* independent policies will be required, one for IB, and another for EB. This idea comes from a principle first stated by Tinbergen (1952) which says that if a number of independent policy targets are to be achieved with a number of effective policy instruments, the number of instruments will, in general, need to be at least as great as the number of targets. In other words, to achieve full employment and BOP equilibrium will probably require at least two policies. It is possible for one instrument to move the economy in the direction of two goals, as in cases B and D in Table 12.1, but it is rare for only one policy *fully* to achieve both.

To see how these policies might be used to achieve simultaneous IB and EB, we can refer to a diagram first developed by Salter (1959) and Swan (1960). This is done in Figure 12.3.

On the vertical axis R represents an index of international competitiveness such that a rise in R equates to a devaluation of the currency, and a fall in R to a revaluation. If R is high it means that a given level of employment can be sustained with a low level of domestic demand or absorption A, since exports will be high relative to income. IB represents combinations of R and A that yield internal balance. Above the line there is inflation, and below there is recession. EB represents combinations of R and A to achieve external equilibrium. Above the line there is a BOP

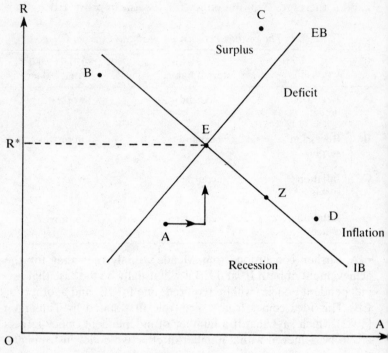

Figure 12.3: Internal and external balance

surplus, and below the line a deficit. Only at point E is there simultaneous IB and EB. We can now represent our cases A–D from Table 12.1 within this figure. For example, case A, where the economy is experiencing both recession and a deficit, is depicted below both the IB and EB lines. In practice, of course, the economy could be anywhere in the figure.

The policy combinations which could be used to move the economy towards E in Figure 12.3 are summarised in Table 12.2. Note that we are assuming the exchange rate is fixed, but can be changed by devaluation and revaluation, and that there are no international capital movements. Under these conditions, to solve case A expenditure-changing policies could be used to raise income and employment and an expenditure-switching policy in the form of devaluation could be used to improve the trade balance. In Figure 12.3 this is shown by following the arrows placed in the vicinity of A, i.e. raising absorption along the horizontal axis and simultaneously moving upwards towards E by reducing the deficit through devaluation (increasing R). The policy mixtures for the other cases could similarly be represented in Figure 12.3. Note that a move from point Z (internal balance with a deficit) would require both a successful devaluation *and* a policy of disabsorption, otherwise the competitive advantage from devaluation would be eroded by inflation resulting from excess demand, and the economy would move vertically up from Z rather than to E. This was the conclusion of the absorption approach in section 12.2.

Table 12.2: Expenditure-changing and expenditure-switching policies

Case		Policy for internal balance	Policy for external balance
A	Recession deficit	expand ($\uparrow$ A)	devalue ($\uparrow$ R)
B	Recession surplus	expand ($\uparrow$ A)	revalue ($\downarrow$ R)
C	Inflation surplus	contract ($\downarrow$ A)	revalue ($\downarrow$ R)
D	Inflation deficit	contract ($\downarrow$ A)	devalue ($\uparrow$ R)

So far we have shown how a mixture of expenditure-changing and expenditure-switching policies could, in theory, move an economy towards its internal and external goals, but what if devaluation were ruled out? Mundell (1968) suggested that if we introduce international capital mobility into the model, it might be possible to reach point E by using monetary policy to achieve EB and fiscal policy for IB. Table 12.3 shows how this could be done for our cases A to D.

In case A, for example, instead of using expenditure switching policies to improve the BOP, the authorities could adopt a tight monetary policy instead to raise interest rates and attract foreign capital. However, since high interest rates might also contract domestic activity and make the recession worse, fiscal policy is used at the same time to expand output and employment.

Table 12.3: using fiscal and monetary policies to achieve internal and external balance

Case		Policy for internal balance (fiscal)	Policy for external balance (monetary)
A	Recession deficit	expand	tight
B	Recession surplus	expand	easy
C	Inflation surplus	contract	easy
D	Inflation deficit	contract	tight

In this way, the government can 'assign' various policy instruments to achieve the twin goals of IB and EB, but upon what basis do the authorities chose to use a particular policy for a particular goal? Mundell's solution to this assignment problem was to suggest a rule which has become known as 'the principle of effective market classification'. This says that the authorities should assign the policy to the goal upon which it is likely to have the greatest relative impact. This ensures that the authorities move in the right direction, and that the net costs of BOP adjustment are minimised. In case A, for example, both fiscal and monetary policy could be used to expand output, but fiscal policy will have the greatest relative impact on this target and monetary policy on the BOP.

12.4 APPRAISAL

The traditional approach to the BOP represents a synthesis between a number of alternative mechanisms for achieving simultaneous IB and EB within a general equilibrium model of the economy. A full representation of this framework is beyond the scope of this book, but for those readers familiar with the ISLM model from macroeconomics, it is tantamount to adding a set of equations to model the BOP. The full model would thus contain a goods market (IS), a money market (LM), and an external sector representing EB. This ISLMEB model thus presents a useful framework for discussing alternative theories about the workings of the economy and incorporates insights derived from all of the adjustment mechanisms we have discussed, including Keynesian income adjustment, the absorption approach and the elasticities approach. Moreover, it can be used as a basis for discussing policy options, including the assignment problem, and as a framework for developing empirically relevant hypotheses.

Although this apparatus is still widely used in BOP discussions, we need to complete this chapter by summarising its major limitations, some of which we shall return to in Chapter 13.

In the first place, the ISLMEB model is essentially short-run and based upon given stocks of money, financial assets and physical capital. Secondly, it takes the aggregate price level as given, and makes no attempt to provide an adequate explanation of inflation or inflationary expectations. Thirdly, its inherently Keynesian bias means that the focus of attention tends to fall on the aggregate demand side of the economy to the relative neglect of supply side considerations. Fourthly, despite Mundell's contribution, its treatment of international capital movements is very limited. This may have been justified to some extent in the 1940s and early 1950s when the international capital market was relatively quiet, but it is quite unrealistic from the mid-1950s onwards. Finally, the traditional approach was designed to meet the circumstances of the day, namely fixed exchange rates and monetary authorities committed to protecting the domestic money supply from the effects of deficits and surpluses on the BOP. By the 1970s, neither of these two assumptions was realistic.

NOTES

1. For example, by allowing reserves of foreign exchange to fall to accommodate a deficit.
2. We shall not be concerned here with longer-term policies which might impinge upon the BOP. For example, the decision by the British to join the European Community in 1973.
3. Johnson (1961) first used the term expenditure-reducing for policies that influenced the level of spending, and expenditure-switching for those which altered its composition. The expression expenditure-

changing is probably more accurate, however, since policies might be used to increase spending as well as to reduce them.

4. For the original work on the Keynesian multiplier in an open economy, see Machlup (1943).

5. Devaluation (revaluation) refers to an official lowering (raising) of the value of a currency fixed in terms of other currencies or an international reserve asset such as gold. The value of a currency can also fall (rise) in the foreign exchange market without official action. In this case a depreciation (appreciation) has occurred.

6. See, for example, Houthakker and Magee (1969), Adams and Junz (1971) and Leamer and Stern (1970).

7. In a more complex presentation we could define domestic objectives in terms of the achievement of as high a level of domestic demand as is compatible with a given rate of price inflation. This, however, would require a detailed specification of the relationship between these two variables. In addition, EB might not be seen as a policy goal. For example, the USA adopted a policy of 'benign neglect' with respect to its BOP under the Bretton Woods system as part of its contribution to maintaining sufficient international liquidity. This is discussed more fully in Chapter 16.

FURTHER READING

For an alternative treatment of the issues raised in this chapter, including a full ISLMEB model, see Stern (1973). An easier presentation can be found in Grubel (1977), including a discussion of devaluation. Finally, some of the more important contributions in this area are available in the readings by Cooper (1969).

13 The Monetarist and Structuralist Approaches to the Balance of Payments

In this chapter we look at two schools of thought which have become increasingly prominent in recent years in connection with balance of payments (BOP) theory—the monetarist and structuralist approaches to the BOP. We begin in section 13.1 with an evaluation of the monetarists' contribution and contrast it in section 13.2 with that of the structuralists. Finally, in section 13.3 we examine the UK BOP historically between 1972 and 1980, and evaluate the contributions of both of these schools of thought, as well as that of the traditional approach discussed in Chapter 12, to our understanding of UK experience over this period.

13.1 THE MONETARIST APPROACH

The monetarist approach to the BOP began to take shape in the 1970s, although its roots go back much further, and was part of a broader 'revolution' in economic theory which has by no means come to an end. In part it reflected growing dissatisfaction with a macroeconomic apparatus which was still dominated by Keynesian thinking and which had failed to provide a satisfactory explanation for current problems; but it also represented a change in thinking about macroeconomic phenomena which in many respects returned to the classical tradition in economic thought.

In terms of the BOP specifically, the traditional approach which we discussed in Chapter 12 was based upon a macroeconomic framework which focused primarily on the short run, an economy which need not gravitate automatically towards full employment, on fixed exchange rates and prices, and (except in the Mundell case) there was little analysis of international capital movements. The BOP would be brought back into equilibrium through a combination of automatic adjustment mechanisms based upon a synthesis of the elasticities approach and the absorbtion approach, and through a judicious selection of demand management policies by the authorities.

Monetarists, by contrast, have been spending more time looking at long-run problems, they tend to assume an economy which displays an in-built tendency towards full employment, price flexibility (including in some cases flexible exchange rates), and they stress the importance of short-term international capital markets for BOP analysis. Payments adjustment is seen much more in terms of monetary adjustment rather than through income or relative price changes, and policy would tend to reflect a more *laissez-faire* attitude on behalf of the authorities.

Clearly, not all recent developments in BOP theory have been due to economists who might call themselves monetarists, and it is as misleading to talk about *the* monetarist model as it is to depict the traditional synthesis as a monolithic representation of Keynesianism. None the less, there are certain key ideas associated with the monetarist revival which have an important bearing upon BOP theory.

Although the traditional approach did not ignore the role of money, since this was represented by the LM side of the analysis, monetarists believe that money should be the central focus of attention in BOP theory. Instead of looking narrowly at the current account, monetarists want to look at the BOP as a whole in terms of an inflow or outflow of money. If you want to understand the BOP, they argue, the best place to start is in the money market to see if there is any imbalance between supply and demand.

The first important insight which comes from this is to re-emphasise the links between the trade balance and the domestic money supply which so intrigued Hume (1969). As we observed in Chapter 2, Hume questioned the macroeconomic basis of mercantilism by showing that a payments surplus would be self-defeating in the long run, while a deficit would be automatically eliminated as a result of the flow of gold between countries. Providing each country fixed its exchange rate in terms of gold, and changes in the domestic money supply were linked to gold reserves, then the inflow of gold into the surplus country would raise the aggregate price level (given the quantity theory of money) and eliminate the surplus. This would follow from the rise in the price of exports and the fall in the price of imports. The reverse would happen in the deficit country.

To see how this process reappears in a modern monetarist's explanation of the BOP, imagine a simplified banking system in which bank deposits constitute the only source of money (M), and all foreign currencies are held by the banks in the form of exchange reserves (R). The total money supply would then consist of R and domestic bank deposits (D):

$$M = R + D$$

The implication of this is that a persistent deficit is a monetary phenomenon which can *only* occur if a deficit in the trade balance (which will lower R) is *not* allowed to feed through to a contraction in M, either because the government won't allow it to contract output and employment and 'sterilises' it by raising D to compensate; or the banking system is unable to control its lending.

Although this is a highly simplified model, the point remains that there might well be difficulties in preventing the trade balance from spilling over into the domestic money supply, which was something essentially ignored in the traditional approach by assuming perfect sterlisation. The further point is that, according to this interpretation of the BOP, a deficit can only be persisitent if it is accompanied by domestic credit creation (increasing D). The view that governments cannot continue indefinitely to absorb a deficit by running down their foreign exchange reserves, but will ultimately have to restrict domestic credit creation, has been part and parcel of the International Monetary Fund's philosphy for many years.

Hume's analysis forms the basis of the gold standard adjustment mechanism which we shall discuss in Chapter 16, but the important point here is that it stresses the links between the trade balance and domestic activity through changes in the money supply *unless* the monetary authorities prevented it by sterilisation. Since if the change in reserves cannot be sterilised (as monetarists assume), it is a fundamental proposition of the monetarists' approach that a BOP disequilibrium is a temporary phenomenon resulting from a stock imbalance in the money market which will ultimately be self-correcting. The importance of these monetary repercussions for the BOP marks the starting point of the monetarist approach to the BOP.

The first application of this approach is to provide an alternative explanation of the mechanisms linking money income, prices and the trade balance for an economy operating under fixed exchange rates in the short run.

According to the traditional approach, an increase in the money supply pushes down interest rates and stimulates an increase in activity, particularly domestic investment. This sucks in imports and leads to a current account deficit. The monetarist mechanism, however, instead of working its way through interest rate mechanics, operates instead through cash balance mechanics. According to monetarists, when people are deciding how much to spend, they are influenced by the cash balances they hold. They spend more when these balances are 'excessive' and less when they are deficient. Hence, when the money supply is increased, rather than holding extra cash balances, people temporarily increase their spending. Since in aggregate they cannot succeed, the excess money supply is translated into an increased demand for goods, whose prices are bid up as a result.

In an open economy, however, this cash will disappear out of domestic circulation, and if the country is a price-taker in international markets (a 'small' country), there will be no discernible effect on world prices. As far as the domestic economy is concerned, however, the rise in demand brought about by the increase in the money supply diverts potential exports to the home market and leads to a trade deficit. Note, in particular, that any rise in domestic prices caused by this extra spending can only be *transitory* until domestic and international prices come back into balance with each other.

This contrasts with Hume's explanation, where it is the rise in the domestic price level which causes the deficit by making exports less competitive and imports cheaper. This cannot persist according to modern monetarists because it implies that identical goods are selling at different prices in different markets, which violates the conditions for perfectly competitive markets. Only if the country is 'large' in international trade can the increase in its money supply increase the world's money supply and international prices in the same proportion. This follows from the quantity theory of money. Hence, although the end result of the increase in the money supply is the same as under the traditional approach in so far as it leads to a deficit on the BOP, the mechanism linking the two together is quite different.

One area where this cash balance approach has been applied is to investigate the effects of devaluation. According to the traditional approach, devaluation improves the trade balance by switching expenditure away from imports and in favour of the country's exports. For the monetarist, however, this improvement can only be transitory until the rise in import prices brought about by the devaluation feeds through to the domestic price level. In other words, for a small country, devaluation will raise its domestic price level by the amount of the devaluation. If, in the longer run, all markets for goods and factors are perfectly competitive and money prices are flexible, all prices would be determined internationally. By definition, therefore, the devaluing country's prices will be determined by world prices, and can only provide a transitory competitive advantage until domestic prices adjust, and devaluation cannot improve a country's competitive position in the long run. The only solution is to control the money supply and the amount of domestic credit created, to ensure that supply equates with demand in the money market and inflation is not allowed to erode the country's competitive position.

The monetarists' contributions we have discussed so far have been derived from a framework which is similar to that of the traditional approach in as much as it is still essentially short-run, but what happens under flexible exchange rates and if international capital is highly mobile?

As far as international capital movements are concerned, the traditional approach assumed that such *flows* were related to interest rate differentials across countries. Hence, one way of helping to overcome a deficit within the ISLMEB approach would be to push up interest rates to attract foreign capital. Despite this, the traditional approach had relatively little to say about the effects of short-term capital movements on the BOP, and by the 1970s the *flow* approach had become inadequate in explaining the highly volatile movement of short-term portfolio capital within the context of floating exchange rates.

The monetarist approach to short-term capital flows—known as the *stock* approach—starts from portfolio theory, which seeks to explain how investors distribute their wealth between available assets to ensure a balance between risk and return.[1] International capital holders will want to ensure that they hold assets denominated in different currencies so that a depreciation in one currency is offset by an appreciation in another. Similarly by spreading out their assets across countries they can ensure that if local factors reduce the return on an asset in one country, the chances are that things may be better elsewhere.

An important implication from this approach is that the increase in interet rates, which under the flow theory would have led to a continuous inflow of foreign capital, now leads only to a one-off inflow as investors rearrange their portfolios to include a higher proportion of the more attractive asset. Expectations about different risks and returns can, therefore, provide a useful insight into the volatility of short-term capital movements in the contemporary world.

A second implication was that changes in interest rates under a floating exchange rate system would have repercussions in the foreign exchange market as the increase in demand for the more attractive assets increased the demand for those countries' currencies and forced them to appreciate against other currencies. We shall look at these repercussions on the foreign exchange market again in Chapter 14.

Finally, in recent years much effort has been expended by monetarists and others to model the long-run relationship between the money supply, the price level and the exchange rate under a system of flexible exchange rates. For example, the quantity theory of money might be used to explain the relationship between a country's money supply and its aggregate price level, while the purchasing power parity theory (which we shall discuss in Chapter 14) is used to explain the relationship between exchange rates and price levels in different countries. These models are still relatively new and are too complex to reproduce here, but they have allowed economists such as Dornbutsch (1978) to speculate on the difficulties involved in achieving simultaneous internal and external balance when countries are inflating at different rates under floating exchange rates. In such a situation it might not be possible for a country to maintain *both* stable prices and stable exchange rates, since the exchange rate may be influenced by the difference between the foreign and domestic price levels. For example, if the UK is inflating at a faster rate than her major competitors, then the pound may have to depreciate to maintain stable prices.

There is little doubt that the monetarist revival has enriched our understanding of the BOP and exposed some of the weaknesses of the traditional approach discussed in Chapter 12. The focus on cash balance mechanics and imbalances in the money market adds an extra dimension to BOP adjustment mechanisms, and re-emphasises the monetary implications of BOP adjustment. It reminds us that deficits and surpluses will have repercussions in the money market.

In addition, the monetarist approach provides another argument for the essentially transitory effects of devaluation policy, and support for the view that the authorities can make a deficit worse if they allow an excessive expansion in domestic credit creation.[2] The return to Hume's gold standard also emphasises how easy it is for domestic credit-creation to spill over into the external sector, and the difficulties which face the authorities when trying to sterilise the effects of the external sector on the domestic economy. This assumption of perfect sterilisation was an important limitation of the traditional approach.

None the less, when the monetarist approach is confined within the fixed exchange rate model with no international capital movements, the differences between it and the traditional approach may not be all that profound, but revolve around differences in emphasis over the relative contribution of price adjustment, income adjustment and adjustment through cash balances. In this sense, both can be integrated within an extended ISLMEB framework.[3] The argument then comes down to empirical questions about such things as the ability of the authorities to sterilise monetary inflows and the extent to which changes in the money supply affect prices and output.

Critics of the monetarist school argue that monetarist models are set at a particularly high level of aggregation and incorporate some particularly strong assumptions. These include full employment, perfectly flexible prices and (in some cases) exchange rates, and a presumption that interest rates and prices are set in competitive international markets. There is plenty of scepticism about the monetarists' explanation for the high levels of unemployment in the industrial countries, as well as about the ability of markets in goods, assets and currencies to clear in the manner described by monetarist theory.

It is perhaps in the longer-run models that the monetarists' contribution is potentially more innovative, in so far as they deal explicitly with questions which were becoming increasingly more relevant in the 1970s, such as how to achieve long-run internal and external balance in a world of greater flexibility in exchange rates and volatile capital movements.

Unfortunately, however, these questions are very difficult to answer, and it is hard to say how relevant the conclusions from these models are to government policies in the shorter run, in as much as long-run monetarist models tend to assume away many of the problems which make the BOP a problem in the first place! It is perhaps this faith in competitive markets and the long-run automatic adjustments of the economy back to equilibrium which sets monetarists apart from their opponents and reinforces their association with the normative goals of free trade and what might be described as the IMF/GATT *status quo*. If, on the other hand, disturbances to the BOP originate predominantly from outside the money market, or the process of monetary adjustment is going to take too long to solve immediate problems, then not only do interventionist policies become more plausible, but the traditional approach once again becomes relevant for short-run policy-making.

There are some economists, however, who feel that both the traditional and the monetarist approaches are insufficient to deal with certain types of BOP problem. This school of thought starts from a belief that markets do not work very well and that structural imbalances within an economy are a potent source of persistent BOP disequilibrium. This is true not only in LDCs where one might expect sectoral rigidities as symptomatic of underdevelopment, but might also be relevant to DCs. In other words, these economists regard the BOP as a structural problem. It is to this school of thought that we now turn.

13.2 THE STRUCTURALIST APPROACH

The structuralist approach to the BOP has its roots in the protest by development economists in the 1950s and 1960s against the uncritical application of neoclassical trade theory to LDCs. In this sense it was part of the philosophy ascribed to the new international trade theorists which we discussed in Chapter 4. It represented not only an alternative way of looking at the BOP within the context of LDCs, but it became associated with a broader opposition to neoclassical economics and the post-war monetarists. The so-called monetarist-structuralist debate was particularly active in connection with the diagnosis of inflation in Latin America.[4]

In more recent years, however, a 'structural' approach has been applied to DCs, and in particular to the UK, as both an implicit critique of both the traditional approach to the BOP and the monetarist approach which we examined in section 13.1. The leading exponent of this school of thought in the context of DCs has been Thirlwall.[5]

Structuralists essentially believe that structural imbalances in the economy are the source of BOP problems. These imbalances in turn arise from the fact that growth and development involve a discontinuous process of structural change. For example, in a developing country agricultural output is often unble to respond to increased demand in the urban sector during a period of rapid growth as a result of structural inertia in supply. These supply bottlenecks can often arise when different regions or sectors grow at different speeds if resources are not sufficiently mobile.

In DCs, on the other hand, the problem might originate in an inability to shift resources away from goods which are no longer competitive internationally and into new goods for which the prospects appear more promising. In this case it is the structural characteristics of goods on the supply side of the market which is causing the imbalance rather than a lack of competitiveness relating to price factors.

What makes these structural imbalances more important is the fact that price adjustment, including variations in the exchange rate, is weak and unable to eliminate the disequilibrium. In this sense both the traditional and monetarist adjustment mechanisms are insufficient to cure BOP problems arising from structural imbalances in the economy, and their associated policies are ineffective. For example, devaluation or depreciation can only be a temporary panacea which makes countries more competitive in the short run in goods with a given set of characteristics which were the source of the BOP problem in the first place!

Finally, structuralists perceive a direct link between the BOP and domestic growth such that growth may be constrained by the BOP. In the context of LDCs, the BOP constraint may arise in the following way. Suppose that in order for the economy to grow a

certain amount of domestic investment is required. This investment may in turn require imports of physical capital such as
machines which can only be purchased if the requisite foreign
exchange is available. If, therefore, export receipts fall unexpectedly, the resulting foreign exchange shortage may entail a
contraction of capital goods imports and a fall in investment and
growth.[6]

The source of the problem originates in the structural characteristics of a developing economy committed to growth. First, there is
the dependence on imported capital goods. This arises because, by
definition, in a developing country there is not likely to be an
indigenous capital goods sector, and because the goods the
country wants to produce may require fairly rigid combinations of
factor inputs.[7] If these essential inputs from abroad are not
available in the correct amounts, domestic producers cannot
substitute other inputs such as labour and maintain output at the
same rate. Secondly, there may be an inability (or unwillingness)
on the part of the authorities to cut back on less essential imports
as a means of rationing foreign exchange in favour of essential
capital goods. Finally, and probably most important of all, the
reason for the setting-up of these relatively capital-intensive
industries in the first place is because the prospects for increasing
traditional exports are believed to be limited or unpredictable.
This is derived from a pessimistic scenario with respect to the
terms of trade and the costs associated with export instability if the
country specialises on a relatively narrow range of goods. We
considered this viewpoint in Chapter 4.

The result of all this is that many LDCs believe themselves to be
caught in a structuralist dilemma: their BOP will not improve
fundamentally until they switch to manufactured goods with
favourable long-run prospects; but because the prospects for their
traditional exports are bleak and volatile, they are unable to
purchase the necessary capital imports and raw materials from
abroad in order to develop these alternative lines of production.
Moreover, fluctuations in their export receipts makes rational
planning impossible and leads to 'stop–go' cycles and crisis
adjustment whenever earnings fall unexpectedly. Traditional
expenditure-changing and expenditure-switching policies and
direct controls could be used to correct the resulting imbalances in
the BOP, but they do not solve the underlying structural

problems; and monetarist policies to maintain equilibrium in the money market might be incompatible with any sort of realistic growth path. Examples of economies which seemed to be constrained by their BOP in the 1960s include Ghana and Brazil.[8]

As a result of the structuralists' diagnosis of the BOP, many LDCs in the 1960s and early 1970s adopted heavily protectionist and inward-looking policies. We examined criticisms of these policies in Chapter 4, including the view that such policies have been very costly and ineffective, and that many LDCs have indeed managed to establish a manufacturing base despite being structurally 'backward'. There are also some fundamental criticisms levelled against the basic structuralist model.[9] First, it is suggested that it adopts too pessimistic a view of the ability of an LDC to switch resources to the export sector in line with changes in comparative advantage, and that it underestimates the extent to which resources can be transferred through the operation of the price mechanism. In addition, its assumptions about the substitution possibilities between domestic and foreign inputs may be too rigid. Monetarists also re-emphasise the need for realistic growth targets and the prerequisite of monetary stability for the maintenance of a satisfactory BOP position.

As far as DCs are concerned, the BOP constraint manifests itself in a slighly different way. The crux of the problem is that the country is trying to achieve internal balance and at the same time to grow fast enough to compete with other DCs. Unfortunately, supply bottlenecks occur in particular sectors which push the BOP into deficit and necessitate a contraction of domestic growth. The source of the structural imbalance lies in the characteristics of imports and exports. On the one hand, if the country's export goods do not have the necessary characteristics to satisfy foreign demand, then the income elasticity of demand (the responsiveness of demand to changes in income) will be low and export receipts in those products will not grow fast over time. Moreover, the underlying problem may not reflect a lack of price competitiveness so much as an inability to compete on non-price grounds. For example, the products may be inferior in quality, after-sales service may be poor, and so on.

On the other hand, the source of the problem may refer not to a low income elasticity of demand for exports so much as to a high income elasticity of demand for imports. This could either be because of a dependence on imports of raw materials and energy sources such as oil, or because domestic consumers prefer foreign goods such as cars and refrigerators to similar goods produced locally.

For these reasons the BOP may act as an effective constraint on growth, since in the long run a country cannot grow faster than the rate of growth consistent with equilibrium in the current account of its BOP. In other words, if a country gets into BOP difficulties before it has reached domestic full capacity, then demand has to be contracted and investment curtailed. This may further exacerbate the country's long-run BOP position if it results in slower productivity growth and export goods become even less attractive to foreigners.

One important and unfavourable side-effect of BOP-constrained growth may be to encourage a process of de-industrialisation and a shrinkage in the manufacturing base. This can ocur if the growth in manufacturing output which is constrained by the BOP is less than the rate of productivity growth. This will imply that labour is being shed in some sectors of the economy at a faster rate than the economy can absorb it elsewhere.[10] This fear has taken on a new meaning in the context of the micro-chip revolution.

According to the structuralist approach, the policy implications are clear for DCs. In the long run the rate of growth of manufacturing output will have to be made consistent with the BOP by switching to export goods with a relatively high income elasticity of demand in order to increase the rate of growth of exports; and the income elasticity of demand for imports must be reduced. This may in turn require a programme of investment to re-equip and revitalise industry aimed particularly at improving its non-price competitive position. Selected import controls might also be used to reduce imports of goods and services, and exchange controls to stem capital outflows, even if they are contrary to the IMF/GATT *status quo*, although economists such as Thirlwall would argue that these policies should not be used as substitutes for more fundamental structural reforms. In direct contrast to the monetarist approach, these policies lay stress on direct government intervention and reflect a view which has relatively little faith in market adjustment, including flexible exchange rates.

13.3 THE UK BALANCE OF PAYMENTS 1972–80

We suggested in Chapter 11 that the movement of the UK BOP on current account into surplus after 1979 had been greeted with mixed enthusiasm by many economists in so far as it concealed some underlying problems in the UK economy, including a deficit in manufactured goods. In this final section, we examine some alternative views on the UK BOP between 1972 and 1980, and in particular compare the interpretations given by the traditional, monetarist and structuralist schools.

Table 13.1 The UK balance of payments and sterling exchange rate movements between 1972 and 1980

			£ million			
	(1) Trade balance	(2) Invisible balance	(3) Current account	(4) Total official financing	(5) Foreign exchange rate[1]	(6) Effective exchange rate[2]
1972	−748	995	247	−1265	0.40	103
1973	−2586	1605	−981	−771	0.41	114
1974	−5351	2078	−3273	−1648	0.42	118
1975	−3333	1812	−1521	−1465	0.45	128
1976	−3939	3048	−881	−3629	0.55	151
1977	−2284	2243	−41	7361	0.57	159
1978	−1542	2481	939	−1126	0.52	158
1979	−3458	2595	−863	1905	0.47	148
1980	1178	2028	3206	1372	0.43	130

Notes: [1]Sterling price of the dollar.
[2]Trade weighted average of 21 currencies including the US dollar, 1971 = 100.

Sources: (1), (2), (3), (4), HMSO UK balance of payments, various years, (5), (6), Bank of England Quarterly Bulletins.

Table 13.1 reproduces some basic statistics for the UK BOP after 1972 and shows how the value of the pound has moved in relation to both the US dollar and a 'basket' of international currencies. The foreign exchange rate in column (5) refers to the cost in sterling of purchasing 1 unit of foreign exchange, in this case the dollar. In other words, in 1972 it cost on average 40p to buy $1. The 'effective exchange rate' in column (6) shows in index form how the cost of a representative basket of currencies including the dollar has varied in terms of the pound. A rise in the index indicates that the purchasing power of the pound has fallen in terms of foreign exchange. The basket is constructed by weighting a number of currencies in terms of the relative contribution of the countries concerned in UK trade. Both the foreign exchange rate and the effective exchange rate will be discussed in more detail in Chapter 14.

From Table 13.1 one or two important facts stand out. First, between 1972 and 1978 there has been a substantial depreciation of the pound against both the dollar and against the basket of international currencies. An all time low was reached in 1976 with the arrival of the 50p dollar. After 1978 the pound then began to recover. The period since 1972 has also been marked by considerable volatility in exchange rates coinciding with the adoption of 'managed' floating by the major industrial countries in 1973.[11]

As far as the BOP is concerned, the current account began to move into deficit in 1973, and that year also saw a record trade deficit coinciding with the rise in the price of oil and the general boom in commodity prices. By 1974 and 1975 the current account and trade deficits were strongly negative, although the effects of domestic recession were by now beginning to be reflected in a fall in import demand. The magnitude of the problem was illustrated in 1976 by the large figure for official financing and the receipt of a $500 million loan arranged by the Group of Ten major trading countries. In 1978 the current account moved into surplus, although the trade balance remained in deficit until 1980 and both were negative in 1979 when the second oil shock materialised.

The underlying position, therefore, is one of weakness, especially with respect to manufactured goods. The evidence suggests a progressive decline in the UK's share of world exports of manufactured goods and an increase in import penetration in the UK market. For example, between 1971 and 1979, when UK manufacturing production grew at an average rate of 0.7 per cent, the volume of exports of final manufactures increased by an average of 3.36 per cent per annum, while the volume of imports of the same goods rose at an annual rate of 13.4 per cent.[12] The spectre of deindustrialisation also found some support from work by Brown and Sheriff (1979), who estimated that the share of manufacturing employment in total employment fell from 34.7 per cent in 1970 to 30.2 per cent by 1980.

Moreover, as we suggested in Chapter 11, the surpluses on current account which occurred in 1978 and continued in the 1980s conceal further weaknesses. In the first case, the current account picture is improved by the inflow of factor payments associated with the exploitation of North Sea oil, which will disappear in the longer run. Secondly, the capital account looks misleadingly healthy since it is bolstered by short-term capital from recycled OPEC oil revenues which are likely to be quite volatile, especially in relation to variations in international interest rates. Finally, some of the improvement in the current account represents the dampening effects which recession and deflationary domestic policies have upon imports. In other words, the payments surplus must be set against the fact that the UK economy was operating at substantially less than full capacity.

So much for the facts, but what interpretations can be found for them?

The traditional approach to the BOP which we looked at in Chapter 12 tended to view UK weaknesses in the 1960s as reflecting a lack of price competitiveness and a lack of flexibility in exchange rates. This lack of price competitiveness in turn was often associated with high labour costs which were reflected in an inflation rate for the UK consistently higher than that of our major competitors. The relatively fixed exchange rate rule adopted by the UK under the Bretton Woods system (to be discussed in Chapter 16) also allowed insufficient room for the exchange rate to adjust to restore competitiveness.

Monetarists, on the other hand, agreed that the underlying problem was the excessive inflation rate and that greater flexibility in exchange rates would be desirable, but they put the blame for UK inflation squarely at the feet of the monetary authorities for allowing an excessive growth in the money supply, rather than on labour costs *per se*. In 1979, when the Conservative Party assumed political power, they set about adopting monetarist-style policies to reduce the rate of inflation by raising interest rates, eliminating foreign exchange controls, and generally attempting to reduce public expenditure and government involvement in the economy.

The structuralist school, however, regards both traditional and monetarist policies as insufficient because they are based upon a failure to diagnose correctly the source of the UK's problems in connection with the BOP. In the first case, they argue that the substantial depreciation of sterling between 1972 and 1977 did little to improve the UK's competitive position, because the essence of the problem was not the lack of price competitiveness, but the failure to compete effectively on non-price grounds. In this sense, a favourable change in relative export and import prices only makes the UK more competitive in the *wrong* goods.

The underlying structural problem is that the income elasticity of demand for the UK's exports is too low in relation to the income elasticity of demand for its imports from the rest of the world. In fact the export elasticity is estimated to be about 0.9, while the import elasticity comes out at something in the region of 1.7.[13] According to Thirlwall's calculations this means that for a growth rate of world income of 5 per cent, UK exports would grow at 5.0 × 0.9 = 4.5 per cent per annum, while the full employment rate of growth of income would be 3.0 × 1.7 = 5 per cent per annum, assuming an annual growth rate for the UK of 3 per cent. Hence, for the growth in imports to be kept in line with the rate of growth of exports, the UK growth rate would have to be slowed to 2.6 per cent. This is the sense in which UK growth is constrained by the BOP, since full employment and BOP equilibrium cannot be achieved without a substantial reduction in real income.

As far as the structuralists are concerned, the major source of the problem is not import dependence, since the income elasticity of demand for UK imports is not especially different from other developed countries, but that the elasticity with respect to exports is much lower than that of the UK's competitors. The UK figure of 0.9 compares with 3.5 for Japan, 3.0 for Italy, 2.4 for West Germany and 1.0 for the USA. The reasons for this low figure, they argue, stem from the inability of UK exporters to compete effectively with foreign producers on non-price grounds including poor after-sales, low quality and the tendency to continue producing goods for which the income elasticity of demand is relatively low. The weakness of the UK BOP, therefore reflects a failure to produce and market commodities of the right quality in the face of rapidly changing technologies and world demand patterns.

To solve these underlying structural imbalances structuralists recommend a planned rearrangement of the pattern of production to switch resources to goods with a high income elasticity of demand, and measures to improve upon non-price characteristics.

Improving productivity alone is not enough unless it also reduces the BOP constraint on growth. The precise strategy to be adopted can vary. Thirlwall himself would favour a programme of government investment backed up with selective import subsidies, although these subsidies should not be seen as a substitute for more fundamental structural changes. Bodies such as the Cambridge Economic Policy Group, who would be broadly in sympathy with Thirlwall's views, would in addition adopt selective import controls.

Thus, although in many respects all three schools of thought we have examined would agree on many of the underlying problems of the UK BOP over this time period, there remain important policy differences.

Traditional policies would tend to reflect the view that the lack of competitiveness of the UK economy can be overcome through appropriate variations in exchange rates and the use of demand management policies to reduce the rate of inflation and maintain internal and external balance. Monetarists also stress the importance of price competiveness and the need to maintain control over the domestic money supply but would emphasise the prominent role of monetary policy in this respect and the importance of viewing demand management policies within the context of international capital movements and flexible exchange rates. They would also have greater faith in competitive market adjustment and less faith in interventionist policies by the government.

Structuralists, on the other hand, do not see the problem primarily in terms of price competitiveness, but in terms of the characteristics of the goods the country is importing and exporting. They have much less faith in the ability of price adjustment to restore equilibrium and are generally opposed to flexible exchange rates on the grounds that they do not bring about the necessary structural adjustments and that they generate harmful side-effects which we shall enlarge upon in Chapter 14. In terms of policies they are more inclined towards government intervention not so much in the traditional expenditure-changing and expenditure-switching sense, as in the sense of direct investment to alter the pattern of production and direct policy action to curb imports and support exports, even if this is in defiance of the international *status quo*.

NOTES

1. For an application of portfolio theory to international capital flows, see Branson (1968). The monetarist approach to capital movements is also explained in Kouri (1978).
2. For some empirical support for this proposition, see Miles (1979).
3. An attempt to integrate monetarist models within the ISLM framework is contained in Williamson (1983, ch. 8).
4. See Thirlwall (1983, ch. 12).
5. See, for example, Thirlwall (1982, ch. 12).
6. The model upon which this reasoning is based is called the structuralist two-gap model and is explained in Thirlwall (1983, ch. 13).
7. Technically, this is called a fixed coefficient production function.
8. For the Ghana case, see Killick (1978).
9. See Thirlwall (1983, ch. 13).
10. See Blackaby (1979).
11. For some evidence on this, see Zis (1983).
12. See Prest *et al.* (1982, ch. 3).
13. These calculations are based on work by Houthakker and Magee (1969).

FURTHER READING

For a more detailed textbook account of the monetarist approach to the BOP, see Caves and Jones (1981, chs. 17, 18). Some of the early writings in this area are available in Frenkel and Johnson (1976). A clear survey of more recent contributions can be found in Kreinin and Officer (1978). For a discussion of the monetarist approach within the context of the ISLMEB framework, see Williamson (1983). The application of the structuralist approach to LDCs is summarised in Thirlwall (1983). As far as DCs are concerned, the structural approach is synthesised in Thirlwall (1982). Finally, for some data and a discussion of the UK BOP, including a review of evidence on the relative importance of price and non-price factors, see Prest *et al.* (1982, ch. 3).

14 The Foreign Exchange Market

14.1 THE FOREIGN EXCHANGE MARKET

In its most general sense, an exchange rate is simply the rate or price at which one currency exchanges for another or for some 'basket' of currencies. Although people still tend to think in bilateral terms, such as the value of the pound sterling in terms of the US dollar, the modern tendency is to look at a country's 'effective' exchange rate or the value of its currency in terms of some weighted average of the currencies of its major trading partners. In which case, it is quite possible for the pound to rise or fall against the dollar, yet remain relatively stable in terms of a basket heavily weighted by European currencies.

To proceed with our analysis of the foreign exchange market, however, we need a more precise definition of the exchange rate. Consequently, we shall define the *foreign exchange rate* as the price of 1 unit of foreign currency in terms of domestic currency. For example, if it costs UK citizens 50p to buy 1 US dollar, the foreign exchange rate will be £0.5 = $1, or 50p. 50p is therefore the sterling price of the dollar, but confusion arises because we could just as easily have quoted the dollar price of sterling as $2 = £1, or simply $2. The choice is arbitrary, but in this chapter we shall always refer to the foreign exchange rate as the sterling price of foreign currency.

It follows from our definition above, that if the exchange rate rises from 50p to 60p for $1, the pound will actually have *depreciated* against the dollar, since it now costs UK citizens 10p more for each unit of foreign currency. Hence, a *rise* in the exchange rate according to our definition means in practice a *fall* in the value of the home currency. This will become clearer when we use a diagram to show the workings of the foreign exchange market in section 14.2.

The foreign exchange market can be thought of as like any other market in economics as the means by which buyers and sellers are linked. In this case it is the buyers and sellers of foreign exchange which are being linked. As we shall see, this applies even when the authorities step in to 'fix' the exchange rate. We shall investigate the properties of this market in section 14.2, but first we need to consider some aspects of the institutional setting within which the market operates, and the type of transactors (buyers and sellers) involved.

People require foreign exchange for a variety of reasons—to purchase goods and services abroad when on holiday, to buy imports to sell in the domestic market, or to purchase a foreign asset. In addition, the monetary authorities will have an 'official' role to play in the market, depending on the type of exchange rate system in operation.

However, by far the majority of foreign exchange transactions are carried out between the major banks and specialised foreign exchange brokers. Much of this trade takes the form of exchanging bank deposits denominated in different currencies, although in practice most of the activity occurs in a small number of important international currencies such as the US dollar, the pound sterling or the German mark. These major currencies are often referred to as 'vehicle currencies'. The advantage of this procedure is that it enables foreign exchange dealers to hold lower transactions balances in only a few currencies which are readily exchangeable. Thus, in the major financial centres of the world, such as New York, London or Zurich, when the hours of business are common to different time zones, business is conducted at a furious pace by means of the telex system.

Foreign exchange dealings are carried out not only for reasons of travel or trade (in goods and assets), but are also intimately tied up with three activities known as arbitage, hedging and speculation. We shall consider each of these in turn.

Arbitrage is a general term used in economics to describe the process of simultaneously buying something where it is cheap, and selling where it is more expensive, thereby yielding a profit to the arbitrageur and at the same time ironing out price discrepancies between different regions. For example, if the price of the dollar in London is 10p cheaper than in New York, an observant arbitrageur might buy dollars in London and sell them in New

York (via telex) and make a handsome profit in the process. As long as other arbitrageurs do the same, their joint actions will push up the price of the dollar in London and lower it in New York until the price differential is eliminated. In a market such as the foreign exchange market where the 'goods' are relatively homogeneous and information about rates in different countries is very good, one would expect profit-motivated arbitrage to be very effective in linking together market prices and ensuring consistency between the various currencies.

Hedging and *speculation* (which could be carried out by the same person) both relate to expectations about the future values of currencies. Unlike arbitrage, an intertemporal dimension is involved. A hedger in the foreign exchange market is essentially someone who wishes to avoid the risks involved in gambling on the future price of a foreign currency. If, for instance, a UK exporter has just received a sum of money in US dollars deposited in a bank account in New York, and he wishes to hold on to the money for a few months, but doesn't want to risk a depreciation of the dollar against the pound, he can sell the dollars for pounds at the current exchange rate and invest his money in the UK. Whether the exporter makes a profit or not by investing his money in the UK is neither here nor there, since the motive behind the hedge was to eliminate the uncertainty of an exchange rate loss in the future. Even though the dollar might in fact *rise* against the pound, he values the certainty of not making a loss more than the gamble of a possible gain.

Speculators, on the other hand, choose to gamble and leave themselves open to risk because they expect future currency movements to be in line with their subjective forecasts. By correctly anticipating the future the speculator hopes to make a profit. For example, suppose our exporter expects the dollar to appreciate against the pound over the next few months, he could invest his money in a US bank and earn some interest, and convert it back (including the interest) into pounds at the end of that time period. If he is correct in his forecast he will have made a profit on the foreign exchange deal. Whether or not he also profits from banking the money depends on the difference between interest rates in the USA and the UK.

Although speculators are often painted as rather shady and unscrupulous characters (e.g. the 'Gnomes of Zurich'), in fact, anyone can act as a speculator when using the foreign exchange market as long as he is willing to leave himself open to risk. In practise the number of 'professional' speculators in the market is relatively small compared with the number of speculative transactions which take place by commerical banks, central banks, multinational corporations and traders. And as we shall see in section 14.3, it is an open question as to whether speculation is harmful or beneficial to the community.

To complete our discussion of the institutional structure of the foreign exchange market, we need to distinguish between the 'spot' market and the 'forward' market.

Trading in the foreign exchange market concerns not only currencies for immediate or 'spot' delivery, but also for 'forward' delivery at a specified future date from when the contract is agreed. If, for example, a UK importer knows he will have to buy raw materials from the USA in 30 days' time, he can contract to buy the necessary dollars (and sell sterling) at an exchange rate agreed *now* for delivery in 30 days' time, regardless of what the spot exchange rate turns out to be on that date.

The advantage from the importer's viewpoint is that he can hedge against the uncertainty surrounding the cost of his dollars in the future and make his plans on that basis. Of course, if the spot price actually falls over the 30 days he will be paying more in the forward market than he would have needed to, but he prefers to 'insure' against the possibility of a rise in costs above all else.

It must be apparent by now that for the foreign exchange market to function smoothly and be able to provide these funds for hedging, there must be people who are willing to take the risks involved in providing the foreign exchange for the later date. This is the role of the speculator in the forward market. The speculator who has sold dollars forward to the UK importer must buy the sterling in 30 days' time in exchange for dollars at the contracted price. If in the meantime the pound has fallen against the dollar in the spot market, he makes a profit on the deal, but if the pound appreciates he makes a loss. Hence, the forward market allows people with different expectations about future exchange rates and different attitudes to risk to engage in mutually beneficial trades.

14.2 THE DETERMINATION OF THE EXCHANGE RATE

One can think of spot exchange rates as either being determined by the supply and demand for foreign exchange, or as being fixed within certain limits by the monetary authorities through official intervention.

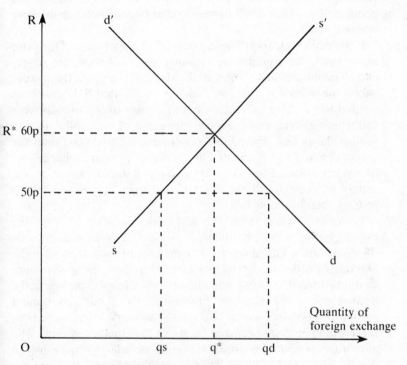

Figure 14.1: The foreign exchange market

Figure 14.1 shows how the exchange rate might be established by market forces. On the vertical axis is the foreign exchange rate R represented by the sterling price of a dollar. On the horizontal axis is the quantity of foreign exchange ($) in the market. dd′ represents the demand by UK residents for dollars arising from any of the motives discussed in section 14.1, including payment for imports, for buying assets (lending abroad) or for hedging/

arbitrage/speculation. The curve slopes down to the right-hand side to signify that a rise in R (a fall in the value of the pound) will lead UK residents to demand fewer dollars because US goods and assets will have become relatively more expensive to purchase. Similarly, the supply curve for foreign exchange ss' shows the supply of dollars at various exchange rates. It slopes upwards to the right-hand side, on the assumption that when the pound falls in value against the dollar foreigners will find it cheaper to buy UK goods and assets and will demand more pounds and supply more dollars.

If the market clears efficiently through the operation of the price mechanism, the equilibrium exchange rate will be where supply and demand are in balance at R*. If, for example, there were excess demand for foreign exchange such that UK residents wanted to purchase qd dollars, but at a price of 50p only qs were forthcoming, one might expect the value of the dollar to rise against the pound (the pound to fall against the dollar) until the excess demand was eliminated at the higher foreign exchange rate of 60p per dollar. The reverse could happen if there was an excess supply of dollars and the foreign exchange rate would fall to restore equilibrium at R*.

If, on the other hand, the authorities decided to 'peg' the exchange rate at 50p per dollar, it would only be by accident that this fixed rate would also serve to match supply and demand in the market. In order to defend this rate, therefore, the government would be forced to intervene to buy or sell foreign exchange at the desired price. For example, in Figure 14.1, if the government wished to keep the rate at 50p while the market rate were 60p, there would be excess demand for the dollar equal to qs − qd. The authorities would, therefore, be obliged to sell qs − qd worth of dollars from their reserves. In practice, the official rate need not be so rigidly fixed, and normally there will be a band within which the currency will be left to fluctuate, with official intervention only when it hits the ceiling or the floor.

There are many ways in which the authorities could achieve this management of the currency other than by selling dollars. For example, the Bank of England could arrange a 'swap' with the US Federal Reserve System by which it transferred sterling to the USA in return for an equivalent sum in dollars. There would thus have been no net capital movement, but the Bank of England would now be in a better position to cope with the excess demand for dollars.

Although we have been discussing the foreign exchange market in terms of two extremes—a fully flexible market and a fixed rate (within some band)—historically there have been many different regimes in operation, ranging from the relatively fixed system under the gold standard from about 1870 to 1914 and briefly restored as a gold exchange standard from 1925 to 1931, to the chaotic floating of the 1930s. After the second world war the major industrial countries re-established a fixed system, but allowed a greater margin for variability. Since 1973 most industrial countries have been engaged in 'managed floating', whereby market forces are left to determine exchange rates within certain limits (much larger than under the previous system) outside of which the authorities will intervene. We shall look at the history of the international monetary system in more detail in Part 5, and look at the pros and cons of alternative exchange rate systems in section 14.3, but for the remainder of this section we shall look more closely at what lies behind the supply and demand curves in Figure 14.1, and at those factors which can be said to determine exchange rates.

The place to start when looking at the determination of exchange rates is the BOP current account and trade in goods and services. If there were no capital movements and the exchange rate floated freely, the current account would have to be in balance for the foreign exchange market to clear. In other words, we would explain R* in Figure 14.1 by applying neoclassical price theory based upon the assumptions of perfectly competitive markets. According to this theory, the price of foreign exchange, i.e. the exchange rate, would adjust to clear the market at the point where the demand for foreign exchange to buy imports and make other current payments equals the supply that is forthcoming from the sales of exports and other current receipts. As long as the supply and demand curves dd' and ss' are correctly shaped, and the market adjusts to restore equilibrium if there is any excess supply or demand, then the market will be stable.

Economists have spent some time examining the stability of the foreign exchange market which seems to be closely linked to the elasticities or slopes of the curves defining the supply and demand for imports and exports. In general the more elastic (flatter) the demand for imports and exports, the more stable the foreign exchange market will be.[1]   Nevertheless, there are good reasons for expecting the market to show signs of instability in the short run. For example, the 'J' curve phenomenon referred to in Chapter 12 shows how devaluation can worsen the trade balance in the short run. In addition, it would be incomplete to consider the stability of the exchange rate without looking at the role of speculation and short-term capital movements. But first we need to look at one of the oldest theories of exchange rate determination which follows on logically from our current account explanation—the purchasing power parity theory (PPP).

The PPP theory was first presented by Cassell (1922).[2] In its *absolute* form it suggested that a flexible exchange rate would adjust to ensure that a pound will buy as much in the UK as in any other country, such as the USA. For example, if we take a number of commodities such that a unit of each costs £2 in the UK (i.e. a pound of salt, a dozen eggs, etc.) and a unit of these same commodities costs $1 in the USA, then the equivalent exchange rate for a dollar would be £2, given by the ratio of the domestic 'price' level to the foreign 'price' level:

$$R^*\pounds UK = P\pounds UK/P\$USA = 2/1 = 2 \qquad (14.1)$$

This idea, known as the 'law of one price', is based upon the notion that goods which are perfect substitutes for each other in international trade would have similar prices when measured in the same currency as a result of competition and arbitrage. In other words, a commodity which sells for a given sum in one country should sell for the same sum in all other countries, otherwise it would pay arbitrageurs to buy where it was cheap and sell where it was relatively expensive, thus bringing regional prices closer together.

If we choose individual commodities which are fairly homogeneous, then this process might work quite well, but when aggregating across many goods and services and using price indices the process is likely to be imperfect, especially with product differentiation and impediments to trade such as tariffs and transport costs. In view of these problems a weaker version known as *relative PPP* has been put forward, focusing on *changes* in prices and incomes rather than upon exact ratios as in (14.1). P£UK and P$USA would now be interpreted as price indices, and according to this version, if the price level doubled in the USA so goods formally costing $1 now cost $2, the equilibrium price of the dollar should fall from £2 to £1:

$$R^*£UK = P£UK/P\$USA = 2/2 = 1 \qquad (14.2)$$

With the move to greater exchange rate flexibility in the 1970s, it has become important once again to consider whether PPP can explain exchange rate differences between countries arising from their differential rates of inflation. Empirically there does seem to be some support for it. Kravis *et al.* (1978) found the absolute version worked well for Western industrial countries, but less so for Japan, and not at all well for LDCs, especially when non-traded goods were considered.[3] Kravis and Lipsey (1978) also found some support for the relative version for pairs of industrial countries between 1950 and 1970 over periods of about two years, but it was less accurate over longer periods. PPP may, therefore, be a useful guide to what happens to exchange rates when countries inflate at markedly different rates, but it should only be taken as a *very rough* guide.

The other area of analysis which has become increasingly important in the 1970s and 1980s in the determination of exchange rates concerns short-term capital flows. As we saw in Chapter 12, the traditional approach to the BOP tended to neglect international capital movements or explain *flows* of capital rather simplistically in terms of interest rate differentials between countries. This clearly became unrealistic after 1973 when international capital became highly mobile. In Chapter 13 we compared the traditional *flow* theory with the more recent *stock* approach favoured by the monetarists. One important implication of this approach is that shifts in stocks of portfolio capital between different countries are bound to have repercussions on exchange rates. For example, if investors decide to increase the proportion of their wealth which they hold in UK assets, then this stock shift will tend to increase the demand for pounds and push up the value of sterling in the foreign exchange market.

Exchange rates are determined, therefore, by many factors and types of transactors, including importers and exporters, hedgers, speculators and arbitrageurs, lenders and borrowers of capital, and government officials intervening to 'manage' their currencies. Whilst trade in goods and services probably exerts the dominant influence in the longer run, the short-run picture has become increasingly complex since the adoption of greater exchange rate flexibility and the growth of short-term capital markets. In particular, portfolio adjustment of financial assets in response to expectations about the BOP and future changes in exchange rates can lead to important and sometimes destablising variations in exchange rates.

14.3 FIXED VERSUS FLEXIBLE EXCHANGE RATES

One of the most debated issues in international economics concerns the choice of exchange rate regime and the pros and cons of fixed versus flexible or floating exchange rates. In practice, of course, neither extreme has ever existed, but it remains useful to use these ideal types as the basis for drawing some positive and normative conclusions of relevance when choosing a hybrid system. In this sense, the debate over fixed versus flexible exchange rates is analogous to that between perfect competition and monopoly in the economic analysis of market structures.

To prevent repeating the analysis, we shall first consider the case for flexible exchange rates (and against fixed) and then contrast it with the case against flexible rates (for fixed). We shall then review the empirical evidence in this area and briefly describe one or two intermediate regimes which countries might adopt combining some of the advantages of each extreme.

Perhaps the most popular argument in favour of floating exchange rates can be summed up by the expression, 'the market knows best'. 'Best' here implies that a competitive foreign exchange market would be both a more *efficient* means of maintaining BOP equilibrium over time, but also that it would be a more *desirable* solution than leaving the decisions to government officials. This latter normative aspect is particularly appealing to those who believe in essentially 'free' competitive markets where decisions to buy and sell are made through individual choice.

The positive side of the argument is based on the efficient market clearing mechanism discussed in section 14.2. For example, if the UK was running a current account deficit, this would imply an excess demand for foreign exchange, which would push up the sterling foreign exchange rate and lead to a depreciation of the pound. This in turn would make imports more expensive and exports cheaper, and providing the relevant elasticities were high enough, the current account would be brought back into balance.

No one expects the adjustment process to be quite as smooth as this, but if arbitrage and speculation are stabilising, it seems to provide an efficient and automatic solution to BOP problems. As one defender of flexible exchange rates put it, it is simpler to make a single price change by altering the exchange rate than revising thousands or millions of individual wages and prices downwards in order to restore competitiveness on a fixed rate.[4]

A second argument in favour of flexible rates is that they give the government more room for manoeuvre when seeking simultaneously to achieve internal and external balance. As we saw in Chapter 12, obtaining IB and EB at the same time is difficult enough anyway, but the advantage of floating is that, in principle, it frees the government from the BOP constraint in as much as the exchange rate automatically adjusts to maintain EB. For example, the government might select an appropriate rate of increase for the domestic money supply compatible with its objectives for IB and let the exchange rate adjust to iron out any discrepancies between the domestic inflation rate and inflation in the rest of the world.

Thirdly, if the foreign exchange market works efficiently under flexible exchange rates, there would be no need for governments to hold official reserves of foreign exchange since official 'accommodating transactions' are not required. In practice, of course, governments will still need to intervene to push the exchange rate in the required direction even if they are committed to floating, but the possibility of economising on reserves is appealing, especially to LDCs who may find the opportunity costs of holding extra reserves to cushion swings in the BOP high in terms of the development opportunities forgone by not being able to use these reserves to purchase scarce inputs from abroad.

One final argument in support of floating refers to the way in which BOP adjustment occurs when a country is suffering from a persistent deficit. Ultimately, under a fixed rate deflationary policies would have to be invoked, since the government cannot go on losing reserves or borrowing forever. Deflation, however, generally involves social costs in the form of unemployment, especially if wages and prices are 'rigid' downwards. Under a fixed rate this is the only way in which the country's competitive position can be restored. Under floating, however, some of this adjustment can be borne by changes in relative prices if the fall in the value of the currency switches resources from the import sector to the export sector.

Some of these arguments were powerful enough to tip the balance in favour of greater exchange rate flexibility in the 1970s and 1980s after a period of almost continuous fixed rates since the second world war. Nevertheless, there are some counter-arguments which are vociferously presented by those who believe that too much flexibility has been permitted and that a return to greater fixity would be appropriate in the 1980s.

In the first case it is suggested that floating rates generate wider fluctuations in exchange rates which increases uncertainty and reduces the volume of international trade. Although one would, by definition, expect floating to increase exchange rate variability, some extra assumptions are needed to establish that this will depress trade flows. First, instability in the sense of greater fluctuations in rates, is not the same thing as uncertainty, since regularly reversing fluctuations could be quite predictable. In fact, advocates of flexible exchange rates point out that in the 1960s apparently fixed rates were in practice frequently changed and often fluctuated quite strongly between certain limits. These changes could also have been quite off-putting for traders. Secondly, the transactors involved would have to be risk-averse and unwilling or unable to use forward markets to hedge the risks involved. Only if they regard future exchange rates as unpredictable and are put off by the risks of fluctuations in these rates will there be adverse effects on the volume of trade.

A second argument against floating concerns its association with destabilising speculation. In general, speculation will exert a stabilising influence on exchange rates, in the sense of ironing out fluctuations over time, if speculators predict the future correctly. Imagine that a large number of speculators anticipate a dock strike in the UK which will increase the current account deficit and lead to a fall in the value of the pound. Then by selling sterling now and buying it back in the future when it is cheaper, speculators will be moving the exchange rate in the 'correct' direction in anticipation of the real event (the strike). If they are correct, therefore, the exchange rate will not suddenly fall when the strike begins to take effect, but will move more smoothly towards its 'true' value. If, however, speculators guess incorrectly and the strike does not take place, they will by their concerted actions in selling the pound have made the currency fluctuate more than it would have done. This is what opponents of flexible rates argue has often been the case.

Proponents of flexible rates reply that speculation can also occur under fixed rates. For example, if it is abundantly clear that the economy is suffering from 'fundamental disequilibrium' and that a devaluation is imminent, speculators can make a killing by selling the currency forward just before the devaluation takes place and buying it back after the change in parity. If they turn out to be wrong, all they have lost is the transaction costs from the forward operation. Under a floating rate, however, there is always the chance that the currency will appreciate in value and the speculators lose money. Friedman (1953) in fact argued that speculation *must* be stabilising since if it were not, speculators would go out of business!

There is a certain logic to this, but it glosses over the fact that exchange rate crises still take place, and it may be the case that 'professional' speculators make profits at the expense of other traders including central banks, for whom speculation may be a peripheral activity. The question of stabilising versus destabilising speculation is ultimately an empirical question to which we shall return later.

Thirdly, floating rates are said to be inherently inflationary. If the value of the currency falls this raises import prices and feeds through to 'cost–push' inflation. On the other hand, an appreciation of the currency is unlikely to be passed on in the form of lower prices. Thus, there is an in-built 'ratchet' effect under flexible exchange rates generating inflationary pressures over time. Moreover, if a depreciation raises exporters' incomes, there could also be 'demand–pull' inflation if domestic output is too inelastic in supply to respond to the extra demand in the economy.

This inflationary argument is often linked to another criticism of floating rates, namely that they impose less discipline on a government to take corrective action to cure a deficit. Under a fixed rate, it is suggested, a deficit would be immediately apparent from the decline in foreign exchange reserves, and corrective action will be speedy. Under floating, however, the authorities might be tempted to let the currency depreciate and suffer the inflationary consequences. Defenders of flexible rates, however, assert that these inflationary effects combined with the fall in the currency would make it *more* apparent and not less that something was wrong.

Finally, there are those who argue that a flexible exchange rate requires a flexible economy in so far as adjustment in the exchange rate must be capable of bringing about real adjustments in the BOP. If the economy is fairly rigid, in the sense that resources are relatively immobile, then changes in the foreign exchange market may not bring about the necessary changes in trade flows to restore BOP equilibrium. We have already discussed this structuralist school of thought, which has relatively little faith in market clearing, in Chapter 13 as an implicit critique of the monetarist point of view.

What then is the evidence with respect to fixed and floating exchange rates?

As far as the uncertainty argument is concerned, it is generally accepted that the wider fluctuations associated with flexible rates do increase uncertainty and that many traders are averse to the risks involved, but there is no hard evidence that this has led to a reduction in the volume of trade.[5] It is true that exchange rates have been quite volatile since 1973, but it may also be that they had something to be volatile about![6]

Part of the problem here undoubtedly arises from the greater complexity of foreign exchange markets in the modern world with the increase in the number of currencies traded and the larger number of dealing centres, often operating around the clock. This hugely complicates international currency markets and creates a network of international 'cross rates' each continuously affecting the others. Whether foreign exchange markets can be efficient in these circumstances is difficult to say. It is very hard to test whether markets use all the relevant information and push exchange rates in the 'right' direction, except after the events have occurred, in which case there is an element of self-fulfilling prophecy involved. This is especially likely when speculators use forecasting practices which amount to jumping on the bandwagon, and any rumours which start begin to feed on themselves.

There seems to be some evidence that exchange rates moved to offset differences in inflation rates in the 1970s and moved trade balances in the right direction, but the picture is uneven. Levich (1978), for example, found that forward market rates were generally accurate in predicting future spot rates in the 1970s with the exception of 1977 and 1978. On the other hand, for some countries volatile movements in currencies had disturbing effects. Examples here might include the rapid depreciation of sterling in 1976 and the dollar in 1977, and the appreciation of the pound between 1980 and 1983.

The evidence on speculation is equally ambiguous and is compounded by the fact that there have been few periods historically when floating prevailed long enough to be able to test the hypothesis. Under the gold standard before 1914 there is no evidence of destabilising speculation, but this had much to do with the fact that the international economy was comparatively stable in its own right. It is in the inter-war period, and especially after the collapse of the gold standard in 1931, that the case against floating is rooted since this period witnessed a high degree of volatility in exchange rates.[7] Until the managed floating of the 1970s and 1980s, the best case of floating for any length of time was the Canadian experience from 1950 to 1962. It seems that the Canadian currency remained relatively stable against the US dollar and that, if anything, speculation was stabilising.[8]

The most important conclusion from the Bretton Woods system between 1944 and 1971 was that it turns out to be quite difficult to defend a weak currency against a concerted attack on a fixed exchange rate. A good example of this was the persistent attempts by the UK Labour government in the 1960s to delay the inevitable sterling devaluation until November 1967. Speculators who had been shrewd enough to sell sterling forward immediately prior to this date made a tidy profit in the process.

At the present time, most industrial countries seem to be content to 'muddle along' with managed floating—a system which falls short of complete flexibility, but is nevertheless a significant departure from the relatively fixed system which operated under the Bretton Woods agreement and had collapsed under great pressure by 1972. It is also fair to say that the move towards greater exchange rate flexibility has not led to the unbridled chaos which many opponents of floating rates expected. On the other hand, the system could not be described as smooth and stable, and many commentators would regard it only as a breathing space as the international community gropes towards a more permanent, and implicitly more fixed, exchange rate system.[9] We shall return to these issues in Chapter 16.

Although we have been conducting our discussion in terms of the ideal types of fixed and flexible exchange rates, in practice there are a number of intermediate regimes besides managed floating which countries may choose to adopt in line with their own particular economic circumstances. For example, Brazil and Colombia have both used a 'crawling peg' system which involves declaring a parity or 'peg', but changing this parity over time in a series of discrete jumps. This enables them to neutralise the effects of their heavy inflations by a sizable depreciation of their currencies, but at the same time to reduce the incentive for speculation. This is achieved by announcing the steps in advance and making the steps so small that speculators do not find it profitable to tie up their resources by buying and selling the currency. For a review of the crawling peg by its inventor, see Williamson (1981).

Some countries also operate on a 'wider band' system, which allows them to fix a parity, but with a wider band around it (usually about 5 to 10 per cent) than was permitted under the 'adjustable peg' Bretton Woods system. Not only does this allow greater market fluctuations to take place, but it also provides the authorities with more room for manoeuvre if things go wrong, thereby reducing the chances of a speculative attack on the currency.

Finally, the real choice which faced the majority of countries, especially LDCs, in 1973 when the major currencies began to float was not whether to fix or float, but against which currency or basket of currencies to fix to minimise the damage resulting from fluctuations between the major currencies. For a small 'open' LDC or a country which specialises on a narrow range of exports, it makes sense to fix the currency in terms of a 'vehicle' currency, such as the US dollar or sterling, in order to cushion the economy from the effects of 'external shocks'. This at least guarantees them relatively stable purchasing power in terms of foreign goods, especially if 'shocks' tend to originate mainly from external rather than internal sources.

This indeed seems to be what most countries have done since 1973 according to Holden *et al.* (1979). It is the less open, more diversified countries at a relatively high level of development which have tended to adopt flexibility, and the others which have pegged against the currency of an important trading partner or a weighted average of major partners' currencies.

NOTES

1. To ensure a stable equilibrium, the absolute value of the price elasticity of demand for imports and for exports must, on average, exceed 0.5. Empirical work seems to confirm that this is indeed the case, but only in the long run and not by very much. For further details on this, see Stern *et al.* (1976).
2. For a recent review of the PPP theory, see Officer (1976).
3. Balassa (1964) has suggested that this could be explained by the fact that higher-income countries had less non-traded goods and therefore more opportunities for increasing productivity than LDCs. Hence, non-traded goods would be expensive in rich countries and cheaper in poor countries relative to traded goods.
4. See Friedman (1953).
5. This was the conclusion of Burtle and Mooney (1978) when they attempted to test the reactions of businessmen to flexible exchange rates.
6. For some data on the increased volatility of exchange rates between 1973 and 1982, see Zis (1983).
7. See, for example, Nurkse (1944).
8. See Plumptre (1970).
9. For a view that the UK government should have engaged in a 'dirtier' float to prevent the 'excessive' fall in the value of the pound after 1972, see Thirlwall (1974).

FURTHER READING

For an alternative textbook treatment of the issues discussed here, see Grubel (1977). Aliber (1969) provides an insight into the institutional workings of the foreign exchange market. Yeager (1976) gives a more detailed account of the historical evidence with respect to international currency regimes. A classic article in favour of flexible exchange rates is that of Friedman (1953). More recent reviews of the debate over fixed and flexible exchange rates are available in Baldwin and Richardson (1981) and Goldstein (1980).

PART 5

The International Monetary System

15 Issues in International Monetary Relations

In Part 4 we discussed the implications of alternative balance of payments (BOP) adjustment mechanisms and economic policies primarily from the viewpoint of individual countries. These processes and policies, however, are bound to have repercussions on other countries, and it is the recognition of this fact that has encouraged governments to seek to coordinate their objectives within an internationally accepted framework of rules and institutions.

In this final part of the book we examine the problems which arise when nations attempt to coordinate their international economic relations, and the rules and institutions which have been devised over the years with this end in mind. In Chapter 16 we consider the major developments which have occurred in international monetary relations since about 1870, including the classic gold standard which operated from about 1870 to 1914 and again in modified form from 1925 to 1931; the Bretton Woods system which lasted from the end of the second world war until 1972; and the current system of 'managed' floating. In Chapter 17 we turn our attention more specifically to relations between developed countries (DCs) and lesser developed countries (LDCs), including a discussion of proposals put forward in the 1970s for a new international economic order (NIEO).

For the remainder of this chapter, however, we shall focus on the role of money in the international economy and on the general issues which arise when countries attempt to settle their debts with each other and otherwise coordinate their BOP policies.

15.1 THE ROLE OF MONEY IN THE INTERNATIONAL ECONOMY

Money is generally defined as anything which is acceptable in exchange for goods and services or in settlement of debt, although in practice certain convenience factors come into play to ensure that money is homogeneous, durable, portable, and so on. In this sense, anything can play the part of money as long as people have confidence in it, and historically many different things have performed this role, including precious metals such as gold and silver, and less obvious items such as cowrie shells and cigarettes.[1]

Economists typically distinguish between three main functions which money can perform: as a medium of exchange, a store of value, and a unit of account. As a medium of exchange money serves to overcome the inefficiencies associated with having to carry out transactions on a bilateral or barter basis, and it greatly facilitates the division of labour. In a money economy goods can be exchanged for money which can then be exchanged for other goods, thus removing the need to ensure a 'double coincidence of wants', i.e. finding someone who wants what you have to offer and at the same time possesses something which you are willing to accept in exchange.

As a store of value money may be held over time as a repository of purchasing power. This is an essential process since, in reality, receipts and purchases are rarely perfectly synchronised. Finally, the units in which money is measured (pounds, dollars, etc.) are generally used as the units in which prices, accounts, debts and financial assets are measured. In fact, in the modern world most transactions are carried out without actually requiring money to be physically exchanged. Accounts are simply altered at the end of a given time period to show the net balance between the two parties.

International money has similar functions to perform between residents of different countries. It generally serves to expand the volume of trade by making exchange smoother and more efficient, and enables debts to be settled on the basis of an acceptable unit of account and store of value. It may be a commodity such as gold, a national currency such as the US dollar or pound sterling, or a monetary unit created specifically by international agreement, such as the European currency unit (ECU) or 'special drawing rights' (SDRs) issued by the International Monetary Fund (IMF).

For the remainder of this chapter we shall elaborate on some general problems which arise in international monetary relations. In section 15.2 we ask two questions: What form should international money take? And in what quantities should it be made available? This raises issues connected with the choice of international 'reserve assets' and the 'liquidity problem'. In section 15.3 we discuss the 'fairness' of the rules and institutions which govern international economic relations and enable countries to adjust to deficits and surpluses on their BOP. In short: Who should issue international money? And to whom should it be distributed? Finally, in section 15.4 we consider the circumstances in which countries might want to move towards closer monetary ties, including the use of a single currency.

15.2 RESERVE ASSETS AND LIQUIDITY

We have suggested so far that international money can take a number of different forms and that it is generally conducive, if not essential, to international trade. But what form or forms can it take? And what determines the amounts available in the international system at any moment in time? To answer these questions we need to look at why countries need to hold reserve assets, i.e. stocks of foreign currencies or commodities such as gold, which can be used by the monetary authorities to influence the foreign exchange market and the BOP. These assets, together with access to international credit, will determine the country's liquidity position.

The picture is easiest to see when a country is committed to defending a fixed exchange rate, since reserves will be essential to enable the authorities to maintain the value of their currency within the agreed limits when disturbances occur to the BOP. The situation is analogous to a household holding a cash balance over a week or a month in order to synchronise payments and receipts which arise before the next salary cheque or wage packet appears. The size of this balance will depend on a number of factors, including the magnitude of fluctuations in the BOP—countries subject to strong and unpredictable swings in export receipts will tend to hold higher average balances to cushion the effects of these swings.

In addition, higher reserves will generally be held if automatic adjustment mechanisms (discussed in Part 4) which operate to offset BOP problems are slow or inefficient, and the government is either unable or unwilling to use other policy instruments to correct payments imbalances, including altering the exchange rate. Finally, countries may wish to hold extra reserves as a precaution against a speculative attack on the currency. In this case, the extra reserves are held to convince speculators that the authorities are prepared to defend the exchange rate without resorting to devaluation.

The picture is less clear, however, when fixed rates are abandoned since, in theory, under a perfectly flexible exchange rate system reserves are not required at all. This is because the exchange rate itself is supposed to eliminate payments imbalances automatically. In practice, under managed floating since 1973 reserves have still been held, but the evidence suggests that less are required than under a more rigid system.[2]

As well as deciding on the size of reserves to hold, a decision will also have to be taken about the *composition* of reserves to be held by the monetary authorities. This will depend upon the types of international money or credit currently available and acceptable under the rules of the international monetary system, and also on the expected risks and returns associated with them. In the modern world the authorities will generally hold a mixture of foreign currencies, gold and SDRs, and have access to a number of forms of international credit.

Table 15.1 shows how the level of reserves has changed since 1960 and the distribution between gold, foreign currencies, reserve positions in the IMF, and SDRs. Notice that gold—which played the major role under the gold standard, and a less important but still significant role under the Bretton Woods system as the backing for the US dollar—has declined in importance since 1970 despite a significant rise in its market price.

By far the largest proportion of reserves nowadays are held in reserve currencies, the most important being the US dollar. As we shall see in Chapter 16, the dollar became the main form of international liquidity after 1945, and despite the abandonment of the dollar-based gold exchange standard in the early 1970s, and the wider use of other 'strong' currencies such as the German mark and the Japanese yen, about three-quarters of reserves are still accounted for by dollars.

Two other types of international money have come into prominence in the last two decades—SDRs and international credit. SDRs were introduced in the late 1960s by the IMF because

Table 15.1: The level and composition of international reserves 1960–79

End of year	Total reserves[1]	Composition of reserves % total			
		Gold[2]	Foreign exchange	SDRs[3]	Reserves in IMF
1960	61.8	61.49	32.69	0	5.82
1965	72.4	57.73	34.81	0	7.46
1970	92.5	40.22	48.11	3.35	8.32
1975	279.9	43.44	48.91	3.14	4.51
1976	303.4	38.60	52.67	2.87	5.86
1977	363.7	37.78	55.02	2.23	4.97
1978	420.5	42.02	52.51	1.93	3.54
1979	629.6	57.18	38.96	1.99	1.87

Notes: [1]Billions of special drawing rights.
[2]Valued at 1 SDR per ounce through 1970 and at the London market price after 1970.
[3]Valued at $1 until 1971 and rose to $1.30 in 1979.
Source: International Monetary Fund (1980).

it was felt that there was insufficient international liquidity, and that an alternative reserve asset was required to supplement the US dollar, which was undergoing periodic crises of confidence reflecting the growing US current account deficit.

The attraction of the SDR was that it could be regulated by the IMF and was not dependent upon any particular country's BOP. The IMF would simply credit the accounts of its members with a certain number of SDRs which they could then use under agreed rules to finance deficits. Unlike gold, SDRs were not dependent on gold discoveries around the world and they were virtually costless to produce and transfer. In addition, they can act as assets by attaching an interest rate to them as a reward for holding on to them.

Before 1971 the SDR was defined in terms of gold on the same basis as the US dollar, but with the move to generalised floating in the 1970s this procedure was changed to allow it to be valued in terms of a weighted average of major currencies which could be revised every few years. The first SDRs were allocated in 1970, and although at present they constitute only a small proportion of international reserves (about 2 per cent in 1979 from Table 15.1), as we shall see in Chapter 16, there are plans to widen their use.

Finally, there is the availability of international credit. Even though countries are still likely to hold some reserves, access to credit to finance deficits represents an alternative means of acquiring international money. Before the formation of the IMF after the second world war, access to credit was quite limited and was only made available on an *ad hoc* basis between governments. In the post-war era, however, credit facilities have been considerably widened, especially in the 1970s. As well as the normal borrowing facilities extended by the IMF (to be discussed in Chapter 16), it currently has a number of other facilities. These include funds for compensating countries whose export receipts are subject to severe fluctuations (the compensatory finance facility),[3] for emergency loans at short notice (stand-by arrangements), and to finance oil import price rises (the oil facility). There are also special facilities to help poorer countries over short-term payments problems (supplementary financing facility) or to carry out longer-term adjustments (extended facility). In addition, some countries have access to credit facilities outside the IMF, the most important being arrangements worked out between central banks.

One of the most important issues in international monetary economics concerns the question of liquidity, i.e. how much international money (reserves plus credit) should be made available to finance international trade. If there is insufficient liquidity, and countries are short of reserves or credit and are unwilling to alter their exchange rates, then they may be tempted to impose controls of one form or another to cure payments difficulties. These controls are likely, however, to have the adverse effects on welfare which we discussed in Chapter 5. On the other hand, if there is too much liquidity about this may encourage countries to grow too fast and generate inflationary pressures in the world economy.

This problem of liquidity is well illustrated after 1945 when the immediate problem was a shortage of foreign exchange to finance recovery in Europe. Since the USA was the only major economy to have come out of the war relatively unscathed, the burden of major reserve asset fell on the dollar. This quickly manifested itself in a 'dollar shortage' as European countries sought to expand their purchases of imports. This shortage was solved in the short run by the transfer of Marshall Aid from the USA to Europe, and in the longer run by the USA being prepared to run a payments deficit with the rest of the world in order to provide the world community with sufficient dollars to finance the growth in international trade. It was precisely a lack of confidence in the ability of the USA to continue in this role in the late 1960s which lay behind the creation of SDRs as an alternative reserve asset to the dollar.

Paradoxically, however, at the very time that SDRs were being introduced to supplement international liquidity, that liquidity was itself expanding and many economists see a direct link between the rapid growth in reserves in the early 1970s and the onset of inflation in the major industrial countries. This problem of finding a balance between insufficient liquidity and excessive liquidity is a major problem in international monetary economics.

15.3 ADJUSTMENT TO PAYMENTS IMBALANCES

If one starts from the proposition that countries will have different objectives with respect to both internal and external balance, and will differ in their willingness to use such weapons as controls over exchange rates or capital movements, one of the key tests of an international monetary system is how far its rules and institutions can accommodate the diversity of interests between its members. It is not enough to say that each country should individually choose its own policy mix to satisfy its own objectives, since this ignores the high degree if interdependence characterising modern international relations. For example, it is possible for one country to increase its reserves by running a current account surplus, but it is impossible for all countries to do so simultaneously. Likewise, an individual country can consume (absorb) more than it produces domestically by going into deficit, but the world as a whole cannot.

Hence, whatever rules are adopted by countries individually or in concert with others, will have implications for the distribution of the burden of adjustment to payments imbalances. For example, under the logic of the gold standard mechanism, a country with a persistent deficit would have to experience a deflation of domestic prices and incomes in order to regain its international competitive position. The principle burden of adjustment under this system, therefore, falls on the deficit country itself. By contrast, under a fully flexible exchange rate system, some of this adjustment would be borne by other countries in so far as the depreciation of the deficit country's exchange rate raises the price of its imports and lowers its demand for exports from the rest of the world.

Under a mixed system such as that devised at Bretton Woods, there was a more deliberate intention of finding an acceptable formula for sharing the burden of adjustment. Some deflation of domestic activity was expected, but exchange rates could also be altered to some extent, and financial help could be made available if payments imbalances were particularly serious. It is this deliberate attempt to devise a set of rules to solve payments imbalances between countries which lies at the heart of international monetary negotiations, and is compounded by wider political issues, as economic circumstances change over time and surplus countries do not always see the advantages of helping countries which appear to be perpetually in deficit.

Two particular problems of equity or fairness in international monetary relations relate directly to the creation and distribution of international money: Who should issue it? And to whom should it be distributed?

The issuing of international money causes problems because it confers 'seignorage' on those who use it first. The term seignorage originates in the right of the medieval sovereign to place its stamp on precious metals, thus giving it a profit over and above the value of the bullion. In international trade, therefore, seignorage becomes the difference between the cost of issuing international money and its value in exchange to the first spender. If we take the case of gold as an example, any gap between the cost of producing it and its value as international money accrues to the gold-producing country. One of the reasons why official gold holdings in central banks were not simply revalued as a possible solution to a shortage of liquidity in the 1960s was that this would confer benefits on gold-producing countries such as the USSR and South Africa, a situation which many countries regarded as morally unacceptable.

With a national currency such as the dollar acting as the main reserve asset, the question of seignorage also arises, but in a more complex way. Some countries, including France, objected to the seignorage obtained by the USA in the post-war period resulting from its ability to issue dollars under the gold exchange standard, which the rest of the world then held in exchange for goods and services or assets. Any benefits to the USA, however, would have to be set against its loss of independence in monetary matters resulting from the need to run a continuous deficit to provide the international economy with liquidity, and the fact that central banks were quite keen to hold dollars. In practice the net benefits to the USA may well have been quite small.[4]

As far as SDRs are concerned, since they bear an interest rate which is well below market rates, their 'cost' is much less than their value as a currency or asset. Hence, seignorage is available to the first users. However, unlike with gold or a national currency, the distribution of seignorage is firmly in the hands of the IMF. This does not, however, preclude disputes over its distribution. Unlike any of the other forms of international money we have discussed, SDRs offer a unique chance to share out seignorage in accordance with some agreed distributive formula. But who should receive this new international money?

Initially it was the developed industrial countries who intended to issue the new money in proportion to their IMF quotas, which was supposed broadly to reflect their respective demands for liquidity. But the LDCs put forward an alternative suggestion which has become known as the 'link' proposal, signifying a 'link' between the creation of the new reserve asset and development assistance.[5] This proposal envisaged allocating the new SDRs disproportionately in favour of LDCs on the grounds that this would both allow DCs to run current account surpluses with LDCs financed by the new reserves, and any seignorage arising from the issue of SDRs would accrue to poorer countries in the form of 'disguised' aid.

unfortunately, however, there has been little progress on this proposal. This partly reflects objections to the scheme by those who feel that the aid issue should be kept distinct from the issue of international liquidity, but it also reflects a belief that such a scheme would be inherently inflationary by encouraging over-expansion by LDCs. Since inflation has become the major international problem in the 1970s and 1980s, and the liquidity shortage has to a large extent disappeared, progress on this question has been shelved for the time being. The problem of seignorage has not, however, disappeared and we shall return to it in our discussion of the evolution of the international monetary system in Chapter 16.

THE OPTIMUM CURRENCY AREA

If there are advantages to be gained from linking together regions of a country into a single monetary area such as in the USA or Britain, then there may be advantages from linking countries together under a common currency and monetary area. In short, what is the 'optimum currency area' defining a region with a single currency unit so that, in effect, exchange rate variations become irrelevant?

The advantages from joining a larger monetary union are, in essence, the same as for a single money and fixed exchange rates. Fixed exchange rates and a common currency eliminate monetary fluctuations between the regions and ensure a stable unit of account from which to carry out transactions. There might also be political advantages from being a member of a larger bargaining unit, and from the pooling of coherent economic policies. This pooling of policies is clearly feasible within regions sharing a common identity, but is less so between different countries.

On the other hand, regional development is rarely smooth, and one might expect some regions to grow at the expense of others as resources are attracted away from the declining regions to the more dynamic growth areas. To this extent, the regions giving up their independent monetary discretion would need to be reassured that any adjustment costs are allowed for. This will be made easier if factor markets are well integrated between the regions so that declining regions can obtain finance for any necessary adjustments, and labour migration can act as a safety valve for unemployment. In addition, some form of fiscal transfer within the larger union is inevitable to cope with these regional imbalances.

A good illustration of the issues involved in monetary unification is offered by the experience of the European Economic Community (EEC), which adopted a broad commitment to monetary union by 1980 under the Werner Report of 1970. In fact, in 1969 the European common margins arrangements (which subsequently became known as 'the snake') had been introduced as a first step towards the establishment of a single exchange rate system among EEC countries and the gradual abolition of fluctuation margins between EEC currencies. The 'snake in the tunnel' analogy came about because the smaller band of member currencies moves about in response to 'strong' and 'weak' currencies fluctuating between their limits (2.25 per cent eith side of parity), within the wider band established between the group as a whole and the rest of the world (about 4.45 per cent either way).

With the breakdown of the fixed exchange rate system in 1973 and the first round of oil price increases in 1973–74, the 'snake' was left to float against the US dollar and the 'tunnel' disappeared. In the end it became a common exchange rate mechanism for the smaller EEC countries such as Belgium, Denmark, Luxembourg and the Netherlands.

In March 1979, however, a commitment to a European Monetary System (EMS) was made, with the ultimate objective of monetary union. This partly reflected a desire to increase European political unity, but also the practical advantages of a number of relatively small countries operating in close geographical proximity adopting a fixed exchange rate system.

The main features of this system included the creation of a European currency unit (ECU)—a common currency analogous to the SDR but based instead upon a basket of European currencies; an agreement by members to make available centrally 20 per cent of their gold and gross dollar reserves on a three-month revolving 'swap' basis, in the expectation that at a later date these resources would be taken permanently into a European Monetary Fund as an embryonic European central bank; and the linchpin of the system—a new exchange rate regime.

Under the new exchange rate rules, each country would have a central exchange rate in relation to each of the other member currencies and the ECU, and is obliged to intervene in the foreign exchange market to keep its currency within a band of 2.25 per cent each side of its central rate with the other currencies. Although there is some similarity here with regard to the snake, the EMS would involve a stronger commitment to pool economic policies within the new monetary area.

Although there has been some success since 1979 in widening the use of the ECU away from simply being a unit of account in EEC transactions and towards being a genuinely commercial currency unit, there has been little success in other areas, and the original intention of proceeding to 'stage two' by March 1981 has been abandoned. There simply was not any firm agreement on the transfer of sovereignty from national governments to a common

European institution, or a willingness by the countries concerned to give up the use of the exchange rate as a weapon of monetary policy, which is a prerequisite of membership of a stable exchange rate system.

The pooling of economic policies between the EEC countries has also been hindered by the divergence rather than convergence of their economic performances since 1979, giving rise to continuous uncertainty about exchange rates within the EMS. This underlines the point that closer monetary ties require not only a commitment to pool sovereignty, but also sufficient similarity in economic indicators to make a common exchange rate system feasible. The picture has also not been helped by the fact that the UK, despite being a member of the EMS, has declined to join the exchange rate arrangements. There seems to be little room for optimism about the development of the EMS in the foreseeable future.

NOTES

1. The use of cigarettes as a form of money is vividly demonstrated by Radford's experiences in a prisoner-of-war camp after the second world war. See Radford (1983).
2. See, for example, Heller and Khan (1978).
3. For further details on this particular scheme, see Goreaux (1977).
4. For some elaboration on this, see Crockett (1982, p. 132).
5. For a more detailed analysis of the issues surrounding the 'link,' see Diaz Alejandro (1976).

FURTHER READING

For further analysis of the role of money in the international economy, see Crockett (1982). The liquidity problem is admirably surveyed in Williamson (1973). As far as the IMF's lending facilities are concerned, these are described in the International Monetary Fund (1979). The original theory of the optimum currency area is ascribed to McKinnon (1963), but a more recent review can be found in Willett and Tower (1976). Two up-to-date assessments of the EMS are available in Lomax (1983) and Ungerer *et al.* (1983).

16 International Monetary Relations since 1870

16.1 THE CLASSICAL GOLD STANDARD

The system of international monetary relations which had evolved by the late nineteenth century has become known as the classical gold standard, to distinguish it from the system which operated between 1925 and 1931, which although similar in many respects (and is often called the gold standard), is more properly interpreted as a gold exchange standard. Although the gold standard is essentially irrelevant as a viable way to run the contemporary international monetary system, despite prognostications to the contrary in the 1960s by certain French economists such as Jacques Rueff, it is none the less useful to consider it here for two main reasons.[1] First, it provides a good illustration of a classical BOP adjustment mechanism at work. And secondly, it exerted an important influence on the negotiations which culminated in the Bretton Woods system after the second world war. We shall consider this system in section 16.3 below.

Each country on the gold standard was obliged to fix its currency in terms of gold. For example, the pound sterling might be valued at 113.02 grains of fine gold, and the 'par' value of the US dollar at 23.22 grains. Hence, if each country fixed its currency to gold, they were all fixed to each other. In the example above, the pound would exchange against the dollar at 113.02/23.22 or approximately £1 = $4.87. The only scope for variation in exchange rates arose from the costs of shipping gold between central banks which allowed rates to fluctuate between what were known as the 'gold points'. Take, for example, the case of a UK importer who is faced with an import bill from the USA. If excess demand for the dollar in London pushed up the foreign exchange rate (the price of a dollar in terms of sterling) above the gold point of $4.90, allowing for 3 cents transport costs, it would pay the importer to buy gold in

London at the official rate of 113.02 grains for a pound and sell it in New York in exchange for dollars at the official rate of $4.87 for every 113.02 grains of gold. Such movements of specie would ensure that currencies remained fixed between their gold points, since no one would want to buy foreign currency at any other price.

In order for the gold standard to operate in this way, a number of conditions had to be fulfilled, in particular gold would have to be acceptable as international money, governments would have to be prepared to provide gold on demand in unlimited quantities at a fixed price, and no restrictions could be placed on the import or export of gold. It was especially important that governments obeyed the 'rules' and did not respond to a gold loss resulting from a BOP deficit by issuing more money, or otherwise 'sterilising' the contractionary effects of the gold loss on the domestic money supply. After about 1870 these conditions were sufficiently fulfilled for the major trading countries to begin operating it.

The theory of how the gold standard was supposed to work is based on the automatic adjustment mechanism put forward by Hume, which he called the 'price specie flow' mechanism.[2] We have already referred to this mechanism in Chapter 2 as a critique of the mercantilist philosophy of international trade, and as an ingredient of the monetarist theory of the BOP in Chapter 13. Essentially what Hume demonstrated was that trying to maximise a payments surplus over the long run is self-defeating, because any payments imbalances between countries would be eliminated automatically by the movement of gold.

The idea behind this model of the gold standard was that a deficit would lead to an outflow of gold reserves which would lower the domestic money supply (in the absence of sterilisation by the authorities), and through the operation of the quantity theory of money would reduce the aggregate price level. This in turn would make the deficit country's exports more competitive and its imports more expensive, thereby stimulating an increase in exports and a contraction in imports and improving the BOP. For a surplus country the reverse would happen.

There seems to be some agreement amongst economic historians that the gold standard worked well in promoting international trade and factor mobility in the nineteenth century and that it provided a relatively smooth adjustment mechanism for payments imbalances, although as we shall see below, it did not operate in quite the way that the price specie flow mechanism would suggest.[3] The existence of relatively stable exchange rates and a consistent unit of account for international transactions undoubtedly encouraged confidence (despite periodic crises) and permitted the simultaneous expansion of a number of countries, both developed and developing, without generating any serious long-run inflationary or deflationary pressures.

Although the basic conditions for the gold standard to operate generally prevailed after 1870, including the free convertibility and mobility of gold, the way in which the gold standard actually functioned was not quite the same as Hume's simple model would suggest. In particular, the stress on *price* adjustment to payments imbalances seems to be somewhat at odds with the facts, and the process of adjustment was probably more attributable to other factors, including *income* adjustment. Under this interpretation a deficit would lead to a contraction in income and employment rather than to a fall in wages and prices and the trade balance is improved by the derived fall in import spending rather than by an improvement in competitiveness.

In addition, there is evidence to suggest that the monetary authorities in the deficit countries raised interest rates to attract foreign capital as a means of improving the BOP, rather than allowing the outflow of reserves to bring about the contraction in the money supply. This explains why surprisingly little gold actually did flow between countries. Although it seems the authorities allowed their domestic money supplies to vary with reserves, they also raised interest rates to attract foreign capital.[4] In this sense, adjustment took place on capital account rather than through the reduction of domestic prices which was generally insufficient on its own to explain the adjustment process. This was especially effective for a country such as Britain where relatively small rises in Bank rate could bring forth a significant inflow of foreign funds, and at the same time force some domestic deflation by reducing aggregate demand, particularly domestic investment spending.

The monetary and banking system which operated in the late nineteenth century was, therefore, more complex than the simple gold standard mechanism would imply. In practice, gold was not the principle medium of exchange but more of a reserve asset against which the domestic banks issued a much larger quantity of money in the form of notes and coin and bank deposits. Under this system, known as fractional reserve banking, banks only need to keep a small fraction of their reserves as backing for the much larger volume of loans and deposits. This meant that any change in international reserves (i.e. gold) could now cause a much larger change in the domestic money supply; and the banking authorities had more scope to adjust interest rates than the gold standard model suggested. In particular, a BOP deficit which led to an outflow of gold could be neutralised by an increase in domestic credit. In practice, however, this did not happen very often.

The gold standard also operated less smoothly for LDCs such as Argentina than for DCs such as Britain. Whilst a relatively small increase in Bank rate in London could attract foreign capital and orchestrate a fairly painless adjustment on capital account, for a country such as Argentina any external imbalance such as a contraction of foreign lending could engender a currency crisis and a painful reduction in domestic prices and incomes. For an analysis of this lack of symmetry in the adjustment burden for countries on the gold standard, see Ford (1962). Triffin (1964) has also argued that, although the system worked quite well for the major industrial countries such as Great Britain and Germany, this was to some extent at the expense of the poorer primary producers who were forced to bear some of the brunt of the adjustment through a deterioration in their terms of trade.

Finally, it is important to emphasise that the relative success of the gold standard before 1914 owed something to the particularly favourable circumstances operating at that time, and to the rather peculiar role played by Great Britain in the system.

The late nineteenth century was a period of relatively free trade when many countries managed to grow without experiencing serious BOP difficulties, so that the sort of adjustment implied by the gold standard was rarely needed. It was also a period when international business cycles displayed a high degree of harmony, with incomes, prices and interest rates moving in unison. The role played by Britain was also essential if the system was to function smoothly. London at this time was the premier international financial centre and was able both to lend large sums of money to the rest of the world and at the same time act as a major import market for expanding primary producers such as America and

Argentina without running into serious BOP difficulties.

It was precisely this misunderstanding of how the gold standard actually worked in the nineteenth century, together with a failure to appreciate the particular circumstances which enabled it to work relatively smoothly, which explains the disastrous decision to restore the gold standard on the basis of the pre-war exchange rate parities in the 1920s. It is to this period which we now turn.

16.2 THE INTER-WAR YEARS

Gold convertibility was suspended for all important countries except the USA during the first world war and after a period of post-war reconstruction, which witnessed severe hyper-inflation in many Eastern European countries, especially Germany, a conference was convened in 1922 to set about restoring the gold standard. This was eventually achieved in 1925 when Britain returned to the gold standard at the pre-war parity and was quickly followed by the other important trading countries. Although the system was similar in many respects to the classical gold standard, many of the less important countries agreed to hold part of their reserves in currencies such as sterling and the US dollar rather than in gold. This system, where some central banks will not exchange their currencies for gold on demand but for a currency which is itself tied to gold, is known technically as a gold exchange standard.

The return to the gold standard in the 1920s, and in particular the British decision to return at the pre-war parity, has been the subject of much debate.[5] It seems that the policy-makers concerned were aware that some adjustments would have to be made to match the new circumstances of the post-war era, but that they seriously underestimated the adjustment costs involved and were perhaps a little over-awed by the success of the gold standard in the late nineteenth century without fully understanding how it had actually worked and the important role that Britain had played at the centre of the system. As far as they were concerned the gold standard had represented a period of relatively stable exchange rates during which countries had confidence in gold as the unit of account. Moreover, the classical interpretation of the adjustment mechanism minimised government intervention and seemed to offer a 'fair' way to settle payments imbalances by making the deficit countries take the necessary domestic action to cure their own payments imbalances. These apparent virtues of the gold standard had considerable influence on those bankers and politicians who were charged with the task of restoring the international monetary system after the first world war.

Unfortunately, however, the war had fundamentally altered the balance of economic power in the world, reflected in the growing strength of the USA and the relative decline of Great Britain and France. The result was that exchange rates were seriously out of line with economic realities, with sterling about 10 per cent overvalued in 1925 and the French franc seriously undervalued. Since under the logic of the gold standard a deficit country was obliged to deflate its prices and wages to restore external balance, Britain was forced into severe contraction from 1925 onwards in order to re-establish competitiveness in a situation where export prices were something in the region of 10 per cent overpriced.

In addition, the commitment to the gold standard rules which had worked fairly well in the previous century had diminished after the war. Governments were now more concerned with maintaining internal balance and the USA, in particular, was not averse to sterilising any inflow of gold as a means of containing domestic inflation. Greater downward rigidity in prices and wages also made deflationary policies less effective, and the confidence that countries could maintain fixed exchange rates began to evaporate after 1925.

The collapse of the system was inevitable and quickly followed in the wake of the 1929 Wall Street crash. The stock market collapse in the USA had led to the virtual cessation of American foreign lending, which meant in turn that Germany could no longer afford to pay war reparations to the other European countries. As a consequence, a wave of bank runs spread across Europe and eventually this led to a run on sterling. Finally, in September 1931, Britain abandoned the gold standard.

The ensuing period from 1931 to the outbreak of the second world war can only be described as chaotic as far as the international monetary system is concerned. Currencies were left to float or were devalued, and only an agreement between France, Britain and the USA in 1936 prevented a degeneration into a further round of competitive devaluations. For the first time, countries were actively using commercial policy such as tariffs and quotas as a competitive expenditure switching device to expand exports and cut imports, and controls were introduced to restrict the use of foreign exchange.

Naturally, these policies were disastrous as far as the international community as a whole was concerned as the volume of trade shrank and international capital movements dried up. In addition, the 1930s saw the growth of bilateral trading arrangements including a sterling area revolving around Britain, and a dollar bloc based on the USA. This period of monetary instability and beggar-my-neighbour policies was to have an important influence on those entrusted with the task of resurrecting the international monetary system after the second world war.

16.3 THE BRETTON WOODS SYSTEM

Active negotiations on the post-war international monetary and trading system had already begun between the allies in 1941 with the clear intention of establishing a set of rules and institutions which would replace the chaotic system which had operated during the 1930s. With some of the groundwork already laid, British, American and French representatives met in July 1944 in Bretton Woods, New Hampshire. Their objective was to draft the articles of agreement for two major new institutions—the International Bank For Reconstruction and Development (IBRD) which later became the World Bank, and the International Monetary Fund (IMF). Plans for a third organisation—the International Trade Organisation (ITO)—failed to materialise in the face of American opposition, but a weaker agreement was later reached at Geneva in 1948 on a framework for reducing trade barriers on a multilateral basis. This subsequently became known as the General Agreement on Tariffs and Trade (GATT).

Since we have already discussed GATT in Chapter 5 within the context of commercial policy, and the World Bank in Chapter 10 in connection with the distribution of foreign aid, we shall confine ourselves here to a discussion of the post-war international monetary system and its central institution—the IMF.

What seemed to be uppermost in the minds of the architects of the Bretton Woods system was not merely the restoration of a workable system along the lines of the gold standard, but one which would restore confidence and remove the dislocation and protectionism of the 1930s, but with more built-in flexibility than the gold standard had provided. What was at stake was not just another set of exchange rate arrangements, but a set of rules by which payments imbalances between countries could be equitably settled, and at the same time could promote the growth of international trade. More specifically, the objectives were to achieve exchange rate stability, but with some flexibility; a return to currency convertibility as soon as possible; arrangements for short-term BOP assistance; and an international trading system which would enable all countries to achieve full employment within the context of free trade and factor mobility.

The IMF itself turned out to be a compromise between the British plan put forward by Keynes for an international clearing union, and an American counter-proposal presented by Dexter-White for a less ambitious international stabilisation fund. The Keynes proposal represented a far-reaching attempt to create an international bank which would have the power to create overdraft facilities for deficit countries, and a proviso that central banks would hold accounts at the clearing union in a new international money to be called bancor. The idea was that bancor would be acquired either by depositing gold or received as payment from a country in deficit. Another ingenious feature of the Keynes plan was to make interest payable on *both* borrowings from the clearing union *and* excessive credit balances, thereby reminding both credit and deficit countries of their obligations to adjust to payments imbalances.

In the event, the British plan was considered too radical for the Americans, who were unhappy about the generosity given to deficit countries and the obligations of surplus countries which, of course, were likely to include themselves. The alternative American plan for an international stabilisation fund was less ambitious in so far as it was based on a pool of *existing* gold and convertible currencies (sterling and dollars) which could be lent out to countries experiencing temporary BOP difficulties.

The IMF system which eventually emerged from the Bretton Woods negotiations was much closer to the American plan than to that of the British. A link with the gold standard was retained in as much as US gold stocks formed the ultimate backing for the dollar, and the US authorities were obliged to defend the dollar by buying and selling gold at a fixed price (initially $35 an ounce) from the central banks. However, as far as other countries were concerned, the link with gold was broken since they were only obliged to defend their currencies by buying and selling dollars. In effect the dollar was fixed in terms of gold but other currencies were tied to the dollar directly, or sometimes indirectly through another reserve currency such as sterling. This meant that the system was akin to a gold exchange standard as countries were willing to hold much of their reserves in dollars in the confidence that the dollar would retain its value in terms of other currencies and would remain convertible into gold. Gold was, therefore, viewed as a reserve asset rather than as an intervention currency.

As far as the exchange rate system was concerned, each country declared its par rate in terms of gold, but the authorities could permit a margin of fluctuation of plus or minus 1 per cent around that value. The point here was to combine the advantages of a fixed exchange rate system with more flexibility than was allowed under the gold standard. With this in mind, it was further possible for a country to alter its exchange rate outside these limits if the IMF agreed that the BOP was in 'fundamental disequilibrium'.[6]

The process of adjustment thus envisaged was that temporary imbalances would be financed from reserves or borrowing from the IMF, while more persistent imbalances would be cured by applying monetary and fiscal policies. Only if the domestic adjustments were considered likely to be large and persistent was there to be a change in the exchange rate outside the 1 per cent limits either side of par. Exchange controls, however, could be used to counter destabilising capital movements.

The IMF, which began operating in 1946, saw itself primarily as a source of short-term assistance to overcome BOP problems and the arbiter of an orderly system of exchange rate adjustments. Each member was given a quota based upon a formula incorporating such factors as the size of its national income or its importance in international trade. This quota then determined the amount the country contributed to the Fund (initially 25 per cent in gold or convertible currency and the rest in its own currency); it defined the size of its potential borrowings; and it fixed its voting rights within the IMF's decision-making body. Deficit countries were then permitted to withdraw foreign exchange by giving up their own currency in return, which they subsequently had to buy back when in a position to do so. Generally, the first tranche of 25 per cent of the quota was made available without questions asked (since this represented the country's original contribution of foreign exchange), but further tranches could be subject to the approval of the Fund and require the country to agree to certain conditions, including a possible visit by IMF officials 'to inspect the books'. Although these rules have changed somewhat over the years, the basic principles of the IMF have remained the same. We shall look at some of these changes in section 16.4 below.[7]

During the period of reconstruction immediately following the second world war the IMF made little impact on events which were dominated by European recovery, and an acute shortage of dollars arising from the chronic European payments deficit with the USA. This was largely solved by the transfer of aid from the USA under the Marshall Plan, and a series of devaluations of non-dollar currencies. In 1956 the IMF began to lend to France and Britain in the aftermath of the Suez crisis. By 1958 the dollar shortage was over and the major European currencies became convertible, thus signalling the effective beginning of the Bretton Woods system.

There seems little doubt that the Bretton Woods system worked well in the late 1950s and early 1960s, during which period there was relatively free trade, a rapid expansion in trade and capital mobility, and little by way of serious inflation or unemployment in the major industrial countries. Unfortunately, however, the system had within it a number of in-built contradictions, one of which had been pointed out by Triffin (1960) as early as 1960.

By the end of the 1950s, many European countries were running substantial payments surpluses, and the USA was running the counterpart deficit. It was essential for continued economic expansion that the USA maintained this deficit because it represented the only way that the growth in international reserves could be sustained in the absence of any other reserve asset including gold. However, if the USA continued to run bigger and bigger deficits while its gold assets remained constant,[8] it was only a matter of time before foreign holders of dollars, including central bankers, doubted the ability of the USA to maintain the $35 an ounce gold price and rushed to convert dollars into gold before the dollar was devalued. The system was thus inherently unstable— either the USA corrected its deficit and created a liquidity shortage, or it continued to run a deficit, and a crisis of confidence would occur.

The Triffin dilemma was not the only problem to bedevil the Bretton Woods system; another one stemmed from the adjustment process to payments imbalances. Although there was a degree of flexibility built-in to the Bretton Woods system, countries were finding the adjustment process difficult. This was either because the BOP was not very responsive to government policies, or because governments were unwilling to take the necessary action to cure their BOP problems at the expense of domestic goals. Not only were 'stop–go' cycles a common feature of the 1960s, but delays in implementing the necessary reforms often made the eventual adjustment more difficult.

In addition, there was a general problem of symmetry between deficit and surplus countries, and between the USA and the rest of the world. In the first case, although the Bretton Woods system set out to share the burden of adjustment to payments imbalances between both deficit and surplus countries, in practice the brunt of the adjustment fell upon deficit countries. Whilst surplus countries could continue to run surpluses as long as they were willing to accumulate reserves, deficit countries could not run down reserves or borrow indefinitely.

The dispute between the rest of the world and the USA arose from the belief in some countries, especially France, that the USA was getting unmerited seignorage to finance its war in Vietnam and direct investment in Europe. This was due to the ability of the USA to print dollars which were subsequently held by the rest of the world in exchange for goods and services, and assets. The USA, on the other hand, felt equally aggrieved at having to maintain the value of the dollar and to forgo the use of devaluation policy to cure its own BOP deficit. The system, it seemed, suited neither party.

Finally, there was also a problem connected with the rapid growth of highly mobile short-term capital, particularly after the development of the Eurodollar market in the late 1950s. This was bound to make the fragile fixed exchange rate system vulnerable to speculative capital movements which anticipated changes in parities. Any payments imbalances which persuaded capital holders that a devaluation was imminent led to a capital flight into currencies which seemed likely to appreciate. Speculative crises had occurred in the 1950s, but by the 1960s the underlying payments imbalances between the main trading countries had become more serious, and governments seemed to be either unable or unwilling to take the necessary domestic action to cure them. Capital controls were tried as another remedy, but they were generally ineffective.

The writing was clearly on the wall in 1965 and 1966 when sterling was under persistent speculative pressure. Inevitably, in November 1967 the pound was devalued by 14 per cent. This shook confidence in the ability of the USA to defend the gold price, and in March of the following year a run on the dollar forced the US to declare the dollar inconvertible into gold, except between central banks. The ensuing years were characterised by a series of speculative crises involving all the major currencies, but usually took the form of runs out of sterling and the French franc and into the German mark. Finally, on the 15 August 1971, the USA made the dollar inconvertible even between central banks, and thereby cut the last remaining link between the dollar and gold, leaving the other major countries with little choice but to float. The Bretton Woods system had come to an end.

Negotiations began almost immediately at the Smithsonian Institute in December 1971 with a new structure of fixed exchange rates. The result was a *de facto* 8 per cent devaluation of the dollar in terms of gold, and some revaluation of the stronger currencies. Seven months later a run on the pound led to the British decision to float, a series of further currency realignments, and another round of speculation. Finally, the industrial countries accepted the inevitable and adopted a general system of floating. This system of 'managed floating' has been in operation ever since.

In retrospect it is not difficult to see the contradictions in the Bretton Woods system. Although undoubtedly successful for much of the post-war period, it is hard to see how it could have survived the economic strains which were to emerge in the 1960s in the form of the 'Triffin dilemma', the lack of a satisfactory mechanism for payments adjustment, and the growth of mobile short-term capital.

Some of the blame should also go to the participating countries for failing to devise the necessary machinery to solve these problems. The need for discussion had been recognised early on with the formation of the group of ten in 1965, comprising the ten major trading countries, but little agreement was reached on the required changes. The Triffin school wanted a new reserve asset and greater control over the growth of existing reserves which was reminiscent of Keynes' plans for an international bank with bancor as the new international money. Other proposals included a return to a gold standard and a revaluation of the price of gold. The first was plainly ridiculous under the circumstances, and probably represented more of a political gesture of defiance by French Gaullists against the USA than a serious economic proposal, while the second would have distributed seignorage to the gold-producing countries such as the USSR and South Africa, and was opposed on political grounds. In the end the Triffin school triumphed by persuading the IMF to introduce the SDR in 1967, but unfortunately it came much too late to save the system.

16.4 INTERNATIONAL MONETARY RELATIONS AFTER BRETTON WOODS

Until the oil crisis of 1973, the consensus was that the Bretton Woods system be restored as soon as possible, but with some minor modifications. Subsequently, however, a growing feeling emerged that managed floating was the only viable policy at the present time and the desire to return to the previous system began to fade. This also had something to do with the growing influence of those committed to a market philosophy based upon flexible exchange rates and a return to greater *laissez-faire* in matters of economic policy.

In 1972 a committee of twenty (C20) IMF members was established to investigate possible reforms to the international monetary system. Regular meetings were held between 1972 and 1974 at which proposals were debated at length, but by about 1974 little had been agreed except an outline of reform for further negotiations. At a meeting in Jamaica in 1976 agreement was finally reached on a series of amendments to the IMF Articles of Agreement, which were to come into force in 1978. Any serious long-run reforms had been long since abandoned and the proposed changes were really only a ratification of events which had occurred since 1971 and an attempt to make the system of managed floating work better.

The principal changes to the IMF Articles concerned its lending activities, its supervision of exchange rates and a change in the international reserve asset system.

As far as lending policy was concerned, the IMF introduced a number of new facilities, including the oil facility, the extended facility and the supplementary financing facility. The first was set up in 1974 to help finance the increased cost of imports following the oil price rise in 1973; the second was designed to help LDCs by providing them with long-term finance (up to 10 years) to deal with structural problems; and the supplementary financing facility was made available to countries experiencing serious BOP problems.

In terms of exchange rates, the revised Articles allow countries to float or to peg their currencies, and although they were supposed to be subject to IMF supervision, in practice this amounted to little except a series of guidelines to encourage good behaviour. If they fix their currencies they can fix in terms of anything except gold, including the SDR or a basket of currencies. There are no limits on the margins within which these rates are pegged and there are no rules about how they should be altered. In reality, countries enjoy a variety of arrangements including managed floating, the modified snake of the European Monetary System (after 1979), fixing to the dollar or another major currency or currencies, and crawling pegs.[9]

Perhaps the most important change in international monetary relations since 1978 has been the attempt to replace gold as a reserve asset once and for all, and to raise the status of the SDR. The reforms have included the abolition of the 'official' price of gold and the removal of any restrictions on its sale in the open market. In fact, the IMF has itself been selling off gold reserves and putting the proceeds in a special fund to help LDCs. The dominant reserve assets at the present time are national currencies, about 75 per cent of which are in US dollars, but since 1978 there has been an increase in the importance of other currencies such as the German mark, the yen, the Swiss and French francs and Dutch guilders. The SDR was redefined in terms of a basket of 16 major currencies since the value of gold no longer had any precise meaning and the 'basket' approach is more realistic in a world of generalised floating. The IMF has also been active in expanding the range of activities for which the SDR could be used, and its interest rate has been raised closer towards a market rate.

In many ways the SDR is eminently suitable to perform the role of international money. It can be issued by deliberate planning, it is virtually costless to produce and, most important of all, its distribution is not linked to any one country's BOP. After all, it was the association of international liquidity with the US deficit which was the major weakness of the Bretton Woods system. The main problem with the SDR at the present time lies not so much in its suitability as international money, as in whether there is sufficient confidence for it to become the main form of international money, and how it can be introduced into the system without encouraging central banks to flood the market with unwanted dollars.

Seen within the context of the more structured arrangements of the gold standard and the Bretton Woods system, the present system is chaotic and reminiscent of the 1930s. A variety of exchange rate regimes are in operation with little effective supervision, the reserve asset system depends on the portfolio decisions of central bankers, and there are no accepted rules for sharing the adjustment to payments imbalances. Yet, unlike in the 1930s, the system is not as unstable as it would appear. It is true that floating has tended to increase uncertainty in international trade, and that many traders, bankers and economists would like to see a return to a more orderly system, but there are others, including the representatives of the main industrial countries, who believe that the system has worked quite well, and who are in no hurry to return to what they regard as the excessive rigidity of the Bretton Woods system.

In this sense, the conclusion of the C20 to patch up the managed floating system is in line with the ideological beliefs of the major trading countries at the present time. This is epitomised by the Reagan and Thatcher administrations' determination to eschew greater flexibility in markets, and to tackle the problem of domestic inflation even if this is at the expense of a growth in international trade. This policy of 'no change at the present time' has continued into the 1980s and there are no immediate plans for a more fundamental reform of the international monetary system.

NOTES

1. Not least because there is insufficient gold to make it a viable proposition. For a definitive analysis of the irrelevance of the gold standard in the contemporary world, see Ford (1965).
2. Hume's original essay 'of the balance of trade' is reproduced in Hume (1969).
3. See Kenwood and Lougheed (1971).
4. This is discussed in Bloomfield (1959).
5. The decision to return to the gold standard at the pre-war parity, which became known as 'the Norman conquest of 4.87', after the Governor of the Bank of England Sir Montagu Norman, is discussed in Moggridge (1972).
6. For the meaning of this term, see Chapter 11, note 7.
7. A history of the IMF is available in Southard (1979), and details of the current operations of the Fund are contained in the International Monetary Fund (1979).
8. The gold stock failed to expand primarily because its official price remained fixed while production costs rose. The supply of new gold failed, therefore, to expand. Commercial demand continued to increase and more gold was bought as a speculative asset. This meant that the central banks actually lost gold from official reserves.
9. We looked at the EMS in Chapter 15 and at the various types of exchange rate regime, including crawling pegs, in Chapter 14.

FURTHER READING

A detailed, but very clearly written history of the international monetary system is Yeager (1976). A classic study of the inter-war years undertaken on behalf of The League of Nations is contained in Nurkse (1944). For an evaluation of the Bretton Woods system and events since 1973, including the attempts at reform, see Crockett (1982) and Williamson (1977).

17 Proposals for a New International Economic Order

As a result of growing diplomatic pressure by lesser developed countries (LDCs) in the early 1970s, a special session of the United Nations General Assembly convened in April 1974 concluded its debate by committing itself 'To work urgently for the establishment of a new international economic order'. This new order is to 'redress existing injustices' and 'make it possible to eliminate the widening gap between the developed and developing countries'.[1]

These resolutions formed the basis for a series of negotiations between the North and the South covering a wide range of issues, including an Integrated Programme for Commodities, reform of the international monetary system, and changes in the way in which trade is conducted between the DCs and LDCs.

In this chapter we examine North–South relations, including these proposals for a new international economic order (NIEO). We begin in section 17.1 with some background on the current debate from the 1960s. In section 17.2 we look specifically at matters relating to trading practices, including proposals for a general system of tariff preferences for LDCs. In section 17.3 we turn our attention to the important area of commodities and evaluate the proposals for an Integrated Programme for Commodities. In section 17.4 we examine various aspects of the international monetary system which impinge upon LDCs, including mechanisms for compensatory finance and arrangements for settling the current 'debt crisis'. Finally, in section 17.5 we take a broad look at the evolution of North–South relations over the last two decades and assess the prospects for the 1980s.

17.1 UNCTAD 1964

Although proposals for a NIEO came to the forefront in the 1970s, in fact many of them go back to the early 1960s when LDCs first began to express their dissatisfaction with the post-war international monetary and trading system, and began to articulate their demands for reform. The major forum for these demands has been the United Nations Conference on Trade and Development (UNCTAD), which was established in 1964 as a permanent organisation within the United Nations Economic and Social Council, in spite of opposition at the time by many DCs. It has met periodically about every four years ever since, and acts as a continuous pressure group on behalf of LDCs and assists them in matters of trade and aid. This organisation has played a particularly important role in the commodity discussions emanating from the NIEO.

Despite the fact that in 1961 the United Nations designated the 1960s as the United Nations Development Decade, in which 'member states and their peoples will intensify their efforts to mobilise and sustain support for measures required on the part of developed and developing countries to accelerate progress towards self-sustained growth', the formation of UNCTAD in 1964 represented a culmination of unease on the part of LDCs with the international monetary and trading system which had emerged from the Bretton Woods Conference of 1944 (discussed in Chapter 16). This protest represented both a theoretical challenge to the current interpretation of the relationship between trade and development, and a series of policy proposals for reforming trading relations between the North and the South.

The theoretical challenge, which we discussed at some length in Chapter 4, was enshrined in a document presented to UNCTAD in 1964 entitled *A New Trade Policy for Development*.[2] This document became the basis of demands by the 'new' international trade theorists for policies which ran counter to the prevailing orthodoxy of essentially free trade and specialisation according to comparative advantage. In essence, the new trade theorists argued that the existing model of trade based upon neoclassical economic principles was inappropriate for the circumstances which faced most LDCs, and that free trade and the pursuit of comparative advantage were not necessarily 'optimal' policies once it was recognised that there might be a conflict between international trade and the goal of economic development.

Although we suggested in Chapter 4 that the new trade theorists and the neoclassical school have come much closer together since 1964, so that the debate is no longer about free trade or protection but the conditions under which interventionist policies might be justified, the views expressed at UNCTAD 1964 were strongly influential in encouraging LDCs to adopt protectionist policies in the 1960s and early 1970s. Indeed, many of those same arguments about declining terms of trade, unequal shares and export dependency have reappeared in the debate over the NIEO.

The challenge to the post-war international monetary and trading system also represented a fundamental attack on the 'liberal' interventionist order envisaged by the architects of the Bretton Woods system, whose guiding principles had been free trade and non-discrimination in international trade. The rules and institutions which emerged from the Bretton Woods negotiations, including the International Monetary Fund (IMF) and the General Agreement on Tariffs and Trade (GATT), were seen by many LDCs as being only incidently designed to cater for their needs. They were primarily designed, they felt, to foster trade between DCs and to provide the richer countries with temporary assistance to achieve their domestic goals within a regime of fixed exchange rates. The implicit assumption was that all countries started on an equal footing and would gain from freer trade and *reciprocal* tariff concessions based upon the principle of non-discrimination in commercial policy.

In fact, LDCs strongly argued that they were not starting from an equal base to DCs since, by definition, they were 'underdeveloped' and couldn't hope to compete in the area of manufactured goods. What they wanted, therefore, was a change in the rules to incorporate policies specifically designed for them, and positive discrimination in their favour. In short, they demanded 'trade not aid' and discrimination and non-reciprocity in tariff negotiations.

The 'trade not aid' slogan was not a call for more trade at the expense of conventional 'open' aid (discussed in Chapter 10), but a call for aid disguised through trade on the implicit assumption that the amount of official development assistance being made available to LDCs at the time was insufficient. Moreover, it was felt that it might be politically easier for DCs to disguise aid through trade than to increase the amount of aid 'openly' published in official aid budgets.

The way in which aid would be transferred through trade was primarily by increasing access to developed country markets: by giving *preferential* access to DC markets in manufactured and semi-manufactured goods on a non-reciprocal basis; and by manipulating international commodity prices to redistribute income from consuming to producing countries.

Other proposals which formed part of the same original UNCTAD package included primary product price stabilisation schemes; compensatory finance arrangements; and the fulfilment of the United Nations targets for the total net flow of financial resources from donor countries of 1 per cent of GNP, and 0.7 per cent in terms of official development assistance.[3] In more recent years other issues have been added to this list, including access to western technology and reform of the international monetary system. We shall consider these issues under three headings: trade preferences, commodities, and the international monetary system.

17.2 TRADE PREFERENCES

LDCs had never been very happy with GATT.[4] This was partly because they felt that it contained so many anomalies and escape clauses that DCs could easily discriminate against them, for example, by invoking the 'market disruption' clause legitimately to apply import controls on low-cost imports from the Third World, or to protect domestic agriculture. In this sense, the South has been active in promoting a reduction in northern protection and in gaining greater access for their exports of manufactured and semi-manufactured goods.

More fundamentally, however, they rejected the principles upon which GATT had been built, namely the reduction of trade barriers on a non-discriminatory and reciprocal basis. What they wanted was *preferential* access for LDC exports along the lines of the Commonwealth Preference agreement established between Great Britain and her Commonwealth associates in 1931, especially in manufactured goods. The idea was that industrial countries would lower duties on imports from LDCs while continuing to impose duties at the same level on goods from other countries. The principle of preferential access was sound, in their view, but the practice of limiting such access to a few countries with which the industrial countries had historical ties, was wrong and 'trade-diverting'.[5] Such preferences should be generalised to *all* developing countries.

The principle of discrimination was justified in so far as LDCs were at a disadvantage in the area of manufactured goods and could benefit along the lines of the 'infant industry' argument discussed in Chapter 5. DCs, on the other hand, could benefit from 'trade-creation' if high-cost domestic producers were replaced by lower-cost imports from the newly industrialising developing countries; and DCs would at the same time be providing a form of disguised aid to poorer countries.

Needless to say, the South's demands for trade preferences were met with opposition from the North. This partly reflected scepticism about the merits of the infant industry argument (discussed in Chapter 5), including the view that it would lead to inefficiencies and the 'feather-bedding' of low-productivity producers; and the fact that a general principle of non-discrimination was being replaced by an *ad hoc* principle capable of a wide interpretation. It could also, according to this view, make eventual liberalisation of trade more difficult to achieve, since trade preferences are more effective the higher the non-preferential tariff. Finally, there were doubts about the wisdom of combining aid with trade and a feeling that it might be better to separate the aid issue from the question of trade.

In spite of this opposition, a limited scheme for a generalised system of preferences (GSP) was agreed in the late 1960s and came into force in 1970. Under this scheme DCs made tariff concessions on imports from LDCs in a range of products. In practice, however, the system covered only 23 per cent of the value of export flows from LDCs, about half of which went to the USA which did not implement the scheme, and other countries exempted some commodities. Murray (1973) concluded that only about 5 per cent of trade was affected, and the GSP tended to benefit only a small number of relatively advanced LDCs.

Any progress in the area of the GSP was also reduced by the clash of interests between those countries, mainly from Africa, which were benefiting from the Lomé Agreement concluded in 1975 between the EEC and 50 African, Caribbean and Pacific countries, and the rest of the LDCs. This gave the countries which were a party to the Lomé Agreement free access to the EEC market in manufactured goods and 90 per cent of agricultural commodities, as well as access to funds designed to stabilise the earnings of a number of key commodities.

In 1975 a UNIDO conference in Lima established a target of 25 per cent of world manufactures to be located in LDCs by the year 2000 (compared with 9 per cent in 1977), and the South has reaffirmed its proposals for reducing protection in DCs and its desire to expand the GSP. In fact, as we suggested in Chapter 5.4, the trend has been towards an increasè in protection in manufactured goods in the 1970s and 1980s and the substitution of non-tariff for tariff barriers, despite the Tokyo Round of negotiations completed in 1979.

17.3 COMMODITIES

If one issue has dominated North–South relations since 1964 it has been that of commodities. The South's proposals in this area have always been somewhat ambiguous, but they have consistently demanded schemes to stabilise international commodity markets and to improve the real incomes which LDCs receive from commodity exports. Stabilisation in this context means the avoidance of 'excessive' price fluctuations in order to reduce the volatility of export earnings. What is meant by improving real income is less clear, but it is tied up with 'remunerative' and 'just' prices for producers. In practice, this has amounted to manipulating the terms of trade through international commodity agreements (ICAs) designed not only to stabilise prices and earnings, but also to stabilise them at a higher level than would have occurred in the absence of market intervention.

The case for commodity market intervention as espoused by the South is justified not only as a means of obtaining aid through trade, under the implicit assumption that conventional open aid will not be forthcoming in sufficient quantities, but also because it is believed that left alone, commodity markets generally work to the disadvantage of poorer countries. This in turn reflects a predominantly pessimistic scenario with respect to the future terms of trade for commodity producers, and the view that fluctuations in export earnings generate uncertainty and impose other costs on society. We examined the terms of trade debate and the question of export instability in Chapter 4, and we looked at commodity stabilisation schemes in Chapter 6. Implicitly, the case for these commodity programmes rests on the assumption that their benefits outweigh any costs, including administrative costs, which would arise as a result of their implementation.

The opposition to these commodity schemes by DCs probably does not stem so much from a dispute over the terms of trade or the costs of export instability so much as from their unease about the mixing of efficiency and redistribution, and about the efficacy of such schemes. To this extent they have always given a better reception to proposals to *stabilise* prices or earnings rather than to those which involve the *raising* of prices as a means of transferring resources from consuming to producing countries. Their view is that if ICAs are to be used at all, they should be limited to improving market efficiency (by eliminating excessive fluctuations), and the question of redistribution should be kept separate and dealt with primarily through open aid or financial transfers such as would be involved in compensatory finance arrangements (which we shall discuss below).

As far as the practical side of these schemes is concerned, DCs, especially the USA and West Germany, are more inclined to emphasise the virtues of competitive markets and the dangers and distortions which arise when agencies attempt to regulate or otherwise intervene in commodity markets. In short, they are not convinced that the schemes which LDCs have put forward will work, and they believe that they will be costly to implement.

Although as we saw in Chapter 6 ICAs have been in operation since UNCTAD 1964, progress in the commodity area was very slow until December 1974, when UNCTAD unveiled its new plan for an Integrated Programme for Commodities. In essence, it amounted to the establishment of a series of buffer stocks to regulate the prices of 17 storeable commodities, including 10 core commodities.[6] Altogether, these commodities constituted about three-quarters of the non-oil commodity trade of LDCs. In addition, to ensure adequate financing for these agencies, the proposal was that a $6 billion common fund be set up and paid for out of subscriptions from importers and exporters of these commodities, but with exemption for the poorest countries. This programme was presented and formally accepted after much argument at the UNCTAD IV conference in Nairobi in May 1976 as an integral part of the NIEO.

In many ways the IPC was a diplomatic success for the South in persuading the North to accept the principles of stabilisation and redistribution which the buffer stocks represented, but the conciliatory attitudes expressed in Nairobi turned out to be the prelude to a series of frustrating negotiations over both the operation of the buffer stocks and the means of financing them. Although the IPC has worked in a limited way, there remains a fundamental division of opinion between the North and the South over the question of commodity agreements. There is also a suspicion that DCs were more readily inclined to concede to southern proposals in 1976 because they were afraid at that time that if they did not do so some primary producers would act in concert to restrict access to supplies of raw materials. This exercise of 'commodity power' invoked fears in the North of a repetition of OPEC's behaviour in the oil market in other primary commodities. In the event, as we suggested in Chapter 6, the potential for replicating OPEC's example in other commodities turned out to be very limited. Oil, it appears, does seem to be unique.

17.4 THE INTERNATIONAL MONETARY SYSTEM

LDCs have generally supported the monetary reforms which took place in the 1970s under the auspices of the Committee of Twenty (see section 16.4), at least as far as the exchange rate system and reserve asset arrangements are concerned. They have, however, pressed for reforms on three main issues: the operation of compensatory financing schemes, the 'link' proposal, and the repayment of international debt.

Whilst the North has generally been lukewarm in its response to trade preferences and ICAs, it has given a better reception to compensatory finance schemes. These are designed to compensate LDCs for shortfalls in their export earnings when they deviate from some longer-run trend or norm, through a financial transfer. In fact the IMF has been operating such a scheme since the early 1960s as part of the compensatory finance facility.[7] This scheme compensates poorer countries when their export earnings fall below a five-year moving average trend.

This favourable attitude which the North has adopted has

something to do with the fact that, unlike trade preferences and ICAs, compensatory finance arrangements (CFAs) leave the market relatively unhampered and thus separate the efficiency aspects of market behaviour from the redistributive aspects involved in the capital flow. Having said this, there are still some lingering doubts about whether short-run compensation provides the best criteria for longer-run assistance, and whether it might be a little tough on countries which take the trouble to carry out corrective measures which obviate the need for compensation.

LDCs have also generally welcomed CFAs but with two important qualifications: first, that these schemes should not be seen as a substitute for trade preferences and ICAs, since they do not really address themselves to long-run problems; and secondly, that the conditions under which they operate should be relaxed. In short they want long-run schemes which provide *automatic* access to finance without any conditionality or strings attached.

As far as the operation of these CFAs is concerned, there has been an easing of the rules in the 1970s as part of the wider reforms in IMF lending policy discussed in Chapter 16. Initially, under the IMF scheme a country could withdraw up to 25 per cent of its original quota at the IMF providing the shortfall in export earnings was temporary, and finance was only made available if the Fund was satisfied that the country concerned was cooperating in an effort to correct its balance of payments disequilibrium. More recently, however, these arrangements have been liberalised and a country may now draw up to 100 per cent of its quota in addition to its drawings on any other facilities, including the extended facility and supplementary financing facility. Conditions are attached, however, for drawings over 50 per cent. In addition, in 1981 the IMF introduced a scheme on the import side to compensate for excess rises in food import prices. Despite these changes, however, LDCs continue to lobby for the removal of existing conditions, especially those which might entail the contraction of domestic credit-creation.

As far as the other two areas of monetary reform are concerned, we have already discussed the magnitude of the debt problem facing LDCs and some of the factors which have contributed to it in Chapter 8, and we examined the link proposal in Chapter 15 in connection with the distribution of international money. Although the South was unsuccessful in achieving a link between the creation of SDRs and official development assistance, it was successful in persuading the North to set up a trust fund in 1976 financed by the sale of some of the IMF's gold stocks the proceeds of which were then lent to the poorest countries at very low interest rates (0.5 per cent) and over long time periods (5–10 years).[8]

At the present time it is perhaps the debt problem which is causing most concern in North–South relations. There has even been talk of a debtors' cartel which would involve a unilateral moratorium on outstanding debt repayments by the largest debtors acting in concert. Traditionally, the North has opposed southern demands for a general moratorium on the grounds that it would be unfair since it would benefit the heaviest borrowers in the past, and it might encourage an irresponsible attitude to debt management in the future. Some concessions, however, have been made towards some of the poorest countries.

The approach to debt adopted by the IMF has generally been to provide lending facilities on condition that the country seeking assistance accepts a package of economic reforms, including exchange rate adjustment and deflationary fiscal and monetary measures. However, as we noted in Chapter 8, the growth of commercial bank lending in the 1970s enabled many LDCs to avoid these unpopular policies, and this has been one of the factors contributing to the current debt crisis facing LDCs.

By 1982 the severe difficulties confronting Brazil and Mexico in servicing their debts brought the IMF directly into the negotiations and established a precedent for the future handling of these problems. Since debt-service payments are typically incurred with a large number and a wide range of creditors, including private suppliers, commercial banks and multilateral development institutions, the solution is to adopt a multilateral approach. This involves directing requests for debt rescheduling to the largest creditors. Since the private agencies involved have neither the power nor the resources to monitor such a programme, and the sums at stake are too large for the IMF alone to deal with, the solution is for the IMF to coordinate a package of reforms, to provide short-term funding to help the country over the worst of the crisis, and to persuade the other parties concerned to continue existing lines of credit. By early 1983, five of the ten largest debtors had either completed or were engaged in formal multilateral debt restructurings with commercial banks.[9] Needless to say, this issue will continue to dominate North–South economic relations in the immediate future.

17.5 PROSPECTS FOR THE 1980s

From the vantage point of the mid-1980s, the last two decades since the establishment of UNCTAD as a permanent forum for North-South relations on trading issues have undoubtedly seen the growing influence of the South in matters connected with the international monetary and trading system, even if progress in the areas of commodities, trade preferences and reform of the international monetary system has so far been modest at best.

LDCs have generally been successful in gaining recognition for their views on the relationship between trade and development, even if some of the more extreme rhetoric of the new trade theorists has been modified in more recent years, and some poor countries have moved towards a less inward-looking stance in trade policy. Similarly, the South has achieved some success in obtaining broader recognition from the North that non-reciprocity and discrimination in international commercial policy might be necessary if the poorer countries of the world are to benefit from international trade.

On the other hand, there remains considerable practical opposition from the North to the sort of proposals put forward in the 1970s as part of the NIEO. This stems not only from a belief that the schemes concerned will not work, but also from a more fundamental objection to the interference with markets which they imply, and to the principle of mixing the goals of efficiency and redistribution. In this sense, the issue of 'trade not aid' remains a basic stumbling-block in North–South relations. Indeed, in the past it led economists such as Johnson (1971), who would otherwise generally be in favour of freer trade and *laissez-faire*, to support interventionist trade policies on the part of LDCs. The argument is that whilst first-best policies, such as trade liberalisation, open aid and the use of ICAs and CFAs for stabilisation purposes, might be preferable, second-best policies, such as trade preferences and ICAs designed to redistribute income from consumers to producers, become justified in the absence of a significant increase in the quantity of open aid. Since there is little evidence that such a fundamental redistribution of resources is likely to be forthcoming in the foreseeable future (indeed our discussion in Chapter 10 suggested the reverse), then interventionist policies such as those embodied in the proposals for the NIEO will continue to be attractive to supporters of the South.

As far as the future is concerned, therefore, despite the publicity which surrounded the publication of the Brandt Report (1980) with its stress on the mutual interdependence between DCs and LDCs in international relations, there is little sign that a fruitful dialogue between the North and the South is imminent. It seems that the original optimism on the part of the South which surrounded the early negotiations on the NIEO has by now largely disappeared, but so too has the worst fears of the North that the success of OPEC would lead to a polarisation between rich and poor countries and a degeneration into resource bargaining. Even the threat of a debtors' cartel seems for the time being to have abated.

NOTES

1. See the United Nations General Assembly resolutions 3201 (s–v1) and 3202 (s–v1).
2. This document is discussed in Friedberg (1968).
3. We looked at the measurement of aid in Chapter 10.
4. For some background on GATT, see Chapter 5.4.
5. The terms 'trade-creation' and 'trade-diversion' were defined in Chapter 7.2 in connection with integration movements.
6. For some details on the operation of buffer stocks, see Chapter 6.
7. The IMF's scheme is discussed in Goreux (1977).
8. The lending policies of the IMF are reviewed in Williamson (1982). For a liberal view of this organisation, see Cline (1976), and for radical interpretations, see Abdalla (1980) and Payer (1974).
9. These countries include Mexico, Brazil, Venezuela, Argentina and Chile. See Brau *et al.* (1983) for further details.

FURTHER READING

For some background on the earlier issues in North–South relations, see

Johnson (1967a, 1971). Various views on the NIEO are contained in Bhagwati (1977) and Helleiner (1982). A forthright case is made against the NIEO by Brunner (1982). A more liberal interpretation of North–South economic relations is available in Cline (1979).

Bibliography

Abdalla, I. (1980), 'The inadequacy and loss of legitimacy of the International Monetary Fund', *Development Dialogue*.

Adams, F. and Junz, H. (1971), 'The effect of the business cycle on trade flows of industrial countries', *Journal of Finance*.

Alexander, S. (1952), 'The effects of a devaluation on a trade balance', *International Monetary Fund Staff Papers*.

Aliber, R. (1969), *The International Market for Foreign Exchange*, New York: Praeger.

Alnaswari, A. (1974), 'Collective bargaining power in OPEC', *Journal of World Trade Law*.

Amacher, R. et al. (1979), *Challenges to a Liberal International Economic Order*, Washington: American Enterprise Institute.

American Petroleum Institute (1971), *Petroleum facts and figures*.

Arrow, K. *et al.* (1961), 'Capital-labour substitution and economic efficiency', *Review of Economics and Statistics*.

Balassa, B. (1963), 'An empirical demonstration of classical comparative cost theory', Review of Economics and Statistics.

Balassa, B. (1964), 'The purchasing power parity doctrine: a reappraisal', *Journal of Political Economy*.

Balassa, B. (1965), 'Tariff protection in industrial countries: an evaluation', *Journal of Political Economy*.

Balassa, B. (1971), *The Structure of Protection in Developing Countries*, Baltimore: John Hopkins.

Balassa, B. (1977), *Policy Reform in Developing Countries*, New York: Pergamon Press.

Balassa, B. (1979), 'Incentive policies in Brazil', *World Development*.

Baldwin, R. (1969), 'The case against the infant industry argument', *Journal of Political Economy*.

Baldwin, R. (1979), 'Determinants of trade and foreign investment: further evidence', *Review of Economics and Statistics*.

Baldwin, R. and Richardson, J. (1981), *International Trade and Finance: Readings*, Boston: Little, Brown and Co.

Ball, D. (1966), 'Factor intensity reversals: an international comparison of factor costs and factor use', *Journal of Political Economy*.

Balogh, T. (1963), *Unequal Partners*, London: Blackwell.

Barnet, R. and Miller, R. (1974), *Global Reach*, New York: Simon and Schuster.

Batra, R. (1975), *The Pure Theory of International Trade under Uncertainty*, London: Macmillan.

Bauer, P. (1971), *Dissent on Development*, London: Weidenfeld and Nicolson.

Bauer, P. and Yamey, B. (1981), 'The political economy of foreign aid', *Lloyds Bank Review*.

Behrman, J. (1979), 'International commodity agreements: an evaluation of the UNCTAD integrated program for commodities', in Cline, W. *Policy Alternatives for a New International Order*, New York: Praeger.

Bergson, C. (1976), 'A new OPEC in bauxite', *Challenge*.

Bergsten, C. *et al.* (1978), *American Multinationals and American Interests*, Washington: The Brookings Institute.

Bhagwati, J. (1958), 'Immiserising growth: a geometric note', *Review of Economics and Statistics*.

Bhagwati, J. (1964), 'The pure theory of international trade', *Economic Journal*.

Bhagwati, J. (1976), 'Taxing the brain drain', *Challenge*.

Bhagwati, J. (1977), *The New International Economic Order: The North–South Debate*, Cambridge, Mass.: MIT Press.

Bhagwati, J. and Eckhaus, R. (1970), *Foreign Aid*, London: Penguin.

Blackaby, F. (1979), *Deindustrialisation*, London: Heinemann.

Bloomfield, A. (1959), *Monetary Policy under the International Gold Standard 1880–1914*, New York: Federal Reserve Bank of New York.

Brandt, W. (1980), *North–South: a Program for Survival*, Cambridge, Mass.: MIT Press.

Branson, W. (1968), *Financial Capital Flows in the US Balance of Payments*, Amsterdam: North Holland.

Brau, E. *et al.* (1983), 'Recent multilateral debt restructurings with official and Bank creditors, *International Monetary Fund Occasional Paper, 25*.

British Petroleum (1981), *BP Statistical Review of the World Oil Industry 1980*, London: British Petroleum.

Brown, C. and Sheriff, T, (1979), In Blackaby, F. *Deindustrialisation*, London: Heinemann.

Brunner, K. (1982), 'Economic development, Cancun and the western democracies', *The World Economy*.

Burtle, J. and Mooney, S. (1978), 'International trade under floating rates', in Dryer, J. *et al. Exchange Rate Flexibility*, Washington: American Enterprise Institute.

Cassell, G. (1922), *Money and Foreign Exchange after 1914*, London: Constable.

Caves, R. (1960), *Trade and Economic Structure*, Cambridge: Harvard University Press.

Caves, R. (1971), 'The industrial economics of foreign investment', *Economica*.

Caves, R. and Jones, R. (1981), *World Trade and Payments*, Boston: Little, Brown and Co.

Central Statistical Office (1981), *The UK Balance of Payments*, London: HMSO.

Central Intelligence Agency (1979), *Handbook of Economic Statistics*, Washington, DC.: Central Intelligence Agency.

Central Intelligence Agency (1981), *The World Factbook*, Washington, DC.: Central Intelligence Agency.

Chenery, H. (1961), 'Comparative advantage and development policy', *American Economic Review*.

Chenery, H. and Carter, P. (1973), 'Foreign assistance and development performance', *American Economic Review*.

Cline, W. (1976), *International Monetary Reform and the Developing Countries*, Washington DC.: Brookings Institute.

Cline, W. (1979), *Policy Alternatives for a New International Order: An Economic Analysis*, New York: Praeger.

Cline, W. (1981), 'El interes de America Latino en la intergracion economica, *Intergracion Latinamericano*.

Cline, W. *et al.* (1978), *Trade Restrictions in the Tokyo Round: A Quantitative Assessment*, Washington: Brookings Institution.

Cohen, B. (1969), *Balance of Payments Policy*, Harmondsworth, England: Penguin.

Cooper, R. (1969), *International Finance*, London: Penguin.

Corden, W. (1971), *The Theory of Protection*, London: Oxford University Press.

Corden, W. (1974), *Trade Policy and Economic Welfare*, London: Oxford University Press.

Council of Economic Advisers (1981), *Economic Indicators*, Washington, DC.: Council of Economic Advisers.

Crockett, A. (1977), Exchange Rate Policies for Developing Countries, *Journal of Development Studies*.

Crockett, A. (1982), *International Money*, London: Nelson.

Davenport, M. (1970), 'The allocation of foreign aid', *Yorkshire Bulletin*.

Danielson, A. (1982), *The Evolution of OPEC*, New York:

Harcourt, Brace, Jovanovich.

Diaz-Alejandro, C. (1972), Trade Policy and Economic Development, *Yale University Economic Growth Centre Discussion Paper*.

Diaz-Alejandro, C. (1976), 'The post-1971 international financial system and the less developed countries, in Helleiner', G. *A World Divided*, London: Cambridge University Press.

Dornbutsch, R. (1978), 'Expectations and exchange rate dynamics', *Journal of Political Economy*.

Dunning, J. (1971), *The Multinational Corporation*, London: Allen and Unwin.

Dunning, J. and Stopfort, J. (1983), *Multinationals: Company Performance and Global Trends*, London: Macmillan.

El Agraa, A. (1980), *The Economics of the European Community*, London: Phillip Allen.

Ellsworth, P. and Leith, C. (1975), *The International Economy*, New York: Macmillan.

Evans, D. (1976), 'Unequal exchange and economic policies: some implications of the neo-Ricardian critique of the theory of comparative advantage', *Economic and Political Weekly*.

Evans, J. (1971), *The Kennedy Round in American Trade Policy: The Twilight of the GATT?*, Cambridge, Mass.: Harvard University Press.

Exxon Corporation (1980), *Middle East oil*, New York: Exxon Corporation.

Ezriel, M. *et al.* (1977), 'Commodity price stabilisation and the developing countries, the problem of choice', *IBRD Staff Working Paper 262*.

Financial Guardian (1984), 'Long wait for justice for the man who took on Roche', *Financial Guardian, Wed. 15th Feb.*

Findlay, R. (1970), *Trade and specialisation*, London: Penguin.

Flanders, M. (1964), 'Prebisch on protection: an evaluation, *Economic Journal*.

Ford, A. (1962), *The Gold Standard 1880–1914: Britain and Argentina*, Oxford: Clarendon.

Ford, A. (1965), 'The truth about gold', *Lloyds Bank Review*.

Frenkel, J. and Johnson, H. (1976), *The Monetary Approach to the Balance of Payments*, London: Allen and Unwin.

Friedberg, A. (1968), *The United Nations Conference on Trade and Development of 1964*, New York: the United Nations.

Friedman, M. (1953), 'The methodology of positive economics', in *Essays in positive economics*, Chicago: University of Chicago Press.

Friedman, M. (1953), 'The case for flexible exchange rates', in

Essays in positive economics, Chicago: University of Chicago Press.

Galbraith, K. (1967), *The New Industrial State*, London: Penguin.

George, K. and Shorey, J. (1978), *The Allocation of Resources, Theory and Policy*, London: Allen and Unwin.

Goldstein, M. (1980), 'Have flexible exchange rates handicapped macroeconomic policy?', *Princeton Special Papers in International Economics, 14*.

Goreaux, L. (1977), 'Compensatory financing: the cyclical pattern of export shortfalls', *IMF Staff Papers, 24*.

Graham, E. (1978), 'Transatlantic investment by multinational firms: a rivalistic phenomenon?', *Journal of post-Keynesian Economics*.

Green, C. (1980), 'Insulating countries against fluctuations in domestic production and exports: an analysis of compensatory financing schemes', *University of Manchester Department of Economics Discussion Paper, 16*.

Green, F. and Nore, P. (1977), *Economics an Antitext*, London: Macmillan.

Grubel, H. (1977), *International Economics*, Homewood Illinois: Richard Irwin.

Grubel, H. (1971), 'Effective protection: a non-specialist guide to the theory, policy implications, and controversies', in Grubel, H. and Johnson, H. *Effective Tariff Protection*, General Agreement on Tariffs and Trade Graduate Institute of International Studies.

The Guardian (1984), *Empty stomachs that fill rich men's stomachs*, *Guardian* Feb. 1984.

Hafbauer, G. and Adler, F. (1968), *Overseas Manufacturing Investment and the Balance of Payments*, Washington, DC: US Treasury Department, *Tax Policy Research Study, 1*.

Haberler, G. (1936), *The Theory of International Trade*, London: W. Hodge and co.

Haberler, G. (1959), *International Trade and Economic Development*, Cairo: National Bank of Egypt fiftieth anniversary lectures.

Harrod, R. (1952), *Life of John Maynard Keynes*, London: Macmillan.

Heckscher, E. (1919), 'The effect of foreign trade on the distribution of income', reprinted in *Ekonomosk Tidskrift*.

Helleiner, G. (1982), *For Good or Evil*, Toronto: University of Toronto Press.

Heller, H. and Khan, M. (1978), 'The demand for international reserves under fixed and floating exchange rates', *IMF Staff*

Papers, 25.
Helpman, E. and Razin, A. (1978), *A Theory of International Trade under Uncertainty*, New York: Academic Press.
Henderson, P. (1971), 'The distribution of official development assistance commitments by recipient countries and by sources', *Oxford Bulletin of Economics and Statistics*.
Hicks, J. (1939), 'The foundations of welfare economics', *Economic Journal*.
Hirsch, S. (1967), *Location of Industry and International Competitiveness*, Oxford: Clarendon Press.
Holden, P. *et al.* (1979), 'The determinants of exchange rate flexibility: an empirical investigation', *Review of Economics and Statistics*.
Holzman, F. (1966), 'Foreign trade behaviour of centrally planned economies', in Rosovsky, H. *Industrialisation in Two Systems*, New York: Wiley.
Hood, N. and Young, S. (1979), *The Economics of Multinational Enterprise*, London: Longman.
Hopkin, B. *et al.* (1970), 'Aid and the Balance of payments', *Economic Journal*.
Hotelling, H. (1931), 'The economics of exhaustible resources', *Journal of Political Economy*.
Houthakker, H. and Magee, S. (1969), 'Income and price elasticities in world trade', *Review of Economics and Statistics*.
Hufbauer, G. (1966), *Synthetic Materials and the Theory of International Trade*, Cambridge, Mass.: Harvard University Press.
Hume, D. (1969), 'Of the balance of trade', reprinted in Cooper, R. *International Finance*, Harmondsworth, England: Penguin.
International Monetary Fund, (1979), *IMF Survey*, Washington: The International Monetary Fund.
International Monetary Fund (1980), *International Financial Statistics*, Washington, DC: The International Monetary Fund.
International Monetary Fund (1981), *International Financial Statistics*, Washington, DC: The International Monetary Fund.
International Monetary Fund (1982), *Survey*, Washington, DC.: The International Monetary Fund.
International Petroleum Encyclopaedia (1981), Oklahoma: Penwell Publishing co.
Johnson, D. (1974), *The sugar Program: Large and Small Benefits*, Washington: American Enterprise Institute.
Johnson, H. (1961), 'Towards a general theory of the balance of payments', in *International Trade and Economic Growth*, Cambridge Mass.: Harvard University Press.

Johnson, H. (1962), *Money, Trade and Economic Growth*, London: Allen and Unwin.

Johnson, H. (1966), 'Trade preferences and developing countries', *Lloyds Bank Review*.

Johnson, H. (1967), 'Some economic aspects of brain drain', *Pakistan Development Review*.

Johnson, H. (1967a), *Economic Policies towards Less Developed Countries*, Washington: Brookings Institute.

Johnson, H. (1971), *Trade Strategy for Rich and Poor nations*, London: Allen and Unwin.

Jones, R. (1979), *Essays in Trade Theory*, Amsterdam: North-Holland.

Kaldor, N. (1939), 'Welfare propositions of economics and intertemporal comparisons of utility', *Economic Journal*.

Kenwood, A. and Loughheed, A. (1971), *The Growth of the International Economy 1820–1960*, London: Allen and Unwin.

Killick, T. (1978), *Development Economics in Action*, London: Heinemann.

Kindleberger, C. and Lindert, P. (1978), *International Economics*, Illinois: Richard Irwin.

Kouri, J. (1978), 'Balance of payments and the foreign exchange market: a dynamic partial equilibrium model', *Cowles Foundation Discussion Paper, 510*.

Krauss, M. (1973), *The Economics of Integration*, London: Allen and Unwin.

Kravis, I. (1965), 'Availability and other influences on the commodity composition of trade', *Journal of Political Economy*.

Kravis, I. *et al.* (1978), 'Real GDP per capita for more than 100 countries', *Economic Journal*.

Kravis, I. and Lipsey, R. (1978), 'Price behaviour in the light of balance of payments theories', *Journal of International Economics*.

Kreinin, M. (1974), *Trade Relations of the EEC: An Empirical Investigation*, New York: Praeger.

Kreinin, M. and Officer, L. (1978), 'The monetary approach to the balance of payments: a survey', *Princeton Studies in International Finance, 43*.

Lall, S. (1973), 'Transfer pricing by multinational manufacturing firms', *Oxford Bulletin of Economics and Statistics*.

Lall, S. (1974), 'Less developed countries and private foreign direct investment: a review article', *World Development*.

Leamer, E. and Stern, R. (1970), *Quantitative International Economics*, Boston: Allyn and Bacon.

Leontief, W. (1954), 'Domestic production and foreign trade: the American capital position reexamined', *Economica Internazionale*.

Levich, R. (1978), 'Further results in the efficiency of markets for foreign exchange', in *Managed Exchange Rate Flexibility: The Recent Experience*, Boston: Federal Reserve Bank of Boston Conference series, 20.

Linder, S. (1961), *An Essey on Trade and Transformation*, New York: John Wiley.

Linder, S. (1967), *Trade and Trade Policy for Development*, New York: Praeger.

Lipsey, R. and Lancaster, K. (1956), 'The general theory of second best', *Review of Economic Studies*.

Lipsey, R. (1970), *The Theory of Customs Unions: A General Equilibrium Analysis*, London: Weidenfeld and Nicolson.

Lipsey, R. (1983), *An Introduction to Positive Economics*, London: Weidenfeld and Nicolson.

Little, I. *et al.* (1970), *Industry and Trade in Some Developing Countries*, Oxford: Oxford University Press.

Little, I. (1982), *Economic Development*, New York: Basic Books.

Lomax, D. (1983), 'Prospects for the European Monetary System. *Nat. West. Quarterly Review*.

MacBean, A. (1966), *Export Instability and Economic Development*, London: Allen and Unwin.

MacDougal, G. (1951), 'British and American exports: a study suggested by the theory of comparative costs', *Economic Journal*.

Machlup, F. (1939), 'The theory of foreign exchanges', *Economica*.

Machlup, F. (1943), *International Trade and the National Income Multiplier*, Philadelphia: Blakiston.

McKenzie, G. and Thomas, S. (1984), 'The international banking crisis', *The Economic Review*.

McKinnon, R. (1963), '*Optimum currency areas*', *American Economics Review*.

McKinnon, R. (1979), 'Foreign trade regimes and economic development', a review article, *Journal of International Economics*.

Mattadeen, A. (1983), '*Reflections after a decade of OPEC pricing policies*', *Nat West Quarterly Review*.

Meade, J. (1951), *The Theory of International Economic Policy, Vol. 1: The Balance of Payments*, London: Oxford University Press.

Meade, J. (1964), 'International commodity agreements', *Lloyds Bank Review*.

Meier, G. (1968), *The International Economics of Development*, London: Harper and Row.

Meier, G. (1984), *Leading Issues in Economic Development*, New York: Oxford University Press.

Mikdashi, Z. *et al.* (1974), A series of articles in *Foreign Policy*.

Miles, M. (1979). 'The effects of devaluation on the trade balance: some new results', *Journal of Political Economy*.

Minhas, B. (1962), 'The homohypallagic production function, factor intensity reversals, and the Heckscher–Ohlin theorm', *Journal of Political Economy*.

Mishan, E. (1968), 'Producers' surplus, what is it?', *American Economic Review*.

Moggridge, D. (1972), *British Monetary Policy 1914–1931: The Norman Conquest of $4.86*, London: Cambridge University Press.

Mundell, R. (1968), *International Economics*, New York: Macmillan.

Murray, T. (1973), 'How helpful is the General System of Preferences to developing countries?', *Economic Journal*.

Myint, H. (1958), 'The classical theory of international trade and the underdeveloped countries', *Economic Journal*.

Myrdal, G. (1957), *Economic Theory and Underdeveloped Regions*, New York: Harper and Row.

Newberry, D. and Stiglitz, J. (1981), *The Theory of Commodity Price Stabilisation*, Oxford: Clarendon Press.

Newman, P. *et al.* (1954), *Source Readings in Economic Thought*, New York: Norton.

Nurkse, R. (1944), *International Currency Experience: Lessons of the Inter-war period*, New York: Colombia University Press.

Nurkse, R. (1967), *Patterns of Capital Formation in Underdeveloped Countries* and *Patterns of Trade and Development*, New York: Oxford University Press.

OECD (1979), *The Impact of the Newly Industrialising Countries on Production and Trade in Manufactures : Report by the Secretary General*, Organisation for Economic Cooperation and Development.

OECD (1981), *Development Cooperation 1981 Review*, Organisation for Economic Development and Cooperation.

Officer, L. (1976), 'The purchasing power parity theory of exchange rates', a review article *IMF Staff Papers*.

Ohlin, B. (1933), *Interregional and International Trade*, Cambridge, Mass.: Harvard University Press.

Ohlin, B. *et al.* (1977), *The International Allocation of Economic Activity: Proceedings of a Nobel Symposium held at Stockholm*, London: Macmillan.

Orcutt, G. (1950), 'Measurement of price elasticities in international trade', *Review of Economics and Statistics*.

Overseas Development Council (1980), *Agenda 1980*, Overseas Development Council.

Papanek, G. (1973), 'Aid, private foreign investment, savings and growth in less developed countries', *Journal of Political Economy*.

Payer, C. (1974), *The Debt Trap*, London: Penguin.

Pazos, F. (1973), 'Regional integration of trade among less developed countries', *World Development*.

Penrose, E. (1976), 'Ownership and control of multinational firms in less developed countries', in Helleiner, G. *A World Divided*, London: Cambridge University Press.

Plumptre, A. (1970), 'Exchange rate policy: experience with Canada's floating rate', *Princeton Essays in International Finance, 81*.

Posner, M. (1961), 'International trade and technical change', Oxford University Press.

Prebisch, R. (1964), *Towards a New International Policy for Development*, New York: The United Nations.

Prest, A. *et al.* (1982), *The UK Economy*, London: Weidenfeld and Nicolson.

Radetski, M. (1976), 'The potential for monopolistic commodity pricing by developing countries', in Helleiner, G. *A World Divided*, London: Cambridge University Press.

Radford, T. (1983), 'The economic organisation of a POW camp', in Samuelson, P. *Readings in Economics*, London: McGraw Hill.

Reddaway, W. *et al.* (1967), *Effects of UK Direct Investment Overseas*, Cambridge, Mass.: Cambridge University Press.

Ricardo, D. (1963), *The Principles of Political Economy and Taxation*, Homewood: Irwin.

Robertson, D. (1940), *Essays in Monetary Theory*.

Rowe, J. (1965), *Primary Commodities in International Trade*, Cambridge: Cambridge University Press.

Salter, W. (1959), 'Internal and external balance: the role of price and expenditure effects', *Economic Journal*.

Samuelson, P. (1948), 'International trade and the equalisation of factor prices', *Economic Journal*.

Samuelson, P. (1980), *Economics*, London: McGraw Hill.

Singer, H. (1950), 'The distribution of gains between investing and borrowing countries', *American Economic Review*.

Smith, A. (1937), *The Wealth of Nations*, New York: The Modern Library.

Southard, F. (1979), 'The evolution of the IMF', *Princeton University Essays in International Finance, 135*.

Spaos, J. (1980), 'The statistical debate on the net barter terms of trade between primary commodities and manufactures', *Economic Journal*.

Stern, R. (1962), 'British and American productivity and comparative costs in international trade', *Oxford Economic Papers*.

Stern, R. (1971), 'Tariffs and other measures of trade control: a survey of recent developments', *Journal of Economic Literature*.

Stern, R. (1973), *The Balance of Payments*, Chicago: Aldine.

Stern, R. *et al.* (1976), *Price Statistics in International Trade – An Annotated Bibliography*, London: Macmillan.

Stern, R. (1977), 'The presentation of the US balance of payments: a symposium', *Princeton University Essays in International Finance, 123*.

Stocking, W. and Watkins, M. (1946), *Cartels in Action*, New York: Twentieth Century Fund.

Stolper, W. and Samuelson, P. (1941), 'Protection and real wages', *Review of Economic Studies*.

Streeten, P. (1973), 'The multinational enterprise and the theory of development', *World Development*.

Swan, T. (1960), 'Economic control in a dependent economy', *Economic review*.

Swann, D. (1970), *The Economics of the Common Market*, Baltimore: Penguin.

Thirlwall, A. (1974), 'The panacea of the floating pound', *Nat. West Quarterly Review*.

Thirlwall, A. (1982), *Balance of Payments Theory*, London: Macmillan.

Thirlwall, A. (1983), *Growth and Development*, London: Macmillan.

Thomas, B. (1972), *Migration and Economic Growth*, Cambridge: Cambridge University Press.

Tinbergen, J. (1952), *On the Theory of Economic Policy*, London: North Holland.

Todaro, M. (1982), *Economics for a Developing World*, London: Longman.

Triffin, R. (1960), *Gold and the Dollar Crisis*, New Haven: Yale University Press.

Triffin, R. (1964), 'The evolution of the international monetary system: historical reappraisal and future perspectives', *Princeton University Studies in International Finance*.

Tsiang, S. (1961), 'The role of money in trade balance stability: synthesis of elasticity and absorbtion approaches', *American Economic Review*.

Tugenhat, C. (1973), *The Multinationals*, London: penguin.

Ulph, A. (1984), 'The price of oil', *The Economic Review*.

Ungerer, H. *et al.* (1983), 'The European monetary system: the experience 1979–82', *IMF Occasional Papers*.

United Nations (1978), *Transnational Corporations in World Development: A Reappraisal*, New York: the United Nations.

UNCTAD (1981), *Handbook of International Trade and Development Statistics: Supplement 1980*, New York: United Nations Commission on Trade and Development.

United States Department of Energy (1981), *1980 International Energy Handbook*, Washington, DC: United States Department of Energy.

Van Duyne, C. (1975), 'Commodity cartels and the theory of derived demand', *Kyklos*.

Vernon, R. (1966), 'International investment and international trade in the product cycle', *Quarterly Journal of Economics*.

Vernon, R. (1971), *Sovereignty at Bay*, New York: Basic Books.

Viner, J. (1937), *Studies in the Theory of International Trade*, New York: Harper and brothers.

Viner, J. (1950), *The Customs Union Issue*. New York: Carnegie Endowment For International Peace.

Willett, T. and Tower E, (1976), 'The theory of optimum currency areas and exchange rate flexibility', *Princeton University Special Papers in International Economics, 11*.

Williamson, J. (1973), 'International liquidity a survey', *Economic Journal*.

Williamson, J. (1977), *The Failure of World Monetary Reform 1971–1974*, New York: New York University Press.

Williamson, J. (1981), *Exchange Rate Rules: The Theory, Performance and Prospects of the Crawling Peg*, London: Macmillan.

Williamson, J. (1982), *The Lending Policies of the IMF*, Washington DC.: Institute for International Economics.

Williamson, J. (1983), *The Open Economy and the World Economy*, New York: Basic Books.

Wilson, P. (1983), 'The consequences of export instability for developing countries – a reappraisal', *Development and Change*.

Wilson, T. *et al.* (1969), 'The income terms of trade of developed and developing countries', *Economic Journal*.

World Bank (1978), *World Bank Atlas*, Washington: World Bank.

World Bank (1978a), *World Development Report 1978*, Washington, DC.: World Bank.

World Bank (1981), *World Development Report*, Washington, DC.: World Bank.

World Bank (1984), *World Development Report*, Washington, DC.: World Bank.

Yeager, L. (1976), *International Monetary Relations*, New York: Harper and Row.

Zis, G. (1983), 'Exchange rate fluctuations 1973–82', *Nat. Westminster Quarterly Review*.

Name Index

Subject Index